Evan Davis was born in 1962 in Surrey. He is the highly respected presenter of the BBC Radio 4 *Today* programme, as well as presenting BBC 2 business reality show *Dragons' Den*. He was the economics editor of ~~the~~ 2008.

The Library at Warwick School
Please return or renew on or before the last date below

1/14

2 2 FEB 2016		

Also by Evan Davis

PUBLIC SPENDING

MADE IN BRITAIN

Evan Davis

ABACUS

First published in Great Britain in 2011 by Little, Brown
This paperback edition published in 2012 by Abacus

A CIP catalogue record for this book
is available from the British Library.

ISBN 978-0-349-12378-3

Typeset in Sabon by M Rules
Printed and bound in Great Britain by
Clays Ltd, St Ives plc

Papers used by Abacus are from well-managed forests
and other responsible sources.

MIX
Paper from
responsible sources
FSC
www.fsc.org   FSC® C104740

Abacus
An imprint of
Little, Brown Book Group
100 Victoria Embankment
London EC4Y 0DY

An Hachette UK Company
www.hachette.co.uk

www.littlebrown.co.uk

ACKNOWLEDGEMENTS

This book was written as the accompanying television series was being filmed, which means that the printed and audiovisual forms of the project informed each other as they went along. Those involved in either have thus been involved in both. The two are best seen as the product of team endeavour, even though I must take responsibility for the facts herein and their interpretation.

The book could certainly not have been published without the help of Tom Bromley. He wrote up the history sections, many of the company examples and other material too amounting in total to at least a third of the text. He consistently delivered quality material on time without fuss.

The book could also not have been written without the help of the teams involved in producing the three television programmes. They came up with bright ideas for the content, persuaded people to take part and researched the background stories. Dan Hillman, Martin Small and Jon Stephens produced the programmes, ably assisted by Sreya Biswas, Sam Goss and Benedict Sanderson. The assistant producers in particular were helpful in collating facts and providing briefs on each visit. Not only were they invaluable to the whole project but they were also a pleasure to work with.

Dominic Crossley-Holland got me involved in *Made in Britain* in the first place, and with the series producer Michael Tuft has provided continual encouragement and helpful feedback as the project progressed. The teams at the *Today* programme and the *Bottom Line* have had less of my time than they should have and have kindly not grumbled. Many others have been involved at the BBC, including Martin Davidson, who deserves recognition for helpfully attempting to push us to be ambitious in scope, Simon Finch, John Kitsis and Pamela Seal. The Open University deserve credit for backing the documentaries from the outset.

Many people were filmed and interviewed in the making of the programmes. All gave me – and the cameras – remarkable access. Companies are often nervous about opening their doors to broadcasters so all of those who did deserve thanks. But I wish to express special gratitude to the many that did not in the end appear in the films. It is frustrating to waste time with documentary makers who then fail to use your contribution. I know that because much of what I had filmed failed to make the cut as well. What I can assure you is that every conversation I have had in recent months has helped shape the thinking in the book.

I'd like to acknowledge historian Frank Trentmann as the man who introduced me to the term 'Free Trade Nation', in the title of his book on the makings of modern British commerce, consumption and civil society.

I must thank my agent Claire Paterson and the publishers Little, Brown. Zoe Gullen edited the book with great speed, all the more remarkable for the fact that the haste did not detract from the quality of her work. The book would have been unreadable had her pen not been liberally applied. Tim Whiting

Acknowledgements

at Little, Brown has exhibited excellent judgement on almost every decision through the process, but above all I thank him for his patience.

And while on the subject of patience, my final thanks go to Guillaume, who has exhibited so much of it at home. If there was a medal for it, he would be on the podium collecting it.

CONTENTS

PREFACE TO THE
PAPERBACK EDITION

It is very hard to be optimistic when everything is going wrong. Unless you are of an unusually stubborn disposition, it is also all too easy to doubt your abilities when you encounter a run of bad luck. So, given the recently troubled state of Western economies, it is really no surprise that there has not been much economic optimism around lately, and that the British have (again) started doubting their ability to produce or sell anything worthwhile.

The purpose of this book is to persuade you that our national capacity to earn a living is greater than you realise. Because I am not deluded, I will not be arguing that everything is rosy. We made some colossal mistakes in the years running up to the financial crash that broke in 2007-08 and are still suffering the consequences today. But it would be tragic to let the flow of bad news cloud our judgement to the point that we forget Britain remains a relatively productive economy despite several years of appalling setbacks. My goal is simply to clarify what has gone right and what has gone wrong in recent years, in terms of our ability to pay our way in the world. The truth is that in the decades running up to the financial crisis a lot did go right as well as a lot going wrong. Indeed, recognition of the good in the nation's performance might give a much-needed confidence boost in facing up to the bad.

The basic story of the UK is one of an economy that has been surprisingly dynamic in recent decades. Contrary to popular perception, we did not idly stand by while China and other countries stole our industries and jobs; in fact, we adapted to the changing environment. Our economy moved up market as we migrated towards industries in which we had a competitive advantage over newly emerging industrial economies that could mass produce goods at prices lower than we could afford to match. We shifted away from manufacturing industries into new ones increasingly based on selling intellectual property, services and specialist goods.

As a result, our economy grew in those years. Far from being complacent, we were mostly regarded as a pioneer in carving out a new role for ourselves. Other European countries watched as, year by year, our economic performance exceeded theirs. If you want one simple fact to remind you of why we were not insane to follow the path we did, just note that our national income grew faster than that of each of Germany, Italy and France in the 1980s, the 1990s and the 2000s. We were clearly doing something right (although in fairness to them, in the last decade the UK population was rising, which pushed up growth). As fast as we exited some industries, we found new ones that raised national income per head. On average, we got richer, not poorer. In addition to that, and contrary to popular perception, there were more jobs in Britain rather than fewer. In 2011, even after three years of crisis, over 29 million people were in work in the UK, one and a half million more than a decade before, and five million more than in 1981. Indeed, so strong was the UK labour market it succeeded in absorbing hundreds of thousands of foreign workers who wanted to find a job.

Nothing that has happened in the financial crisis has undermined these contentions. That we did make that move up market in the years running up to the financial crisis remains unarguable. Manufacturing's share of our output declined considerably, yet our economy got bigger not smaller. And even as we let our manufacturing sector shrink relative to everything else the value of our manufactured output was actually growing, until hitting its all-time peak in the first quarter of 2008.

In 2011 the Centre for Economic Performance at the London School of Economics published a statistical analysis of the economy in the years of the Labour government (1997 to 2010). It bears out all these findings:

> Overall, we find that British performance was impressive between 1997–2010 compared to other major countries both in terms of productivity and the labour market. The productivity performance was not primarily driven by the 'bubble' sectors of finance, property or government services. Rather, human capital, ICT and efficiency improvements were the dominant forces especially in the business services and distribution sectors ... Analysis of other indicators of business performance, such as foreign direct investment, innovation, entrepreneurship and skills, supports our view that the gains in productivity were largely real rather than a statistical artefact. This evidence points to a more positive reading of the supply side of the economy than the current consensus.

Our national move up market was not some kind of mad departure from all economic logic, but a natural response to the environment surrounding us. Some deindustrialisation made manifest sense. If we could get the Chinese to make our manufactured items, we could then do more lucrative things like designing and marketing the manufactured items the Chinese made. We didn't have to take leave of our senses to engage in this process. It was part of our economy's evolution from blue collar to white collar.

Not only did the process have a clear logic, it also reflected well on the ability of the British economy to adapt as conditions changed. In fact, the structure of UK industry and employment changed very radically indeed. For example, in the two decades from 1990 the share of the UK economy accounted for by manufacturing halved, from 22 per cent to 11 per cent. That is a dramatic change for such a short period in a country generally regarded as conservative. Fusty old Britain has not been stuck in its ways after all. In the 2000s no other developed country had such a large shift away from traditional industries towards financial and other business services.

Looking at particular industries, you get the same picture. Take the changes in the City of London over the last twenty-five years: since the big bang of 1986 we have seen the takeover of the old British merchant banks, the rise of the big American investment banks and then the re-emergence of dominant British banks. I don't necessarily consider these developments to be positive, but they do make the point that we are quite willing to change when the incentive is there.

What drove all of this? Many critics think that it was all determined by Margaret Thatcher and that she led a modern attack on the old industrial working class. She was certainly content to watch British manufacturing fade and she did also enthusiastically promote the growth of the City. She might have been intent on class war, for all I know. But the funny thing is that even after she, and her party, left office the trends continued. Government has had a role in easing the changes that have occurred, but it has not been the main player in driving them. In my own view, what has been more important than politicians in shaping the economy is the exchange rate. People often underestimate just how significant it is in coordinating the direction an economy takes. A strong exchange rate entices companies to move lower-value activities off shore because they become relatively expensive to pursue in the UK. In the last decade in particular, the strong sterling exchange rate combined with the falling price of manufactured goods caused by China's industrialisation told British consumers to buy imported goods and British manufacturers to make things elsewhere. That is what they did.

So far, so good: a broadly positive account of what occurred in the UK. A flexible economy adapted to the price signals it faced and gravitated towards higher-value industries. The statistical evidence is that it succeeded in doing those things. What could possibly go wrong? The answer, of course, came with the financial crash. It was not just a random piece of bad luck, it exposed two hugely important failures of the new British economy.

First, it highlighted the weaknesses of the financial services industry, which had been the pin-up sector of the new economy. Much of its success turned out to be illusory. It had expanded in part by taking extra risks (which it had not itself understood) and thus had not created nearly as much valuable output for the UK as bankers and everybody else had generally supposed. As a result of the crash it ended up a subsidy junkie, obtaining taxpayer support on a scale that old manufacturers such as British Leyland could only have dreamed of enjoying.

But there was a second and more significant problem. Although the UK had changed a lot and achieved strong economic growth, its new economy simply didn't have an export sector big enough to sustain the lifestyles to which the nation had become accustomed. Our economy was still exporting a lot, in up-market sectors, but it was not exporting enough. For all the successes, the domestic-facing sectors of the economy were too big relative to the export-facing ones. Prior to the crash, the nation had spent, had borrowed and had imported on an unsustainable scale. It was this unsustainable spending that underpinned the activity which allowed the economy to grow as fast as it did. That meant that when the crash came along the borrowing came to an end, as did the spending, and something had to change. We either had to build a bigger export sector or accustom ourselves to a different, less sumptuous lifestyle. We suddenly realised that the story of UK transformation wasn't quite as remarkable as we might have thought; we needed to import unsustainably in order for the whole thing to work.

At the risk of caricaturing the story, it is as though the UK made two sudden discoveries in the 1990s: factories were not very profitable as a result of the international competition prevailing at the time; and shopping centres were highly profitable and the staff highly productive because they could sell a lot in each hour at work. As an economy we responded to those two observations by closing factories and opening new shopping centres. The economic data looked good as more profitable and higher-value jobs were created. It seemed like a winner until the reality dawned that an economy can't thrive for ever by simply selling foreign goods to itself. Opening shopping centres only created a good investment in new high-value jobs for as long as the borrowing to pay for imports to fill the shops could last.

This stylised account captures at least some of what the UK did in the decades running up to the crash. We simply went too far in reducing the size of our tradable sector: that is, the one containing industries which either export or compete with imports. In its place we allowed the non-tradable sector to grow too big, not so much creating jobs in shopping centres but in many services aimed at domestic consumers (including, incidentally, government services). A dysfunctional chain reaction turned what started out as a relatively healthy adjustment in the UK to an unhealthy over-adjustment: the economy initially grew well as Britain obtained benefits from moving into higher-value sectors and relied on cheap manufactured imports (especially and latterly from China); the growth led consumers and governments to be optimistic about their long-term prospects; that in turn led them to over-estimate the degree to which their incomes could grow; and the over-optimism led to a willingness to borrow unsustainably. The borrowing fuelled spending which fuelled more transformation and more economic growth, seeming to justify the optimism underpinning it all. But at some point it had to become clear that the borrowing was too high, that incomes were not always going to grow that fast. That was the point at which the mistakes of the past became evident.

The fall in the value of sterling as the crash hit is a telling indicator that we allowed too much of our industry to go off shore. At an exchange rate of £1 to €1.45 (the approximate rate that prevailed in 2006), the UK is not a great place to make things for export but it is a great place to buy and import them. At a rate of £1 to €1.15 (the rate in 2011), it is a much better place to make them and a less good place to buy them. The overly strong exchange rate in the earlier part of the decade had duped us into closing down too many factories and opening too many shopping centres.

You might well ask what grounds there are for optimism in that account of our economic development. You could look at the whole pre-crash evolution of the UK economy as a sign that the country went wildly astray. But, appalling as much of it looks in hindsight, it is worth remembering that good things in economics often go too far. The evidence is simply that of a country performing perfectly respectably at the task confronting it. Back then, a high exchange rate and formidable manufacturing competition were the challenges. As the economy exhibited a healthy reflex to the conditions then prevailing, there is no reason to think that it can't now adapt to its new circumstances. Or, to put it another way, if we aren't as dim and unproductive as people often think we are, then we are probably better able to land on our feet than most people think.

Some numbers may help in putting the scale of our mistakes into perspective. The bad news is perhaps best illustrated by a comparison of the performance of the economy in the five years after 2006, set against the predictions made that year by the then chancellor, Gordon Brown. Back then, he anticipated the economy would grow by 13 per cent over the next half-decade; in fact, it is barely bigger at the end of that period than it was at the beginning. It's a long way that our expectations have fallen. Even allowing for the facts that Mr Brown was probably unduly optimistic back in 2006 and that the economy is operating well under its potential at the start of 2012, one can still say that, when the shock of the crisis hit, our national income turned out to be permanently about 10 per cent smaller than we had thought it was going to be. It is as though we've handed back the equivalent of all the economic growth we enjoyed between mid-2004 and 2007. Other countries have also found themselves having to lower their expectations, but few have faced an adjustment on the scale of the UK.

But now put this in context: the economy grew 33 per cent in the decade running up to the crash. In fact, you can take seven percentage points off that thirty-three and you would still have the UK economy growing faster than the economies of Germany, Italy and France. So while the mistakes were bad, they need not be fatal to our sense of economic self-worth.

That is in no way intended to minimise the scale of the task now at hand, which is to rebuild our tradable sector. That will almost inevitably involve shrinking part of the non-tradable sector and it is hard to imagine we can do this without a greater emphasis on manufactured goods as these are far more export-oriented than services. For the next few years, therefore, the British need to discover their inner German and get back to skills such as engineering and manufacturing.

No one should underestimate how formidable a challenge this will be, for several reasons. First and most obviously, it is easier to export more when other countries are importing more. Unfortunately, the news recently has been dominated by the problems in our big markets – the Eurozone and the United States. They have major problems of their own and do not appear ready to shop for more British goods. Indeed, they are also hoping they can export their way to recovery. Annoyingly, the countries where we'd like to sell – the emerging markets like China and India where demand is growing fast – are not ones where we do sell very much.

A second reason that it will be difficult to shift direction is that it always takes many years for adjustments to occur when they involve the supply side of the economy. We can change the way we choose to spend money very quickly, but we can't change what we produce nearly as fast. The former is just a matter of taking a decision on what to buy. The latter, though, requires skills to be nurtured, factories to be built, companies to be created. If it took a decade or two for the economy to de-industrialise too far, it must take about as long for us to reverse that process. And bear in mind that production is more frag-mented around the world than it used to be, so it is not just a matter of a few successful companies opening up new factories. It is a task of rebuilding whole supply chains too.

The third and final reason is that it involves a painful assault on our living standards. Think back to my caricature of a nation opening too many shopping centres and closing too many factories; at the time, the shopping-centre jobs created may have been better paid than the old factory jobs that disappeared. But if they are unviable in a world where unsustainable borrowing is forbidden, then they will disappear and the jobs replacing them may not be as well paid. A similar argument applies to government jobs. If some of them could only be afforded before the crash on account of unsustainable government borrowing or unsustainable tax revenues from an artificially inflated financial services sector, then after the crash it should not be a surprise if some of those jobs are lost, are less well paid or are financed by higher taxes on the rest of the economy.

All the grim economic news that has emerged since this book was originally written a year ago has demonstrated that Britain's rebalancing is not going to be quick or painless. If you were hoping that I would tell you we'll be out of the woods soon, I'm afraid you will be disappointed. My optimism is not based on the idea that we will have a return to strong economic growth very soon, but on the simple observation that we live in an industrious, flexible and productive economy that will return to growth at some point. Over time, we have proved to be as good as any country in the world at adapting our economy to the prevailing conditions. There is no reason to suppose we can't continue to do so.

INTRODUCTION

This is a book for anyone who is interested in Britain's econ omy, and how our nation earns its living. You may be interested in these things because you wish to know how secure our standard of living is, particularly in a world that is changing as rapidly as ours. You may be someone who worries that we don't make anything any more, and who can't fathom how on earth we pay our way in the world. Or you may simply be the kind of person who feels a surge of delight when the nation wins a gold medal or a Nobel Prize, and a shiver of insecurity when the French do better than us at something, and who thus has a patriotic interest in how we stack up against our rivals. Whatever your motive, the goal of the book is to help you look beyond the difficult years facing us now to assess how effective we are at producing and selling things.

This book is not going to please those who take comfort in how useless we are at everything and at how much better the rest of the world is at teaching, football, running railways, maths, democracy, clearing snow off the roads, preventing crime or saving the planet. I'm afraid you will be sorely disap-pointed: we are really quite good at being a modern, affluent economy and that is why we enjoy as high a standard of living as we do. But equally, this is not for those of you who are patriotic to the point of being closed-minded. If you want an account of our economic characteristics that just shows how great we are – a kind of economic equivalent to the history that some people want our children to be taught at school – then this is unsuitable reading. I have generally taken the view that we are strong enough economically to take the facts as they are, rather than as we'd like them to be, so the book strives to be open-minded. What I have tried to assemble is an objective account of our national economic strengths and weaknesses. There are good bits and bad bits.

Of course, it is extremely difficult to compile an objective account of one's own country. It is almost impossible to know whether personal hopes have played a part in selecting facts or deciding how much importance to attach to them; or indeed whether one has been over-compensating in an attempt to be fair. All you can do is to try to be balanced and to anchor assessments to those of external commentators and those who have less direct interest in the conclusions.

The starting point for this book, and for the accompanying BBC 2 television series, was a trip that was designed precisely to garner an outside perspective. We went to China to visit the 2010 Shanghai Expo. It was in full swing as we started filming: four hundred thousand visitors a day queuing to get a glimpse of 187 national pavilions (and a lot else besides). The Expo is a chance for each country to spend a few million pounds on the construction of a temporary building to show off to the rest of the world. It is not meant to be a competition, but of course that doesn't stop countries vying for prestige and attention. It is the sort of event that arouses a curious mix of nationalistic pride and inferiority.

Two observations struck me at that Expo. First, it was clearer than ever that there is a lot of world out there and Britain doesn't appear terribly important to anybody else. For the Chinese visitors we were just another cool pavilion to visit, parked between Italy and France. The second observation was that we appear to have a rather weaker sense of our national economic identity than do other similar nations. The contrast was right there on show. The French and Italian pavilions were huge and packed with national symbols, many of which were commercial in nature. For Italy, a Ducati motorbike, a massive designer shoe, a ceramics display. France had included a wine section, Louis Vuitton bags and a Michelin exhibit.

The British pavilion had nothing Made in Britain about it. Our modestly sized offering, designed by British architect Thomas Heatherwick, was less about product and more about art. Happily, I can report that it won an Expo gold medal for pavilion design and really did shine out as one of the most visually striking and original sites in the whole compound. We had every reason to be proud of it. Unfortunately, visitors to the Expo, who typically queued for several hours to enter a pavilion, were left a tad bewildered by the fact there was nothing inside except a structure of sixty thousand acrylic needles, each of which contained seeds from Kew Gardens' Millennium Seed Bank at Wakehurst in West Sussex. While they could enjoy posing for photos by a Ferrari in the Italian pavilion, what could they do in ours? There was clearly a demand for something more cheesy. (Fortunately, a life-sized model of David Beckham was available outside to satisfy the punters.)

Our pavilion scored well in the high-concept stakes, but there was clear nervousness among the British staff as to whether that had been the right approach. Even before we arrived it was being explained to us that the Expo was not meant to be a trade fair and that our pavilion was very much in the intended spirit of the event. The implication was that other countries had perhaps cheated by trying to flog their wares. Nonetheless, there was an obvious sensitivity that although ours was clever it was also insubstantial.

Clever yet insubstantial. These are two important words, because for many who worry about Britain's economic direction in recent decades, our pavilion represented as good a symbol of our economy as anything the Italians and French were using to symbolise theirs. Britain's economy is flashy on the outside, its critics would say, but it's empty within. There's a gaping hole in the middle because we simply don't make enough.

That empty pavilion was a great place to start an exploration of what we do as a nation to pay our way. What on earth would we have put inside a more commercial pavilion, had we chosen to build one like the French and Italians?

Well, the answer is that despite the fact that we have only 1 per cent of the world's population, and 5 per cent of the developed world's population, we do have a number of world-class industries and firms. We might have chosen pharmaceuticals (Britain has two of the ten largest pharmaceutical companies in the world); we could have put up an exhibit on our defence and aerospace industries (we are large players in both, with a 9 per cent share of the global market in defence and about 17 per cent of aerospace). We could have had a large display on BP, Shell and North Sea oil and gas extraction. And then, of course, we could also have had a large stand dedicated to our world-renowned banking and insurance industries. They may not be visually very impressive but, love them or hate them, they remain two of our big earners. Finally, we might have tried to dazzle the crowd with some of our cars. I say *our* cars, but our most impressive mass-produced vehicles are perhaps the Japanese models we manufacture and export so well, like the Honda Civic (made in Swindon) and the Nissan Juke and Qashqai, which are made in Sunderland.

Introduction

So yes, we can match the world's best, but for many reasons the average Briton is probably barely aware that these industries could showcase the country abroad, let alone is proud of them in the way that the Germans delight in their cars and the Italians are smug about their fashion. This book, along with the BBC 2 series, tries to show that although we may not have as many cash-generating industries as we might like, we could still at least fill the Albert Hall with the ones we've got, let alone an Expo pavilion.

Over the course of filming and writing *Made in Britain*, I have been rather lucky to see and experience some of the most interesting products that the British are involved in making. The new McLaren MP4-12C sports car, for example: Britain's answer to the Ferrari. Designed for use on the roads (fitted as it is with cup holders) and on the track (accelerating from zero to 100kph in 3.3 seconds), it will go on sale for about £170,000. Everybody said it would be fun to drive, and it was, but that was not half as much as fun as it was to be driven by one of McLaren's own drivers, who knew exactly what they were doing. I never realised a car could take a bend so fast.

The MP4-12C could be seen as an absurdly niche product of no interest to ordinary folks at all. How can Britain earn a living by making things that have such narrow appeal? The answer is that McLaren's car is entering a very lucrative niche. I found myself doing some arithmetic to compare the size of the potential market for the MP4-12C to the turnover of another company I visited, Berwin & Berwin. It is Britain's biggest suitmaker, with a plant in China that is responsible for satisfying a sizeable proportion of the entire UK demand for men's suits. There is nothing niche at all about Berwin, but interestingly McLaren only need to sell three hundred of its supercars in a year to have a turnover to match Berwin's. Ron Dennis, executive chairman of McLaren, is aiming eventually to sell about four thousand a year.

Another highlight of the filming was a ride in the back of a Eurofighter Typhoon. The trip was organised by BAE Systems partly to demonstrate the capability of the plane to the cameras and partly to do some testing of on-board systems that had recently been upgraded. The company's press office had assured me there are seventeen thousand highly skilled and well-trained engineers at BAE Systems. As I put my life into their hands and nervously climbed into the cockpit I remembered that they hadn't told me how many unskilled, untrained engineers were employed there. I needn't have worried. The plane is a remarkable piece of engineering. It can fly at the speed of Concorde and with the agility of Peter Pan. Because it imposes high levels of acceleration force on pilots – G-force – they have to wear anti-G suits to ensure blood continues to flow to the brain. The suits inflate and deflate as the force increases, tightening around the body to ensure that blood does not stop circulating. Having been taken up and down, as well as upside down and sideways on that flight, while being sporadically squeezed to different levels of intensity, I came off the plane feeling as though I had been enjoying a mid-air ballet dance while simultaneously enduring a rough Turkish massage.

The Typhoon is not British; it is a collaboration of four European partners, with the UK having had a somewhat bigger share than the others. It is an understatement to say that it has a long and complicated history that has cost taxpayers dear. The point I drew from my ride in the Typhoon is not that Britain should buy more of them (or that we shouldn't); it is merely that when we muster the resources we clearly have the capability to do some very advanced things.

We picked the MP4-12C and the Typhoon because they are the kinds of products that are more interesting to show off than the many others we are involved in making. But one of the purposes of this book is to stop people trying to assess the value of what we do by looking at physical production alone. It's not the weight or size of an object that makes it valuable and, more than most other advanced economies, Britain has found ways of earning a living that are beyond manufacturing. We have probably taken this too far for our own good and have too small a manufacturing base, but if that is the case the argument is that we just need to make some adjustments to our course rather than reverse the direction we have taken.

My own view is that we have many reasons to congratulate ourselves for our economic achievements, but we have few reasons to be arrogant. Unfortunately, it is hard to contain our sense of self-worth within these very reasonable boundaries. Our view of our economic prowess seems to swing between deep gloom and annoying self-satisfaction. Born in the sixties and, as a youngster, aware of the daily news in the seventies, I was brought up with a sense that we could do almost nothing except go on strike. Our industries were declining, beset by demarcation arguments. Our cars were outclassed by those of the rising Japanese sun in the east, and overtaken by those hard-working continental Europeans. Even then it was being said that we could no longer make things.

Somehow that had all changed by the late nineties, the era of Cool Britannia. By then we thought we had it cracked. Far from lacking confidence, we were getting decidedly smug. The British were creative and smart; the Anglo-Saxon economic model was prevailing over the Rhineland one; Germany and Japan had stagnated; the Europeans didn't understand that services (particularly financial services) were all-important, that manufacturing was old-fashioned and that economies had to be flexible. One decade, a banking crisis and a severe recession later, we are back wondering quite what we do. It is pretty clear that the economy needs to re-balance away from its dependence on financial services and it also needs to export more. Suddenly, we find ourselves asking what it is that we can sell abroad.

This is not just a question about our economic destiny. As I wandered around the Shanghai Expo I sensed the link between business activity and national identity. What the British pavilion had not attempted to do in the way that the French and Italians had was set out what it is that we think of ourselves as bringing to the world. It's not necessarily the job of an Expo pavilion to do that, but it *is* the job of this book. It expands on the arguments and facts presented in the television series and it sets out to answer some important questions: do we manufacture too little? Are we really clever and creative? And can we build a strong trading nation on exports of intangible services?

Before we get started, I should also say what this book does not do. It does not do much of the macroeconomics. The kind of stuff you see on the news each night. You'll notice there is little of the Bank of England, interest rates or house prices, or the usual topics which make up most of the daily economic news we read. This is not because these things are unimportant. The month-by-month ups and downs of the economy matter hugely, and the attempts of the Treasury and the Bank of England to use fiscal and monetary policies to manage them can have an enormous effect on employment levels and incomes. They have the complex task of ensuring there is sufficient spending in the economy to give us all things to do without there being so much spending that prices rise unduly. If they get that job wrong the economy will fail to function.

But while the authorities have the power to screw things up and make us poor, they would be the first to admit they do not have the power to make us rich. All they can really do is entice us to save less and borrow more if overall short-term spending is too low, or encourage us to save more if spending is too high. But over the decades it is not the *demand* in the economy that matters, it is the *supply*. It is what we make and sell rather than what we spend. That's why this book focuses on the long-term and on the supply side. On what we produce and why we produce it, rather than what we spend.

There is one enormous disadvantage of taking a long view here, or anywhere, in fact. In the short term, it is the short-term story that seems more interesting than the long-term one. A book such as this may appear entirely irrelevant if you are reading it in the midst of a bout of double-digit inflation or during an apparently never-ending slump. All I can say in defence is that in the long term the short term always loses. And let me defend my ignoring of the yearly fluctuations of the British economy by simply reminding you that you can get ball-by-ball commentary on that everywhere. Daily news is inevitably preoccupied by the short-term blips, and it struggles with the enduring trends. So this book is more interested in the latter.

The second thing about which this book will have rather little to say is ethics, or fairness. We are a nation strong in defence, pharmaceuticals, financial services and oil and gas extraction. All industries that from time to time attract negative headlines, to say the least. I'm sure there are many who would rather we were world leaders in cuddly toys and landmine clearance. For the sake of this book, though, I make no judgement on the ethics of our major export sectors or the companies that lead in them. There is an interesting discussion to be had about all that, but it is not the one I have here.

The third thing about which this book says little is the environment and natural resources. A significant omission, for you will read in these pages quite a bit about how well off we are, how productive our economy is and how China is not a threat to our affluence despite taking so much of our manufacturing. All this sounds very reassuring in terms of our economic security, but please bear in mind that I have not attempted to assess whether the modern world has sufficient raw materials to sustain the lifestyle we enjoy, particularly once China starts living at western levels of consumption. That is an important question, but it so important it is not one I can squeeze into this book on top of everything else.

There is one final thing the book does not offer: unambiguous assertions where issues are fuzzy or complicated. Annoyingly, many of the questions that are commonly asked about our economy have rather ambivalent yes-and-no answers. Economic life is often grey rather than black and white. This is a pity. I've noticed that it is easier to be exciting when you take an extreme view rather than a balanced one, which is why the best newspaper columnists are those who strive not to see the other point of view. My goal here is to find the right balance between complacency and panic when it comes to our economic place in the world. It is important for us not to underestimate the value of what we currently do, nor to overrate our skills and abilities relative to those of everybody else.

PART 1

WHERE WE STAND

1

How Great is Britain's Economy?

Think about how much you consume each day.

You get out of bed in the morning and put your feet on the carpet. (Someone had to make the carpet.) You go downstairs (someone also had to make the stairs); you put some water in the kettle (courtesy of the water company and, of course, the kettle manufacturer) and you pick up the newspaper from the doormat. Before long, your brain is aching with the sheer number of things that our economic system allows you to enjoy. Just think about all the work that has been done in getting them to you.

Of course, you can rightly say that a kettle only has to be manufactured once for the probable ten years that you use it (implying that you consume just 1/3650th of the kettle each day). But then I haven't mentioned the electricity that powers the kettle, the lorry driver who got it to the shop, the oil company that provided the diesel for the lorry, the retailers who sold the kettle to you, nor the chap in personnel who made sure the shop assistant was trained in kettle-selling.

Think of it like that and it's easy to see our economic system as a miracle of both production and organisation. Britain is a great nation in allowing you to live as well as you do. And, just in case you are inclined to take it all for granted, remember how lucky you are to be living here in the twenty-first century. You are not only better off than most people elsewhere in the world today, you are also very likely better off than virtually anyone who lived in centuries past. Not even the royals had cheap flights, anaesthetics or Radio 4 in medieval times. As the best estimates suggest that just over 100 billion human beings have ever lived on the planet, we can confidently assert that, even if you are relatively poor, you are in the most materially fortunate 1 per cent of human beings who have ever lived on the planet.

So yes, Britain is great. Our economy is a miracle.

But, on the other hand, we also know there is nothing miraculous about it. It simply delivers to us the product of our labour, our ingenuity and (perhaps rather too much) of nature's raw materials. If it seems remarkable that we can consume so much, it is equally remarkable that we can *produce* so much. Economists spend quite a bit of time studying this very topic, not least because it is interesting to see how production rates differ between countries. In Britain, we produce items to an average value of about £20,000 for each of us, per year. But that figure includes those who do not work, such as children, pensioners and the incapacitated, which accounts for about half of the population. Therefore, the average person who does work is producing far more.

What we also need to know, though, is not how much we produce, but our relative standing in the world. The Organisation for Economic Cooperation and Development (OECD) is a large international body based in Paris that acts as a think tank for governments in the developed world and it produces some of the best estimates of comparable incomes. You can see the results in Table 1.1. I have included the G7 nations – the biggest established industrial countries – along with a smattering of others to give some context. And there we are, right between Germany and France.

This table is about as authoritative as any, and in ranking us all it takes into account the different price levels of the various countries to ensure that we don't value, say, an apple in an expensive country like ours more than in a cheap country like China.

I've often been rather fixated on these statistics because, even though I know that income isn't everything, I can't help but see Britain's international ranking in per-capita income as the best single measure of its relative economic effectiveness. In fact, I often have to stop myself reading too much into the table. Look at it too hard and you take spurious pride in the fact that we come out above France, and feel disappointed that the US is so far ahead.

In reality, put the US aside and the difference between our measured incomes is small relative to the statistical errors that inevitably

1.1a How Rich We Are
Annual GDP per capita, 2010
G7 economies

Dollars adjusted for difference in prices

	US dollars
United States	46,588
Canada	39,070
Germany	37,411
United Kingdom	35,504
France	34,148
Japan	33,751
Italy	31,814

Source: OECD Database on Productivity March 2012

1.1b How Rich We Are
Annual GDP per capita, 2010
Selected emerging economies

Dollars adjusted for difference in prices

	US dollars
Poland	19,747
Brazil	11,239
China	7519
India	3339

Source: OECD Factbook 2011–12

appear in those measurements. The best approach is to see that the interesting thing is how similar so many countries are, rather than being preoccupied by the statistical gaps. Austria, Belgium, Denmark, Finland, France, Germany, Italy, the Netherlands and Spain all lie within 20 per cent of our per capita output. Think that if our economies typically grow at about 2 per cent a year, the difference between us is equivalent to just a decade of economic development – which, in big-picture terms, is nothing.

Even though it is clear that the United States is way ahead of the European countries, Table 1.2 reveals at least part of the reason. Americans work more hours. In fact, the typical American works 14 per cent more each year than the typical Frenchman, and 8 per cent more than the average Brit. From the grand menu of economic choices, the US has opted for a higher income but less time to enjoy it than Europe. We too could be richer if we worked more, but we may not feel better off: there is no shame in choosing to have less stuff and more leisure.

This point about the hours we work is important. You might

1.2 How Much We Work
Hours worked per year per person
in employment, 2009

	Hours
Italy	1772
United States	1768
Japan	1714
Canada	1700
United Kingdom	1643
France	1554
Germany	1390

Source: OECD *Factbook 2011–12*

find it particularly galling that we appear to work so much more than the French and Germans. And, even more annoyingly, Table 1.3 shows that they are more productive for each of the hours they do work. I suspect the reason for that is that both the French and the Germans have invested more in capital equipment over the years so they have more tools to do their jobs than we do. But I'm defining tools rather broadly here. Nuclear power stations, for example. Or railways. France has a lot of both. And Germany has a lot of well-equipped factories. Overall, in 2008 France had about £51,000 of capital per worker employed, Germany had £57,000 and Britain was on £49,000.

Perhaps the best way to look at the difference is that we spent less on investment in physical capital in years gone by, which left us with more money to spend on ourselves. But we have to work more hours to compensate for the fact that we have fewer machines at our disposal to help us produce.

So much for the balance countries draw between standard of living, leisure time and machines. What conclusion should we

1.3 How Effectively We Work
Value of output produced per hour worked, 2010

	US dollars
United States	59.0
France	57.7
Germany	53.6
United Kingdom	46.2
Canada	45.2
Italy	43.9
Japan	39.4

Dollars adjusted for difference in prices
Source: OECD Database on Productivity March 2012

draw, pulling together Tables 1.1 to 1.3? Well, we can (and indeed will) argue about the finer points, but taking a broad perspective there is one obvious message. It's one that you should be clear on from the outset: *Britain is not a basket case.* We don't need to invoke our industrial heritage, our success in the war or the great British inventions of yore – from penicillin to the hovercraft – in order to have a sense of self-worth. We are entitled to call ourselves Great Britain. At the same time, we have no grounds for snootiness. If we are not a basket case, neither are our close counterparts. We are in the premier league but we have no reason to think we are at the top of it.

You may be wondering how it can be that we are so close in overall living standards to economies that, on the surface, look so much more impressive than ours. The Germans and Japanese, for example, who make so many more cars than we do. Or the French, whose trains run so much faster. In terms of the anecdotal performance ratings that countries achieve in discussions in pubs around the land, these visible manifestations of success are taken very seriously.

But we are wont to move beyond the anecdotal. In a typical sophisticated modern economy, there is so much going on, and it is all entwined in such complicated ways, you cannot rely on intuition or casual observation to guess at what we do and at how important it is in national output.

The correct way to judge the size of an industry is not by how big it appears to the naked eye, but by how much value it produces according to robust statistical measurement. In producing such data, statisticians use the concept of gross value added, or GVA. The GVA of the hotel sector, for instance, is the value of what it sells – nights in hotels – minus the value of what it buys in – the eggs and bacon it serves for breakfast.

The great thing about GVA is that it makes sure we are not double-counting any output. We don't want to count the sale of eggs and bacon as output of the hotel sector and also as output of the agricultural sector. We have to count those eggs once and once only. So for each sector the only value that is counted is that which *it* added, not which it bought in. It is strictly and consistently compiled, and so we should trust GVA to measure the relative importance of an industry to an economy.

Of course, the statistics are far from perfect, and they tend to be revised from time to time. But as an example of what oddities they can throw out, they show that even though Britain produces over a million vehicles a year (coming just outside the top ten world producers) our car sales sector is a more significant contributor than our car manufacturing one. Using GVA to count the output of car retailers, we take the value of the cars they sell and subtract the value of the cars they buy, thus looking at the value they add to the cars by selling them. And the result is that the selling of cars is 1.3 per cent of the output of our economy. The manufacture of motor vehicles is about 0.8 per cent.

In fact, not only are car dealers more valuable than car manufacturers, they are more significant to our economy than agriculture, hunting, forestry and fishing combined.

You may not like it; you may think it represents an odd world where this is the case; you may rightly argue that agriculture would be more useful to us if we had to revert to a primitive lifestyle. But in terms of simple value generation, car dealing trumps farming. And that is one of those facts that underlines the danger of making judgements on the basis of personal hunch.

Another reason not to jump to conclusions is found in the detailed table of gross value added by sector compiled every few years by the Office for National Statistics (to save paper, I have spared you the whole thing, but the most recent figures for the broad categories are delineated in Table 1.4). The detailed table shows just how many sectors there are. For example, below is a list of ten sectors of our economy isolated in the official UK data.

These each account for (very) approximately one thousandth, or 0.1 per cent, of the UK economy. (If the UK produces the equivalent of £100, they each produce about 10p. Or, to put the figures more realistically, the UK produces about £1.5 trillion a year, so these ten each produce value of about £1.5 billion.) Add these ten together, and you have 1 per cent of UK production:

Manufacture of grain mill products: 0.09 per cent

Manufacture of rubber products: 0.10 per cent

Manufacture of medical and surgical equipment and orthopaedic appliances: 0.13 per cent

Manufacture of paints, varnishes and similar coatings, printing ink and mastics: 0.11 per cent

Manufacture of tanks, reservoirs, radiators, boilers and steam generators: 0.08 per cent

Manufacture of cutlery, tools and general hardware: 0.11 per cent

Manufacture of rusks and biscuits: 0.12 per cent

Market research and public opinion polling: 0.12 per cent

News agency activities: 0.12 per cent

Processing of nuclear fuel: 0.07 per cent

One per cent is not very much of our national income; we still have to account for the other 99 per cent. But then, it is likely that these ten are sectors you had barely registered.

When you look at all the different little things which contribute to our output, you find that in a large economy a number of quite big things that we consider important don't amount to very much. For example, there are few sectors anywhere that, to a casual observer, would appear to be as important as cars are to Germany. Yet automotive production only accounts for about 3 or 4 per cent of the German economy. Reduce German car production to the UK level and replace it with nothing, and

How Great is Britain's Economy?

1.4 What We Produce

	percentage of total output
Agriculture, hunting, forestry and fishing	0.7
Mining and quarrying	2.5
Manufacturing	10.3
Electricity, gas and water supply	2.6
Construction	7.6
Wholesale and retail trade (including motor trade)	10.9
Hotels and restaurants	2.9
Transport, storage and communication	11.2
Financial intermediation	8.9
Real estate, renting and business activities	20.3
Public administration and defence	5.1
Education	6.5
Health and social work	7.4
Other services	3.2
All industries	100

Source: *Office for National Statistics Blue Book 2011*. GVA weights 2008

the country's standard of living drops appreciably, but the German lifestyle would still be perfectly comfortable.

This is not to say that if Germany lost its car industry the rupture wouldn't be felt for many years. But in the national economy, 3.5 per cent is only 3.5 per cent. Similarly with the French train sector. The manufacture of trains accounts for less than 1 per cent of French output. Overall, France manufactures about the same as Britain does.

The thing about modern economies is that most of the work goes into the same old things. In the UK, retailing and wholesaling account for 11 per cent of our national output; construction over 7 per cent; and healthcare and education combine at 14 per cent. In comparing economies, these sectors are always very important and that is why there may be big differences in our performance in certain very visible industries while there are relatively small differences in our overall standard of living. Compare British car brands with German ones and we may not look too smart, but if you appreciate how the different parts of the economy add up – and most importantly understand their actual *value* – we compare very favourably with the best in the world.

There is therefore no need to worry about how we are performing as a modern economy. We are up there. We may not be the greatest economy on earth, but we are pretty good all the same. The rest is really just detail.

However, there are some quite significant details to outline. I have mentioned how much we consume and I have talked about what we produce. The next step is to connect the two and to consider importing and exporting.

We can't possibly produce all the things that we need, so we import some things. Similarly, we produce more of some things than we need, so we export those. In the UK over the last decade, we have exported about 30 per cent of what we produce. And we have imported about 32 per cent of our national income. The gap between the two represents the trade deficit.

It is important to understand what that deficit is. It is the difference between what we sell abroad and what we buy from abroad. But it is also useful to see it more intuitively, as the difference between what we produce as a nation and what we consume. If we produce more value than we want for ourselves, we tend to export the difference and run a surplus. If we produce less than we want, we tend to import the difference and run a deficit. This is a highly simplified account in a world of investments and capital flows, but it gets you most of the way to the right intuitions on trade.

There is a slightly broader measure of our international surplus or deficit: the current account of the balance of payments. This adds various other things to the trade gap, such as the money we earn from investments abroad, which count as a credit, but it doesn't change the most salient fact: being a nation of good consumers, we in Britain tend to run up a deficit. That makes us rather typical of the Anglo-Saxon nations. Table 1.5 gives the balance of payments positions of several important countries.

One really important question is how far that trade deficit matters. Does it tell us that something is going wrong with our economy? Does it tell us that the world doesn't like what we

1.5 How Far We Pay Our Way Internationally
Balance of payments current account
deficits as a proportion of national income
Average 1990–2008

	percentage of national income
Japan	2.9
Germany	1.6
France	0.6
Canada	-0.2
Italy	-0.5
United Kingdom	-1.9
United States	-3.3

Positive numbers represent a surplus, negatives a deficit
Source: OECD Factbook 2010. Author's calculations
based on balance of payments data

make any more, or that we can't sell? How worried should we be about it?

You might be old enough to remember how monthly trade figures were reported on the news. Exports, imports, the trade deficit (or, less often, a trade surplus). Enormous attention was paid to this data. And, even though the figures were pretty erratic (if a British airline bought a jumbo jet, it would show up as a surge in imports for a month), elections were won and lost on them. Now we don't really bother with them. One of the reasons that trade disappeared off the bottom of news bulletins was pragmatic. As the EU became more integrated, the monthly figures were broken down into two separate releases: trade with the EU and trade with the rest of the world. Twice a month seemed too often to talk about trade so instead of trade getting two news hits a month, it soon got none at all. Also, the two figures often moved in different directions so the figures became too complicated to explain.

But we didn't stop reporting trade just because it became onerous. More significant was the fact that even as the volume of trade itself grew over the years, we came to think that the gap between imports and exports mattered less and less. There was a tussle between two views of trade and whether deficits should be seen as a sign of national success or failure.

The old view (for want of a better term) had been that avoiding trade deficits was an end in itself. Successful countries, it was assumed, are those that manage to sell things, just as successful companies are those with lots of customers. The more we sell, the more successful we are. This view was underpinned by how money comes and goes. When a nation exports things it generally earns foreign currency, and when it imports things it generally spends foreign currency. Logically, that means if you export less than you import, before long you will run out of foreign currency to pay for imports and won't be able to buy any more – a national humiliation to be avoided at all costs.

However, in the eighties, more weight started to be attributed to an alternative view – for the sake of clarity, let me call it a new view – which argued that we should not measure national success by how much we sell because, contrary to popular belief, it is not the quality of our products and our ability to sell them that drives the deficit at all. It is instead something completely separate from our national wealth-generating capacity: whether the citizens of our nation are in the mood for borrowing or saving.

This account of trade deficits is generally a complete shock to the system. It jars with the common-sense perception of national success and failure in the world of commerce, so it is worth explaining why a trade deficit might not be as important as you think.

Imagine none of us wants to borrow and none of us wants to save. We all aim to consume exactly what we produce. There will be no 'excess' production or 'deficient' production, so there will be no excess imports or exports. Whatever imports and exports there are must be in balance. Similarly, imagine that exactly half of us feel like borrowing, and the other half feel like lending. Again, the economy remains in balance as, in effect, one half of us lends to the other. As a country we match our consumption and production, even though within the country some people are consuming more, and others less, than they produce. But now imagine that a majority of us feel like borrowing – that is, consuming more than it produces.

In that case, the borrowers can't get all the goods they want from the nation's lenders. They have to get some from elsewhere, which takes them to the rest of the world. The borrowers consume more than they produce, which means they must import more than they export. As they account for the majority of the nation, what the borrowers do determines what the economy does overall. The nation borrows and it runs a trade deficit. When we are in the mood for borrowing, we spend more than we earn and thus suck in imports. When we are in the mood to save, we spend less than we earn and thus chuck out exports and run up a surplus. The point of the new view on the trade deficit is that our decisions on borrowing and saving drive everything. Not our national ability to sell things.

Of course, there is no inconsistency in logic between the old and new views of trade, but there is a difference in emphasis and perspective. You might see the contrast between the two rather as you might distinguish between a psychiatrist and a psychologist in dealing with a troubled child. The psychiatrist looks for the underlying cause in a chemical imbalance in the brain, while the psychologist searches for difficulties in the child's relationship with the father. In the case of trade, one group sees a nation's deficit as a problem of competitiveness in the world economy. The other thinks it is driven by savings decisions that are really quite independent of trading effectiveness.

It is worth asking yourself which one you instinctively support. When I was an economics correspondent at the BBC I often received letters from people (usually older than myself) asking why news bulletins did not give more attention to the trade deficit. They always took the old view. And, I suspect, the majority of casual observers do. Unlike, I suspect, the majority of professional economists. And my own personal view is far more new than old: I think it is very important not to just see the trade deficit as a sign of our national failure to compete.

Let me give you a small analogy to back this. Suppose you are comparing the spending habits of a profligate premiership footballer with a thrifty cleaner. The cleaner, being keen to save, will spend less than he earns and will thus run up what can rightly be seen as a personal trade surplus. The footballer, on the other hand, spends more than he earns and effectively runs up a personal trade deficit. Looking at the material welfare of the two though, it is not really very helpful to focus too hard on the deficit or surplus. The deficit-running footballer is clearly better off than the surplus-generating cleaner.

Scale up the cleaner–footballer analogy a billion times over and you have China versus the UK. Which would you rather be? China is prudent and saves a huge proportion of its national income, generating a huge trade surplus. Britain is less prudent and runs up a significant trade deficit. In economic terms, however, Britain is the more successful nation as its citizens are on average six times richer than the Chinese. They are the prudent cleaners; we are the spendthrift footballers.

There is another reason why I encourage you away from the old view of trade deficits. It entices concern that, somehow, we will end up producing almost nothing at all. When the trade figures worsen, as they do from time to time, you will find yourself having nightmares about us becoming more and more dependent on foreign production and less and less able to pay our way. After all, we saw British Leyland shrink from being one of the world's mass car producers in the late sixties to being a tiny little company producing Rover cars in the nineties, and then to nothing at all. If it can happen to British Leyland, surely it can happen to Britain too?

It can't. We will not become a nation that imports more and more and exports less and less for one simple reason. The nations whose goods we buy will want us to pay for them, and to pay for them we will have to earn some foreign currency, and to earn some foreign currency we will have to export some things. For example, it is highly unlikely that China, having taken all our low-value manufacturing jobs, will take all our high-value manufacturing jobs as well. Why? Because well before that happens we would have stopped being able to afford to buy things from China. That puts a natural limit on the trade deficit.

The benefit of the new view is that it knows the problem will sort itself out at some point. If you think of a trade deficit as akin to borrowing, there is a limit on the trade deficit that reflects the amount of borrowing you can get away with. At some point, foreigners will stop lending to us if we try to borrow too much, and at that point the trade deficit will improve.

What is remarkable is that even poor countries like Vietnam – those which are less effective at almost every economic activity than rich western nations – still manage to pay their way in the world. They do this by making themselves very cheap. They do it because they have to. If they have a problem it is not that their lack of competitiveness manifests itself in a trade deficit; it is that it manifests itself in poverty.

All this discussion tells us not to treat the trade deficit as an end in itself. It should not be an objective of economic policy to make the nation run up surpluses, any more than it should be an objective of cleaners to save as much as they possibly can. We should not judge our ability to make things in Britain by the trade gap. Nor should we generally think of trade figures as something that should determine who is prime minister.

However, while the new view moves ideas on from the trade deficit and competitiveness, it does not mean that there aren't problems with our savings and borrowing. That profligate football player may be better off than the low-paid but thrifty cleaner, but that doesn't mean he has nothing to worry about. He may be putting too little aside for his old age, for example. The point of the new view is not that the deficit never matters; it is that the source of any problem is to be found in the savings habits of the nation. If we save too little, the deficit will be too big. But the deficit is the symptom, not the cause, of the problem.

All of which neatly leads us to ask what the UK's trade performance has been. The figures will always fluctuate, but we would be more concerned about looking for an underlying problem if we consistently spend more than we earn, just as any individual who spends more than he or she earns should probably worry too. It is to this gap between what we earn and what we produce that I turn next.

Over the last three decades Britain has had an average balance of payments deficit of about 1.5 per cent of national income: the annual totals are in Table 1.6. Until the early seventies our balance of payments bounced up and down between surplus and deficit and then it took a pretty sharp turn into negative territory. It still bounces up and down, but now it goes from negative to very negative.

On average, you might loosely think of this as demonstrating that for every £10,000 we earn, we are spending £10,150, with foreigners providing that extra £150.

Unfortunately, it is clear that a nation has to add about as much value to the world as it subtracts; it can't indefinitely consume what it does not produce. Or to put the same point in a different way, nations need to earn as much as they spend. Which implies there is something a little suspect about Britain's semi-permanent deficit.

I use the world 'suspect' as I don't like to jump to conclusions. It could all be all right. It might be that we are a nation of borrowers for good reason. Perhaps we are borrowing not because we are addicted to shopping, but because we are investing in our futures. Maybe British companies are sucking in imports as they build new factories. Or British students are borrowing in order to invest in their education, hoping to be more productive as a result of their years at university. In all these cases, we import more now and will be better able to export later. Maybe we are borrowing rationally in order to smooth the bumps and flows of money over our lifetimes. Young adults tend to borrow as they buy their first house, but then save more as they grow towards retirement. The demographic profile of a

1.6 How Far We Pay Our Way Internationally
Balance of payments current account deficits as a proportion
of national income Britain's post-war history

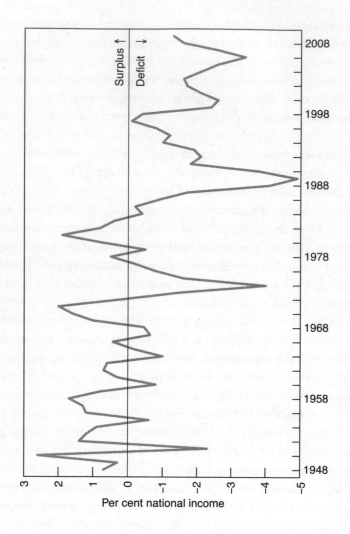

Source: *Office for National Statistics*

population can often determine whether a country is borrowing or saving.

I would love to believe that our trade deficit did represent the collective outcome of a nation's rational borrowing decisions. Alas, as I will explain in more detail in Chapter 6, I find it hard to persuade myself of that fact. The whole story of the economic cycle up to the financial crash in 2007–08 was one of households and banks making poor decisions about how much it was sensible to lend or borrow. I see no reason to assume that we are saving the right amount.

Equally, I would love to believe that the persistent balance of payments deficit is some kind of statistical fluke. That it is not really there. This is certainly not impossible. We British have all sorts of pots of wealth around the world; we have second homes and shares in foreign companies. As these grow in value we get richer. And if they do so outside the sight of the statisticians, we may be getting wealthier each year without them measuring it. In that case, there's no balance of payments problem at all. Our apparently unsustainable lifestyle is in fact sustainable.

But to look closely at the data does not give you grounds for confidence. The statisticians may not have caught it all, but they have picked up a great deal. There is the huge amount of wealth we have parked overseas and the huge amount of wealth for- eigners have accumulated in Britain over the years; there are the debts we owe and the debts owed to us which go back years. And it is clear that our financial position has got worse not better with respect to the rest of the world.

So I take no solace there.

Finally, I would love to dismiss a long-term 'overspend' of 1.5 per cent of national income as rather trivial. After all, that 1.5 per cent leaves us earning 98.5 per cent of what we spend. It doesn't sound too bad when put like that, does it?

It really doesn't sound much. But let me put it like this: to produce our way out of that modest deficit we would need to build an industry bigger than our world-beating pharmaceutical and aerospace industries combined.

No, I worry that the deficit is symptomatic of a problem. I don't panic, but I can't deny being pleased when I see the exports go up and the imports go down. Since the financial crisis, two things have become obvious. We have been borrowing too much and saving too little, and balance needs to be restored. We have thus been exporting too little and importing too much relative to where we want to be. We need to reorient resources away from domestic consumption towards the production of items that can help pay our way in the world.

We don't need to reinvent ourselves completely (we are not a basket case, after all) but we do need to renew. We need a little bit more Made in Britain.

2

How We Got Here

At twelve minutes past six on the evening of 12 August 1985 Japan Airlines Flight 123 set off from Tokyo International Airport to begin the hour-long journey to Osaka. It was just before the Obon festival, when the Japanese traditionally return to their family homes and pay homage to their ancestors. It was then no surprise that the Boeing 747 was full, with 509 passengers and fifteen crew on board.

Flight 123 was never to reach its destination. Twelve minutes into the journey, as the plane flew over Sagami Bay, there was an explosive decompression at the rear of the fuselage. Passengers reported a white mist in the plane, which was the outside air rushing into the cabin. As the oxygen masks came down, everyone on board knew that they were in serious trouble.

The captain of the plane was Masami Takahama, a hugely experienced pilot who had flown for the airline since 1966, and had returned from international to domestic flights in order to help train new pilots. Takahama radioed back to Tokyo to request an emergency landing as the cockpit controls indicated that the problem was a cabin door which had broken, causing the pressure to drop. In fact, things were far more serious. What Captain Takahama and his crew didn't know was that the tail fin had been ripped from the back of the plane and, coupled with the collapse of the plane's hydraulic system, there was no way that they could control the direction of the plane.

In the inquiry that followed, it turned out that the plane had been involved in an accident seven years earlier, which had caused damage to the rear pressure bulkhead on landing. The plane had come in at the wrong angle and scraped its rear end on the runway. For whatever reason, the repairs to that damage were not as thorough as they should have been: it was only a matter of time before crucial replacement rivets worked themselves free.

In the minutes after the decompression, the cockpit calls to the control tower in Tokyo became more frequent, with the same word repeated over and over again: 'uncontrol'. It was testament to Takahama's flying skill that he was able to keep the plane airborne for as long as he did. The plane rose and dived for another half hour, before crashing into the mountains near Mount Osutaka, an isolated area known as the Tibet of the region, about 100 kilometres from Tokyo. Out of the 524 people on board, only four passengers survived. It was the worst single-plane disaster in aviation history.

I find the story of Flight 123 particularly poignant for two reasons. Because of the length of time the captain managed to keep the plane in the air, some passengers – aware of their doom – had time to write letters to their families. Secondly, the cockpit voice recorder shows how the pilots heroically tried to control the plane using the thrust of the engine. It was all they had. But it was futile. They were not really in control of the plane at all, as it was suffering so-called phugoid oscillations – natural cycles of changing speed and altitude. Once a large chunk of the tail fin had fallen into the sea, the cockpit team were victims of the laws of physics rather than pilots of an aeroplane.

I often think about the actions of those pilots. It is only human to imagine that there is something we can do to control our destiny. Yet sometimes we are at the behest of natural forces beyond our control. And in all areas of life there is a good case for distinguishing between the things that are more or less inevitable in the circumstances and the things that are not.

The reason I mention this story is that the effort of the pilots is a good analogy for our commonly held beliefs about the British economy. We like to think that we have the power to be in complete control of economic events, a perception reinforced by the public statements of prime ministers and chancellors. But just as Captain Takahama's accumulated experience was nothing compared to the natural forces he faced, so even the most talented of our politicians and economists cannot define events to the extent that they sometimes claim.

Yet the idea that someone is in control of this beast is pervasive. For example, I had a chat with someone who worked at a museum of industrial history. He told me how terrible it was that we had lost the industry of the past and let it go elsewhere. In his head was a model of our economy as an aeroplane being piloted from a cockpit and, in this case, being piloted badly. Somehow everything had gone wrong. Britain was a great industrial nation and had strayed off course at some point.

That is a commonly held view and a commonly held assumption. We generally suppose that our economy has either gone wrong or that it is all right. We rarely think that neither is the case. The truth is that the British economy has often just behaved as economies in these circumstances tend to behave. When most of us look at the progress of the economy, we often assume it has followed the course it has owing to human volition. Usually we strive for explanations of our performance that accord to some prejudice or other that we hold: that we are superior to other peoples (which explains our success) or that we have some uniquely British failing (that explains our weakness). We shy away from accounts of our economic performance that draw on explanations which say very little that is interesting about ourselves.

I can see why we tend to think that we are in the driving seat, but it overstates our role. Yes, our economy is in some respects shaped by our decisions, but in many other respects it is also down to forces that are hard to resist given the conditions we face. Or, to put it another way, our economy is a blend of two things: ways in which we are special as a nation and those in which we are quite ordinary. We are special in having achieved some great things before any other country, and we are also special in having notched up some dismal and distinctive failures. But at the same time, we are very ordinary in having followed a course that most reasonably functional economies would have followed in the same circumstances.

So, before we go into specifics about the British economy today and the things we produce – manufactured goods, intellectual property and services – let us look at the history of our great industrial past. How did Britain get to where it is today? But let us also consider whether the man in the museum is right by thinking about what underlying forces were driving the rise and fall of old industries. What was great, what was lucky and what was simply inevitable?

The story of the modern British economy begins with an innovation: the factory. This was the most important of the changes that occurred in the British economy between the middle of the eighteenth century and the middle of the nineteenth – changes that were profound, not just for Britain itself, but also for the future direction of the entire world economy. I am talking, of course, about the Industrial Revolution. If there was one industry that symbolised the shift from the old economy to the beginnings of modern manufacturing more than any other, it was cotton. This was the game-changer for the British economy, as the dramatic growth of the cotton industry both revved up the Industrial Revolution and changed working practices forever.

The story of the Industrial Revolution is often told as a tale of its many inventions, such as the steam engine and coke smelting. You may well remember from school history lessons the specific machines that transformed the cotton industry. In 1764 James Hargreaves, a weaver and carpenter from Lancashire, invented the spinning jenny. This device was essentially the mechanisation of the spinning wheel. Eight cotton threads could be drawn out on a moving frame, and then spun and wound as the frame returned. Hargreaves faced great hostility from workers worried about their jobs: his house was attacked and he was forced to leave the area, but by 1780 twenty thousand copies of his invention were in use in the county.

The next leap in progress came via Richard Arkwright, a former barber and wig maker who was also originally from Lancashire. While Hargreaves's invention had changed hand spinning in a domestic setting, Arkwright's water frame worked on a more industrial scale. Arkwright's insight was that the method of drawing cotton into a thread was both slow and labour intensive, and this could be speeded up. His aim was therefore to mechanise the spinning process. The first water frame, built in 1769, consisted of four spindles, but Arkwright realised that he could make something much bigger, holding up to ninety-six spindles, but which still only required one person to operate it.

Arkwright's machine used water wheels to provide power, and in 1771 he borrowed the money to set up and build his first mill. At the end of the same decade came the third key innovation in cotton manufacturing, when Samuel Crompton invented the mule in 1779. This was, in essence, a fully mechanised spinning jenny, but on a much larger scale. Unlike Arkwright's water frame, the mule wasn't protected in terms of patents and was quickly and widely reproduced.

The spinning jenny, the water frame and the mule transformed the process of cotton manufacturing, but a fourth invention was to prove even more influential: the factory itself. As important as creating a machine to improve the process of manufacturing cotton was, a further leap was still required to turn it into a thriving industry. The machines needed to be spatially organised, the flow of materials co-ordinated, the generation and distribution of power sorted out, a division of labour created and a timetable of working hours drawn up.

These are things that sound commonplace today, but in the eighteenth century they were revolutionary concepts. For all of Arkwright's technological innovation in coming up with the water frame, it was the building that housed his invention that is his lasting legacy. Indeed, such is the historic importance of the Derwent Valley, where Arkwright built his first mills, it is now a UNESCO World Heritage site.

Arkwright had chosen the area for a number of reasons, the most important of which was its geography. A ready supply of water was needed to power the water frames, and the narrow part of a valley was ideal as dams could be built for water storage and a powerful flow of water could be created. The fact that the location was remote also helped in terms of keeping the factories out of the way of angry textile workers who, fearful for their jobs, might attack the machines. This leads to a third reason for locating the factories here, which was that there was an untapped pool of labour in this area of Derbyshire. With the local men working in the lead mines, there was an abundant availability of women and children, whose nimble fingers were suited to the work, and whose wages, it should be added, were potentially lower.

Arkwright opened his first mill at Cromford in 1771. One of his partners was a hosier, Jedediah Strutt from nearby Belper, who invested £500. The quality of the cotton produced by Arkwright's machines was perfect for the stockings he made, and within a couple of years Strutt had built his own mills in Belper. This short stretch of the Derwent Valley was soon home to its own production line of factories – two of Arkwright's at Cromford, another at Matlock Bath, Strutt's mills in Belper and another just to the north, in Milford – and the Derwent became the hardest-working river in Europe.

If the Derwent Valley was the birthplace of the factory, the area that really reaped the rewards was Lancashire. As the steam engine arrived to replace the waterwheel, mechanised mills rapidly multiplied and the north-west of England was the perfect setting. The damp Pennine air helped the cotton fibres cling together and so reduced the strain placed on them by the machinery (this made a difference of 10 per cent in production costs compared to drier conditions); land was cheap, with coal and soft water – essential for bleaching, dying and printing the cotton – plentiful; and Liverpool was close by, the ideal port both to get the raw cotton in and to ship the finished goods out. All of which brought huge growth and prosperity to the region – engineering skills were concentrated here, with the building of the Liverpool & Manchester Railway and the Manchester Ship Canal. In addition to an increase in the local population from labourers moving to the area to work in the factories, there was an influx of associated professionals: engineers, builders, bankers and financiers.

The growth of the cotton textiles industry was nothing short of remarkable. In 1803, cotton overtook wool as Britain's leading export, and would retain this position until just before the Second World War. In 1830, cotton goods and yarn brought in just over half of Britain's overseas earnings: the industry employed 425,000 people in 16 per cent of all manufacturing jobs and generating 8 per cent of GDP. In the 1880s the industry accounted for a third of overseas earnings, and even by the start of the First World War it was still contributing a quarter. Its peak in terms of output was in 1912, when 7.3 million metres of cloth were produced.

But if the tale of British textiles in the nineteenth century was one of extraordinary growth and success, the story of the industry in the twentieth century was very much a narrative of decline. Textiles is an industry with relatively straightforward technology, one that requires modest levels of capital to set up. It was, in other words, the perfect industry for developing countries to replicate, and they could enjoy the sort of economic growth spurts that Britain had all those years earlier. The British Empire, which had once been one of the textile industry's blessings (in terms of the huge market for exports), soon became its curse for it left the industry over-reliant on a small number of markets such as India that were fast disappearing. Having had these captive markets for so long had left the British textiles industry somewhat complacent and uncompetitive.

Courtaulds was once the giant of the British textiles industry. It is only just over thirty years ago that the company was the third biggest in the country, with over eighty thousand employees. Today, it is a shadow of its former self, with employees in the low hundreds. So what happened? The short answer is that the company stored up problems that had been affecting the industry for years. The textiles industry was in long-term decline, with foreign companies replicating and bettering the British model.

The problem for Courtaulds was that the biggest buyer of its goods was Marks and Spencer, which had a policy of buying British. This was a long-standing staple of the company's business model and so, while Courtaulds could see the advantages of transferring production to cheaper facilities overseas, its main customer wouldn't countenance such a move. It was a vicious circle: the more Courtaulds went into decline, the more it was reliant on Marks and Spencer; the more it was reliant on Marks and Spencer, the more it went into decline.

This mutually assured economic destruction was ultimately unsustainable. The eighties high-street boom found Marks and Spencer under pressure from younger retailers such as Next and Topshop. These stores took advantage of ever-changing fashions and used cheaper foreign imports to make the most of them. In a modern, increasingly globalised economy, Marks and Spencer's policy of selling mostly British-made goods was outdated: consumers were more driven by price than where the clothes came from. With its reputation as the nation's best-loved retailer under threat, Marks and Spencer realised it was time to look abroad and ended its relationship with its British suppliers. For a company such as Courtaulds, the decision was devastating: without its major buyer, the company's decline, and that of the industry, went into freefall.

Many of us are perhaps disappointed by the loss of jobs and physical production that we suffered as a result of this. As we have seen, Courtaulds went from a workforce of eighty thousand to a few hundred. An appalling record, perhaps, but in my view this is a good example of something that is not down to us or our failings. We could not sustain a mass-market textile industry in this country given the competition that we faced from other countries, however well we had run our textile companies or however hard we had worked. The efforts of Marks and Spencer to continue a 'buy British' policy was flawed in attempting to keep the industry in the UK for as long as it did. It was always a lost cause, and the tale is ultimately a salutary one.

There is, in short, nothing special about Britain's failure in textile manufacturing. Like much of what one observes about the economy, the rise and fall of this industry is best thought of as the result of what one might call 'big forces' rather than individual human decisions. The diminution of the importance of agriculture, the expansion of manufacturing, the rise of the service economy: these are all natural steps for economies to follow. There is nothing special in our country having chosen to tread this path.

So what are these 'big forces'? I stand by three basic rules that determine the direction of most reasonably functional economies. Nations can and do defy them, and may sometimes be successful in contravening them. But in the long term, the rules will generally prevail.

Rule number one is that thriving nations build their economies around the resources they have at their disposal. There is a reason that Saudi Arabia exports oil: it has little else. It would be silly for it to attempt to build a thriving broccoli industry. Equally, there is a reason that China exports cheap manufactured items. It has a ready supply of unskilled labour suitable for manufacturing. The French climate and countryside, meanwhile, offer the perfect conditions for vineyards and making wine. It was the rich clay of Perugia and the volcanic clay of the Amalfi Coast that led to the birth and development of Italian ceramics.

Another way of expressing this is to say that you are best advised to start from where you are rather than where you want to be. Nations might sometimes wish they were endowed with resources other than those they have: a large supply of graduate engineers, for example, or perhaps a world-beating financial services centre. But if they do not have these things, they will not succeed by pretending that they do.

Of course, countries can sometimes create the resources they lack. They can attempt to train graduate engineers or offer tax incentives to banks to cluster into a new financial district. On occasion this makes sense. But it is hard to make an impression in an industry in which you are starting from scratch, particularly if lots of other nations are also trying to do the same thing. We are familiar with the smaller emirates attempting to take their economies beyond oil, by importing labour and creating physical infrastructure on a lavish scale. Whether they will succeed remains to be seen, but they will spend a lot of money doing so. We will never know whether the money could have been better spent in other ways.

The second rule is that properly functioning nations tend to deploy their resources in the highest value activities they can find. If you have a workforce that can either produce textiles or pharmaceuticals, you are well advised to put them to work on pharmaceuticals. Plenty of people can make textiles, but only relatively few can make pharmaceuticals, so the returns there are likely to be far greater. There is, for instance, a reason that Britain does not export many of the things that China does: although we have a large supply of labour that could work in factories producing cheap electronics or toys, unlike the Chinese we have other, more lucrative, options.

Ultimately, unless there are some very perverse incentives, national economies will tend to gravitate towards high-value industries as ordinary workers, companies and investors will themselves find that is where they get the best returns.

There is an important implication of this rule. Many of us have a tendency to see what other nations succeed in doing, and yearn for us to do the same: 'the Germans have made lots of money by exporting machine tools; shouldn't we develop a machine tool industry too?' Probably not. It is precisely because the Germans have made a success in that industry that our companies have decided to steer clear of that well-occupied turf and pursue something different.

These first two rules that nations use the resources they have and do so in the highest-value activities available – in theory should go a long way to explain the patterns of trade between countries. We expect to export what we are set up to export, and to import the things that we cannot produce very well for ourselves.

In practice, trade is determined by many other factors, but economists have long attempted to explain trade as I have outlined it, with vastly more sophisticated variants of the two rules I have outlined. The most important refinement by far is a concept that has a very prominent place in the economists' tool box: comparative advantage. It is so central to arguments about what makes national economies tick that it is worth outlining it here.

An understanding of comparative advantage starts with the idea that nations will strive to trade as profitably as they can and to specialise in activities that are as lucrative as possible. To do so nations will not necessarily do things they are particularly good at, but will instead ensure they do things they are least bad at.

America can export civil aircraft to the rest of the world. Alternatively, it could devote its resources to the manufacture of T-shirts. It may even be capable of making T-shirts more efficiently than anyone else in the world. But as long as aeroplanes are more profitable than T-shirts, it makes more sense for the United States to focus on aircraft and to let Mexico make T-shirts, *even if Mexico is less efficient at it than the United States*. In this example, Mexico is said to have a comparative advantage to the United States in T-shirt manufacture, even though the US could beat the pants off Mexico if it wanted to.

This concept explains why a nation can appear to be bad at everything but still trade profitably. As long as it is less bad at some things than others, it can specialise in those things and allow other countries to specialise in production of the things in which they have the biggest lead. That is to everyone's advantage: trade can occur between countries on that basis to mutual benefit.

The third of the three rules that guide successful national economies is that as things change, nations adapt. It might be that an industry that seems lucrative in one decade becomes unattractive in another – as quickly as you find your niche, you lose it.

The Courtaulds story rather makes the point. And the implication is that the more successful nations will generally be those that can innovate and do not cling on to the past for too long. In fact, they will ride a cycle: they invent something new and carve a scarce and profitable position for themselves; they find others replicate what they are doing and the profits fall; then they move on to invent the next thing.

This is probably the most important rule of all. But the three taken together are simply meant as a guide to what influences the direction an economy takes. Market economies will naturally tend to follow them as prices, wages and returns guide individual players. As it happens, the rules apply as much to companies and even individuals as they do to countries.

What is interesting about Britain's long history as an industrial nation is that it can largely be written as an account of a country following these three rules. Indeed, other successful developed economies have followed a qualitatively similar route. But Britain's history of industrial success – and later of some industrial failure – has of course also been shaped by some distinctively British developments.

So while the decline of the textiles industry is a classic example of Britain behaving exactly as an ordinary economy ought to, at the same time we shouldn't overlook the special, specifically British circumstances that started the industrial ball rolling. After all, in the mid eighteenth century we had a small industry by world standards. Britain spun about three million pounds of cotton yarn each year, which was about the same as in France, but Bengal produced about eighty-five million pounds.

So why was Britain, of all places, the birthplace of the

Industrial Revolution? One reason was the simple economics of supply and demand. British success in the early global economy had led to a comparatively high level of wages in relation to other countries. This mixture of expensive labour and cheap energy led to a 'demand' for technology: if the high price of labour could be replaced with the low cost of energy in the production process, then the costs of making goods such as textiles could be substantially reduced. These relatively high wages also acted as an incentive for product innovation as there was a potential mass market for consumer goods, if only the technology could be found to produce the goods at a viable cost. They also had an effect on the 'supply' of technology: the population was better placed to buy education than in other countries, and these higher rates of literacy and numeracy again contributed to invention and innovation.

The second important factor was the role of the scientific revolution and the Enlightenment. The knowledge of scientific developments was crucial to technological success, and Britain in the eighteenth century was a country ready to learn: scientific lectures were popular; there were bestselling books on the likes of Newton. Perhaps most important of all was the formation of social groups and learned organisations, such as the Royal Institution or the Lunar Society, to discuss ideas.

This dissemination of ideas was vital because one of the other attributes of the Industrial Revolution was the background of its key players. A number of them came from modest families, such as Richard Arkwright and James Hargreaves, and others from nonconformist backgrounds. Non-conformism restricted educational opportunities, not least because the leading universities were closed to those who were not members of the Established Church.

A survey of the seventy-nine leading inventors of the Industrial Revolution, and the occupation of their fathers, showed that 12 per cent came from the aristocracy and gentry, 33 per cent were children of merchants and capitalists, 36 per cent were from a shopkeeping, manufacturing or artisan background, and 19 per cent from a farming or labouring family. These splits were significantly different from the population at large, where just 5 per cent made up the merchants and capitalists class, and 55 per cent were labourers. The industrialists were better educated than in previous generations but were restricted in how far they could take this in traditional ways. The result was to turn their attention to manufacturing.

There was one final element that this group brought to the process. The scientific revolution and the Enlightenment didn't just give these men knowledge; it gave them a way of looking at the world and an empirical methodology. This process of experimentation, of meticulous checking and rechecking, was a world view that trickled down into all parts of the culture. A greater credence was given to naturalistic explanations, and this informed how the inventors worked. They were keen to explore and experiment for themselves, an attitude that could only help creativity and innovation.

In modern economic parlance, we would call this process research and development. Certainly, a number of the key inventions didn't have a single 'eureka' moment, but continued to be adapted for years before reaching the definitive model. Someone like Richard Arkwright was no different from an inventor turning up on *Dragons' Den* today – he needed money to fund developing his idea, which led him to signing up partners like Jedediah Strutt. One estimate suggests that the total cost of developing his water frame came to £13,000: an astronomical sum in those days, but one that Arkwright was to get back many times over.

What the story of the birth of the Industrial Revolution shows is that, despite the big forces that ultimately guide an economy, there are still occasions when individual human decisions can create change, for better or for worse. The beginnings of the

Industrial Revolution is one example of a British manufactured success. But there are also examples of failures that were by no means inevitable. One interesting case study is that of indigenous UK mass car production.

Britain is unique among the big industrial nations of the world in not maintaining a successful mass-market car producer of its own. Germany, Japan, France and Italy – countries that are not too different in complexion from the UK – have all managed to do so. In 1968, when British Motor Holdings and the Leyland Motor Corporation merged to form the British Leyland Motor Corporation, Britain was one of the largest car manufacturers in the world. Even in 1970 there was no inevitable reason for the UK to suffer relative to its competitors.

It was in the decade after that the situation became beyond rescue. Sir John Egan worked with General Motors in the sixties; he joined British Leyland in 1971 and became chairman of its subsidiary Jaguar Cars in 1980. He told me the story from the inside.

'What went wrong with the UK car industry?' I asked.

'Everything,' was his answer.

We all know that industrial relations were a disaster in the seventies. The very day he took up his job at Jaguar, Egan found the factory to be on strike. He immediately realised it was a fight to the death between the trade unions and the management at British Leyland, and he feared Jaguar would collapse, which would have made him the only person to be appointed a senior executive of a car company that had failed to make a single car on his watch.

The Jaguar strike was not terminal, but it was typical of a nation clearly in a habit of industrial confrontation that did not make it easy for companies to be run well. In fact, it didn't serve anyone well. Egan tells a story of observing a strike vote back in the days before secret ballots: the union official asked the enormous crowd of workers whether they wanted to accept the management's latest offer: 'All those in favour of accepting the management's miserable offer, go and stand over there,' he shouted. 'All those against, stand firm.' It wasn't the best way to gauge genuine worker opinion.

But Egan is clear that it was not just bad union practices that were to blame. Management was poor, investment low and the vulnerability to takeover of stock-market-listed British companies made it hard to think long term. The UK's boom–bust macroeconomics didn't help either. The government used to regulate the availability of hire-purchase finance in order to control the overall level of spending in the economy. That made the economic cycle for British car manufacturers particularly volatile. In addition, Egan is scathing of the chain of British companies available to supply parts. He tells of one component that was used in the Jaguar which failed 40 per cent of the time. When he spoke to the proprietor of the firm that made the part, he found that he had bought the company in order to gain from property assets that came with it.

Our failings came at an unfortunate time for UK producers. The automotive world was being transformed. First the Germans applied their engineering skills to mass production and significantly raised the prevailing standards of car design. And then the Japanese developed more sophisticated and successful manufacturing processes. The British car industry, busy fighting fires that it had itself ignited, didn't really know what had hit it. Sir John Egan summed it all up in telling me that he didn't think that once British Leyland had been formed it ever launched a single successful car.

Not even the Austin Allegro with the square steering wheel.

Unlike the case of the textiles industry, there was no economic inevitability about the decline of the British car industry. I would argue that if different decisions had been taken by senior executives, union officials and the government, the outcome might have been very different indeed. An example of history that was not determined by 'big forces', but simply by the fact that we weren't very clever when it came to mass car production.

Overall, we have far more to be proud of than embarrassed about in our industrial past. By luck and judgement Britain was a great industrial nation. The shape of the modern British economy is also a result of our openness to foreign goods and companies that marks our country out as being different from many of its economic rivals. Indeed, our attitude to globalisation has given new life to the car industry, which is alive and well but is just not occurring in British-owned companies. It is to this subject, and to where these unique attitudes come from, that we turn our attention next.

3

An Open Economy

Every year, the German Marshall Fund of the United States, which has the lofty goal of promoting understanding and cooperation between North America and Europe, carries out an international poll. 'Transatlantic Trends' extends across thirteen countries, measuring broad public opinion to find out where we all tend to think the same, and where we tend to think differently.

One of its questions has interested me:

'There are different views about the rise of China. In economic terms, some people see China as more of an opportunity for new markets and investment, while others see it as a threat to our jobs and economic security. Which is closer to your own?'

Think of your own answer before you read on.

Most countries are distinctly negative about the rise of China. The two countries most favourably disposed to it are Britain and the Netherlands. In the 2010 findings, over 50 per cent of respondents in each country saw China as an opportunity. The least well-disposed towards China was our closest neighbour, France, where 63 per cent saw it as a threat, and only 24 per cent an opportunity.

This was not an anomaly. The pattern reflected the 2007 poll, which asked the same question.

It highlights something that does seem to mark Britain out as, if not unique, at least a bit distinctive, with our tendency towards trade, openness and a relatively benign attitude towards global integration. I am devoting this chapter to the openness of our economy and our cosmopolitan culture because these things have played a large part in shaping our overall direction. The subjects of the next three sections – manufacturing, intellectual property and services – all have been influenced by the benevolent attitude we have towards globalisation. One reflection of this is that our leaders – of both Labour and Conservative governments – have tended to take a liberal view of global trade and a sceptical attitude towards protection for British producers.

That is nowhere more true than in our country's attitude towards the EU Common Agricultural Policy. By and large, the British have hated it. Quite a few other European countries (led by the French) do not. The British have also taken a relatively laissez-faire approach to global corporate takeovers.

We do have our own streak of economic nationalism, but it has never seemed to get very far. One of my favourite episodes in recent social history is that of the 'I'm Backing Britain' campaign, which sprang up in the late sixties.

The year 1967 had been mixed, to say the least. This was the Summer of Love and culturally (and chemically) Britain was on a high. June had seen the release of the Beatles' *Sgt. Pepper's Lonely Hearts Club Band*, but while the Fab Four were singing 'Getting Better', things in the British economy were getting anything but. The British finances had their largest deficit since the Second World War (to the tune of £1500 million), and each month the trade deficit was getting wider.

British exporters weren't helped with events beyond their control, such as the Arab–Israeli Six Day War, which disrupted trade due to the closure of the Suez Canal. In September a strike saw the Liverpool, Hull, Manchester and London docks all shut up shop. As the trade deficit continued to grow, British exports piled up in the ports but could not be delivered.

All of this created huge pressure on the pound. With investors selling sterling, the Bank of England had to dig dangerously deep into its reserves to maintain the exchange rate. The situation was unsustainable – as a future prime minister was to say, you can't buck the market – and the inevitable conclusion was that the pound would have to be devalued. On 18 November 1967 the government announced that the pound was to be devalued from $2.80 (which it had been since 1949) to $2.40, a drop in value of just over 14 per cent. In a television broadcast the following day, Harold Wilson, the then prime minister, attempted to explain the decision:

> From now the pound is worth 14 per cent or so less in terms of other currencies. That does not mean, of course, that the pound here in Britain, in your pocket ... has been devalued. What it does mean is that we shall now be able to sell more goods abroad on a competitive basis. This is a tremendous opportunity for all our exporters ... it will also mean than the goods we buy abroad will be dearer, and so for many of these goods it will be cheaper to buy British.

For all the economic inevitability and Wilson's upbeat talk of tremendous opportunities, the devaluation of the pound had a sapping psychological effect on Britain. Edward Heath, then leader of the opposition, called it a 'defeat for Britain' and for many people that was what it felt like: the Queen, watching Wilson's statement with various members of the Privy Council, sat in a 'long, long silence' after the broadcast. Christopher Brooker described the British mood as one 'of aftermath, of exhaustion'.

Not everyone, however, was taking this 'defeat' lying down.

On 13 December John Boyd-Carpenter, Conservative MP for Kingston-upon-Thames, wrote to *The Times* to offer his solution. 'Before the war, Saturday morning was a regular working half-day, both in City offices and on the factory floor,' he noted. Now, though, 'much of the vast capital equipment of the United Kingdom stands idle from Friday evening to Monday morning'. What Britain needed was a 'practical gesture': 'If a number of people, particularly in responsible positions would set an example by sacrificing say the first Saturday of every month and working on that morning without extra pay ... it would give an example to others at home and show the world we are in earnest.'

One person who picked up on this idea was one of Boyd-Carpenter's constituents, Frederick Price, the marketing director of the Surbiton-based Colt Ventilation and Heating. In a post-Christmas company memo about the economic situation, he argued that if the half-day idea was taken up, Britain's balance of payments deficit would soon disappear.

Five secretaries at the company's head office were inspired to respond. 'Everybody understands that our country is in a very difficult financial position,' they wrote to Price, asking, 'how can we put this right?' Their solution was to set the example that Price and Boyd-Carpenter had suggested: 'What about starting this scheme of a five-and-a-half-day week? Let us be the first company to start the ball rolling.' The idea was put to a vote, and the head office staff agreed to start work each morning at half-past eight, instead of nine, for no extra pay.

The initiative was quickly picked up by the media. Frederick Price told *The Times* that the idea would immediately lead to a 7 per cent increase in the company's productivity: 'think if that was the same all over the country ... I think this is the answer to the country's problems.'

Another person who was impressed was Prince Philip, who sent the secretaries a telegram describing their decision as 'the most heartening news I have heard in 1967. If we all go into 1968 with that spirit we shall certainly lick all our problems.' As other companies contacted Colt to take part in the scheme, the company saw the beginnings of a national movement: they announced they would be making 100,000 badges with the slogan 'I'm Backing Britain' emblazoned across a Union Jack, to help advertise the campaign.

As 1968 began, the scheme began to snowball. At Ruskington Foods in Lincolnshire, workers agreed to work extra hours for free to stop a planned increase in the price of their pork pies and sausages. George Apter, owner of a group of Buckinghamshire garages, was one of many who took a voluntary pay cut. The Treasury was inundated with cheques sent in to help pay off Britain's debt.

Perhaps the cheesiest contribution came from the great Bruce Forsyth, who released a single to spur the campaign on. One verse suggested staycationing before the word had been invented: 'Holidays in Blackpool, Plenty of fun, Buy a British car and look for the sun ...'

The suggestions of what British people could do to help continued to come flooding in. Margaret Forest in *The Times* suggested a change in drinking habits: 'Women should switch, surely, from gin to Scotch? Britain is doubly backed because every time you buy a bottle of Scotch you give the Chancellor 37s 6d.'

Meanwhile, a 'How to Help Britain and Yourself' campaign, spearheaded by the then Labour MP Robert Maxwell, offered a hundred 'non-cranky' ways to bolster the country. Farmers were advised to 'grow more wheat. Raise more pigs'; if you are a motorist, 'why not take the family on a motoring holiday of Britain?'; children could set up a 'Help Britain Pen Pal Club', which would create 'new friends for yourself, new future business contacts for your country'; mothers, meanwhile, should offer to do the shopping for neighbours who go out to work – 'Many offices virtually close down at quarter to five because married women have to rush off.'

It was a lively campaign, and certainly well-meaning. But it was completely misguided and I'm not unhappy to report that it got nowhere. The Bruce Forsyth single failed to trouble the top forty. The British Productivity Council wondered about the campaign's effectiveness, making the point that increased output was not the same thing as improved productivity. The trade union movement quite sensibly resisted measures to get its members working extra half-hours for nothing. The Amalgamated Engineering Union described the scheme as 'a protective blanket around inefficiency'.

On the other side of the political spectrum, Enoch Powell dismissed the scheme as 'ineffably silly' and said it should be called 'Help Brainwash Britain'. The key thing, he argued, was the competitiveness of British exports, something that the extra hours put in had no impact upon.

As quickly as it started, the campaign began to fall apart. Back at Colt Ventilation and Heating, the Amalgamated Engineering Union banned its members who worked at the company's Havant factory from taking part: the shop stewards who tried to defy them were suspended and normal working hours resumed.

The ultimate humiliation for the campaign was the news that the 'I'm Backing Britain' T-shirts proudly worn by campaigners had been made in Portugal.

On the high street, the effect of the campaign was negligible: two months in, the branch of Safeway on the King's Road in London described the change as 'very little … it doesn't show up in the sales or stock figures'; the Victoria branch of Tesco 'had not noticed people preferring domestic produce', according to *The Times*.

A straw poll of other local supermarkets found as many foreign goods on special offer as British ones. 'How does that help Britain?' one store owner mused. 'Well, I suppose it helps the housewife get cheaper products.'

Exactly.

And that is the root of the problem with these protectionist campaigns. Buying British is not a virtue if British isn't what you want to buy. Yes, it serves the interests of British producers, but does so at the expense of British consumers. If, on the other hand, I buy a Portuguese T-shirt, I benefit as a T-shirt consumer (that's presumably why I chose the Portuguese one over the British alternative) but I also hurt the British T-shirt producer.

What ultimately did for the campaign is the fact that Britain has a strong tradition of viewing things in terms of the consumer interest, rather than the producer. Far from being a nation of shopkeepers, we have seen ourselves as a nation of shoppers.

Another very significant problem for the campaign was that it was actually quite difficult to 'Buy British' in the modern economy. Marks and Spencer, for whom almost all of its goods were British made, was very much the exception. At the Ford plant in Dagenham, the shop steward who led his men to reject the scheme, argued that when two-thirds of British industry was foreign owned, it didn't really mean anything.

The Times used the case of Heinz Baked Beans to illustrate the point: the beans came from North America, the tomatoes from Portugal, the cornflour from US maize, the sugar from the West Indies and the spices from the tropics. The only things about the beans that were British were the salt and the metal can they came in. Heinz was 90 per cent American owned, yet the can of beans, simply because it was all put together in the UK, was considered British.

For me, the biggest objection to the 'I'm Backing Britain' campaign is that it assumed that the objective of us going out to work and choosing what to buy is to serve some abstract concept of the British economy. It isn't. The economy is there to serve us. Most of us go to work in order to enjoy a higher standard of living than we otherwise would; and most of us buy things in order to consume them. But the campaign was in effect one to cut our standard of living. Exhorting us to holiday at home and buy cars that are not the ones we really want, and getting us to work harder without extra pay are all ways of making us poorer not richer. The campaign was a submission to our economic failure, not the solution to it.

It is of course true that it can sometimes be helpful to cut our living standards, just as it is sometimes helpful for a company to cut its prices even if its objective is to make bigger profits. (In Chapter 6 I will argue that we have tended to over-consume as a nation.) So in that sense the campaign had a certain logic to it. But cutting our standard of living is not an end in itself.

Crucially, if these cuts are to make us more competitive, there are better ways of doing it than by making arbitrary gestures to support a random selection of British firms. Who was to say that whisky distillers and car makers were most deserving of our support? Maybe we should have been directing our patriotic largesse towards British sausages and mash.

But such arguments get you nowhere. It is absurd to define a nation's industrial structure on the basis of charitable shopping. No, the better way to cut the living standards of British people and reduce imports was through the devaluation of the pound. That made imports more expensive and exports cheaper.

I tend to think that what really undermined the 'I'm Backing Britain' campaign was not the intellectual weakness of its case, but its clash with our instincts and history. Britain has a tradition of openness and internationalism, of putting the interests of consumers above those of producers and, of course, of importing goods when it makes sense to do so. In his book *Empire*, the historian Niall Ferguson quotes Daniel Defoe writing in 1725: 'England consumes within itself more goods of foreign growth, imported from the several countries where they are produced or wrought, than any other nation in the world.' The imports that the British couldn't get enough of in the eighteenth century were items like tea, coffee, sugar and tobacco, showing a penchant for foreign products that has never really subsided.

For all the campaigners wrapping themselves up in the Union flag, the simple truth was that in terms of British identity matters were a lot more complicated than they had thought. The shop steward at the Ford plant may have been over-egging things, but foreign ownership of British companies was significant in its extent and not something that exercised people to any great degree. Again, Britain had history in this: Niall Ferguson describes the Glorious Revolution, when William of Orange arrived from Holland to become King William III, as having 'the character of an Anglo-Dutch business merger', in which William was accepted as, 'in effect, Britain's new Chief Executive'.

The instincts of the 'I'm Backing Britain' movement went against the national grain, and like other similar initiatives – Gordon Brown's 'British jobs for British workers' pledge, for example – once that became clear the patriotism it attempted to draw on felt jingoistic at best. Britain might have been smaller in terms of economic might, but by resisting such nationalist overtures it showed we were bigger in ways that were arguably more important.

But if Britain is a free trade nation, where does this instinct come from? The answer is again to be found in our history as an industrial nation. If one event could be said to have forged the relationship between the British people and the concept of free trade, it would probably be the repeal of the Corn Laws in 1846. This was one of those once-in-a-generation moments, whose significance and symbolism lasted far longer than the arguments surrounding the legislation itself.

In some ways, the ideas behind the Corn Laws were not dissimilar to those of the Common Agricultural Policy. They were designed to protect the interests of the country's agricultural sector, and hence of the landholding aristocracy. The 'corn' that the legislation sought to protect was in fact all grain – rye, barley and wheat – and severe restrictions and high duties were placed on foreign imports, to the benefit of British producers. Between the mid seventeenth century and the final repeal in 1846, over 120 corn laws were passed in Britain.

For much of this period, however, their existence on the statute book did not arouse much interest. The British agricultural sector was strong and the country was largely self-sufficient. Indeed, so strong was British farming that we actually exported grain to the continent during this period. But while advances in agriculture broadly coped with the rapid rise in the size of the British population, there were periods of poor harvests and the interruptions of conflicts such as the Seven Years' War of 1756–63. The result was simple: with increased demand for grain, and with no foreign imports permitted to provide the necessary additional supply, the price went up. Grain, which had averaged forty shillings per quarter ton for much of the eighteenth century, reached one hundred shillings per quarter ton in the 1790s. Great news for the producers, but far less so for consumers, who saw the price of bread rocket accordingly. The result was food riots.

At the start of the nineteenth century the situation was exacerbated when a succession of new corn laws reinforced the position of the producers. The 1804 Corn Law set out a sliding scale of duties for foreign imports, with the duties so high when the price was below sixty shillings as essentially to make it uneconomic for foreign producers to sell at those prices. In other words, the law effectively created a minimum price for grain, set at a level well above the historical average and far closer to the exaggerated level of wartime prices. In 1815, with crowds rioting on London streets, the sliding scale of duties was dropped in favour of a total ban on foreign imports under eighty shillings.

A battle was unfolding; one that anyone with one eye on the economic news will recognise today: a clash between those advocating protectionism and those pushing for a more liberal, free trade policy. What is different, of course, is who is on which side of the free trade fence. In the early nineteenth century, it was the campaigners out on the street who were shouting and rioting for a more liberal regime, while the policy makers were arguing for ever tighter restrictions.

In terms of politics, one of the problems for the campaigners was that their views were under-represented in Parliament. With universal suffrage over a century away, a limited electorate got to choose MPs – the 1832 Reform Act ruled that only men with assets above forty shillings could vote. As a result, the aristocracy, whose ownership of the land made them the dominant force in agriculture, were represented in abundance.

The Corn Laws, though, were an economic rather than a political issue and it was, appropriately enough, an economic factor that tipped the balance against these vested interests. The Industrial Revolution, as we saw in Chapter 2, transformed Britain. By the turn of the nineteenth century, self-made men were beginning to wield an influence of their own. The more successful the industrialists became, the less important agriculture was to the British economy: indeed, some went as far as to suggest that it was hindering its development. In 1815 the economist David Ricardo published a pamphlet that argued that corn laws were holding the country back. British labour and capital were being wasted in agriculture, and by importing foreign grain these resources could be freed up to work in the more productive industrial sector.

It was the changing economic balance of Britain, as much as anything, that tipped the scales in favour of the free trade argument. In 1838 the Anti Corn Law League was formed: a slightly strange amalgamation of the Manchester cotton manufacturers, led by the charismatic Richard Cobden, and the Chartist movement, whose main goal was electoral reform and widening the electorate beyond the tiny current franchise. The Anti Corn Law League were helped in spreading their message by developments such as the expanding rail network and the launch of the penny post: Cobden was able to travel the country to champion his cause in a way that would have been impossible twenty years earlier; with the postal system now cheap and universal, the League was able to bombard the electorate with a succession of carefully argued pamphlets.

Cobden's argument for repeal of the Corn Laws was threefold. First, there were clear economic benefits for everyone from their repeal: the influx of foreign grain would lead to a corresponding widening of export markets for British goods; this in turn would lead to a greater demand for labour, with accordingly higher wages and cheaper food. Cobden also suggested that increased trade between nations would make them more interdependent and thus less likely to go to war with each other, and with all the economic disruption that went with it (not least, it should probably be noted, for a company exporting cotton textiles abroad). The League's second main argument was political: the Corn Laws benefited the landed aristocracy to the detriment of everybody else. John Bright, one of the leading voices of the movement, described the battle as between 'the middle and industrious classes' and 'the sordidness of a large section of the aristocracy'.

It is perhaps the third tenet of the League's beliefs that is the most interesting. Cobden and his colleagues suggested that there was a moral case for free trade. They argued that being able to buy goods as cheaply as possible was a civil liberty, and that governments should not intervene to stop this happening. The interests of the consumer, in other words, should be more prevalent than those of the producer. This was an argument that resonated with Richard Cobden's audience, and is a belief that has continued to blossom in British minds ever since. Britain was a consumer society before any other nation, and the interests of this group continue to dominate the economic landscape.

The Conservative prime minister Robert Peel knew that the economic tide was turning against him. His attempts at defusing the situation with revised Corn Laws in the early 1840s failed to stem support for the Anti Corn Law League, even though historians suggest that these earlier changes and reduced duties had a bigger impact than the final repeal. The League's focus was the anticipated 1848 election, at which they hoped to back enough candidates to get a free trade majority in Parliament. But the terrible harvest of 1845 brought matters to a head: Peel realised that the import of foreign grain was essential to avoid starvation, and that once the barrier had been lifted it would be all but impossible to raise again. So, despite being the leader of the landowners' party, he moved to repeal the Corn Laws. This decision led to his downfall as prime minister, split the Conservatives in two and pushed the party out of power for years.

The repeal of the Corn Laws was a watershed. Cobden's campaign had sown a seed of support for free trade, the influence of which on policy and public opinion still lingers. In the late nineteenth century the growing economic might of the United States and increasing military tension between nations led to a sharp and sustained return to high tariffs and protectionism. France, for example, increased duty on foreign grain to stop their farming industry being overrun by American imports. In Britain, however, the instinct was different: consumers liked the lower prices, and so little help was offered to the declining agriculture sector.

At the start of the twentieth century the rising tariffs of other leading nations were having a detrimental effect on the British economy. Unemployment was going up, as were prices. Could

Britain continue with its free trade policy while other governments were stepping in to protect their industries? Led by Joseph Chamberlain, a powerful political lobby began to argue for what they called Tariff Reform – helping home industry via protectionist policies on foreign goods. Protectionism versus free trade rose up once again to become one of the major political questions of the era: it was the defining issue of the 1906 general election, and also critical in the subsequent elections of 1910.

The pro Free Trade movement of the Edwardian era was every bit as persuasive in its campaigning as the Anti Corn Law League had been sixty years earlier. Indeed, it was the Britain of the 1840s that the group successfully invoked: the 'hungry forties', in which the working man was made to go without because of the protectionist greed of the grain producers. A best-selling book of the same name was published, recounting unvarnished recollections of how hard life was back then – stories of men stealing turnips at night to feed their children because bread was too expensive. White bread was a luxury that only a lucky few could afford to buy.

Free Trade was portrayed as the knight in shining armour that liberated the working man from such oppression. The repeal of the Corn Laws was cast as the beginning of Britain's march towards freedom, the first in a line of progressive acts that made the country more liberal, more democratic, and where everyone's interests were represented at the top table. The role of the British as consumers was one that had been taken to the nation's hearts. 'By ensuring cheapness,' Frank Trentmann argues in his book *Free Trade Nation*, 'Free Trade guaranteed a fair price for basic goods for the people, especially groups formally excluded from politics, like the poor, women and children.' Trentmann quotes a Conservative from Yorkshire, who said, 'The poor people hereabouts look upon Free Trade as we do upon Trial by Jury ... as an absolute fundamental right.'

Whatever the rights and wrongs of the pro-Free Trade campaigners' version of history, there is no doubt that as with the Anti Corn Law League, the movement was hugely successful in defining public opinion. The 1906 election in particular was a landslide for Free Trade supporters and was an important swing factor in the 1910 elections as well. For all the efforts of the tariff reform movement, the arguments for free trade remained the received wisdom of the wider electorate.

As the twentieth century progressed, and Britain's empire began to retreat from its high-water mark of economic might, so the nation's attitudes were buffeted by the prevailing economic winds. In the inter-war years, the difficulties faced by the world economy led to Britain following other countries in adopting protectionist policies: by 1932, there was a 10 per cent tariff on most foreign goods, and trade barriers were erected beyond the British Empire. Adopting such policies was understandable, but they serve to underline the detrimental effect of such actions. Between the start of the First World War and the end of the Second, the levels of trade in the world economy remained stagnant, in stark contrast to its growth in preceding and subsequent years. The economic mantra of these years was 'autarky' – self-sufficiency within an economy. Back in the 1840s, Richard Cobden had argued that trade and peace were interwoven: as the world's interdependent links unravelled, and we were plunged into two devastating wars, his warnings felt unfortunately prescient.

The story of free trade since the Second World War moved on to the world of multilateral agreements and trade negotiations. Britain has again found itself at the free trade end of the spectrum in negotiating a succession of General Agreements on Tariffs and Trade (GATT) and in the creation of the World Trade Organization, which has had the effect of moving the world economy away from protectionism and towards a more liberal system. The original GATT agreement in 1947 saw a reduction in 45,000 bilateral tariffs, which covered 20 per cent of the world's trade. The result has been a return to the levels of growth in world trade seen before the inter-war years: in the second half of the twentieth century, world trade grew at an average rate of 6.4 per cent a year.

Britain has not only been one of the EU member states most keen on signing multilateral trade agreements, it has also been a relatively good citizen in terms of the spirit of the WTO rules. It is always tempting for nations to tax imports by arguing that they are being dumped at below-cost prices. In the mid-noughties, the then EU trade commissioner Peter Mandelson found himself in the middle of what the media dubbed 'bra wars': French and Italian clothes manufacturers wanted quotas on Chinese imports to protect their industries, while British retailers wanted the goods to satisfy our demand for cheap products.

The importance of the British consumer remains central to our economy and our way of life. We are a nation that bemoans the homogeneity of the British high street, but at the same time takes advantage of the low prices that such large chains bring. We might voice concern at the effect that internet retailers have had on British bookshops, but the number of people buying from Amazon vastly outweighs those dedicated souls paying full price at their local independent store. The consumer instincts instilled by the Anti Corn Law League all those years ago still prevail, even if the intellectual arguments for them are rarely articulated at a popular level.

Those instincts perhaps explain why the Marshall Fund's Transatlantic Trends data finds us better disposed than almost anybody towards China's economic advance. We identify ourselves as consumers buying cheap Chinese exports, whereas the French view themselves as producers threatened by those very same products.

Of course, I do not want to overstate the differences between us.

In practice, almost no country is unambiguously supportive of free trade. All countries have elements of economic nationalism in their behaviour and those countries – such as France – that purport to be against globalisation often embrace it in their actions.

But, for all this, Britain does appear to be untypically globally integrated for a nation of its size. Not only do we trade very heavily: many of our service industries are internationally facing, a higher proportion of British employees work in foreign-owned companies than do workers in our closest neighbours (although, interestingly, the French are not far behind), and entities from other countries have been allowed to buy up more of our nation than elsewhere while we in turn have bought large amounts of other countries.

In short, our history has shaped our attitudes towards trade and openness. Our attitudes have shaped our policy, and policy has helped shape our economy. In turn, the economy that has evolved here has entrenched our attitudes and policy.

Perhaps the neatest way of exemplifying how different we are is through a comparison of car markets in some of the different European countries. The conspicuous features of the UK, in con-

3.1 How International We Are
Proportion of employees working for organisations under foreign control, 2006

| | percentage of total employment | |
	Manufacturing	Service sector
United Kingdom	28.4	12.6
France	26.3	11.3
Germany	16.5	6.4
Italy	10.1	6.9

Source: *OECD Factbook 2010*

trast to its similar-sized European counterparts, are the lack of a local mass-car marque; the importance of foreign-owned plants; and the foreign ownership of British car brands from Rolls-Royce to Mini. That makes us very different from France and Italy, where both car production and car purchasing are affected by the presence of national companies.

In the first quarter of 2010 French car-maker Renault had a market share in Italy of 8 per cent and in France of 29 per cent. At around the same time, Fiat had a market share in France of about 4 per cent but of 30 per cent at home in Italy. The British consumer is at something of an advantage to the French and Italians in being able to make an unbiased choice of car. In Britain, both Renault and Fiat had shares below 5 per cent.

Wait, I hear you say. At least the French and Italians have a Renault and a Fiat. What have we got? The answer is that our global openness has given us a pretty good car industry, even if it is not one that produces millions of cars emblazoned with our own flag. Looking at data from 2007, just before the financial crash, our car industry measured in terms of the gross value added produced was only marginally smaller than that of France, and was rather bigger than that of Italy.

Amazing as that might seem, while the French and Italians made money from building their own brand cars we made money from building Hondas and Nissans.

There is another, more subtle, point to be made. The integration of productive activity across different countries disguises what we produce. We may look at the brands of cars being driven around the world's streets and think that Britain doesn't make that many. But there are two ways to be big in automotive: you can make 100 per cent of 1 per cent of the world's cars, or you can make 1 per cent of 100 per cent of the world's cars. Britain is closer to following the second of those models.

So, while the value of our automotive output was not too

different from that of France in 2007, France produced a far greater number of actual vehicles – 2.5 million compared to only 1.5 million in Britain. If we produce the same value overall but fewer cars, we must be producing more expensive cars (which seems plausible as both Land Rover and Jaguar are important producers here) and, in addition, we must have been producing more *parts* of vehicles.

As it happens, that is very likely. A British company, GKN, has a global turnover of about £2 billion in the automotive sector but it doesn't make a single car. It does, however, have a 30 per cent share of the market for drive shafts – the bit of the car between the engine and the wheels. GKN is the clear world leader in that little piece of the engine. You might see a Volkswagen or a Toyota in the street, but you don't see the drive shaft. But the GKN product is there, turning the wheels of many of those cars. (Although it should be conceded that the company makes most of them outside the UK as they are too heavy to transport across continents sensibly.)

The car industry is but one example of Britain's relative openness. The important question is whether we should become more like the French – more nationalist, and more inclined to buy British?

You might have detected a degree of scepticism about economic nationalism in my account of the 'I'm Backing Britain' campaign, and it is fair to say that some of the flaws in that effort are more obvious today than they were then. Most particularly, it is getting even more difficult to decide in an economy as extrovert as ours, which nationality to ascribe to anything.

For a company to be British, is it the ownership that matters, or the jurisdiction in which it is registered, or is it where the bulk of its activity occurs? And what if there is no single centre for its activities?

What passport would you issue a product made in China

which was designed by a British person living in the United States who worked for a company owned by investors around the world? Such complicated arrangements are not untypical, and they make it almost impossible to settle on a neat definition of nationality.

Even one existing Buy British website, buybritish.com (strangely, it doesn't use the .co.uk domain name) has to have a page explaining its Britishness ratings with a five-dimensional classification to alert you to exactly how British each product is.

In short, even if it was a mistake for us to be as global as we are, it's probably too late to do much about it. We are already entwined and the cost of cutting existing links to clarify what is ours would be absurdly costly.

And even if we could define Britishness, there is another reason not to retreat into autarky.

The rest of the world has a lot to teach us and the more closely we encourage companies that are operating in the UK to also operate elsewhere, the more likely it is that we keep up with the best standards available.

A very good example was the influence of the Japanese on British factories in the eighties. When Nissan opened in Sunderland it didn't just create one factory's worth of new jobs in the northeast of England, it revamped the supply chains. It shook the UK parts makers out of their low standards and, in doing so, gave the entire British motor industry a future.

Other factories soon adopted Japanese production methods, which were unambiguously a good thing for UK industry: there was less 'them and us' than the prevailing British norm, and systems were introduced that were designed to expose production problems of any kind. Japanese words like *kanban* and *kaizen* came to British factories.

GKN's plant in Castle Bromwich – making those drive shafts for many UK manufacturers – had to raise its game when the

Japanese auto-makers came to town. The machines were painted white (thus better exposing any leaks and giving a lighter air to the whole atmosphere); the apartheid management–worker canteen system was removed; the supervisors were taken from mezzanine offices down to the same level as the plant floor; and a more sophisticated production flow system was introduced, which minimised the need to carry half-finished items around the factory.

Typical of these Japanese innovations was the introduction of the just-in-time system. In the old days, each stage of the production process would have boxes of spare parts ready so that if a problem arose somewhere else in the flow, everyone had enough to be getting on with while it was sorted out. In the new system there was no such buffer. If something went wrong everyone knew about it and soon a permanent solution would be found to prevent such problems arising again.

Continuous improvement and high quality were achieved. At Castle Bromwich, GKN reckon to have gone from three or four hundred duds out of every million shafts produced, down to fewer than ten.

This would have been achieved even if the UK was not as open an economy as it is. But the more we let foreigners in and the more we let Brits out, the sooner we hook up to these kinds of best practices. It would be nice if we invented everything ourselves, but in the absence of our doing so it is probably better for us to join the competition than to stand aside.

While most would accept that inward investors have improved British manufacturing, there is another area of concern that derives from the openness of the UK economy: the degree to which foreign corporations have been allowed to buy up British companies – Cadbury being taken over by Kraft in 2010, for example, or Rowntree by Nestlé in 1988. To what extent should we be worried by these cases?

Even this kind of trade does bring unrecognised advantages.

Most obviously there is the money – if foreigners want to buy things at high prices from us, as a first approximation, one would assume that by selling them we get richer rather than poorer. Indeed, one might think that one way that Britain pays its way in the world is to create companies and then sell them and create some more.

If a global company such as Nestlé wants to buy a smaller UK company like Rowntree because it thinks it can sell great Rowntree confectionery in different countries, would we not welcome that? Who would turn down the chance to make the KitKat the world's favourite chocolate bar?

But while all this is true and while it is the case that if we had to choose whether to be completely open or completely shut we would probably opt for the former, in practice we do not have to make an all-or-nothing choice. And there is one important point to be made against opening Britain too far. Britain needs economic diversity in order to flourish and, being a relatively medium-sized country with an unusual degree of freedom for foreign companies to come and go, the country has to be careful that its balanced economic ecology is not trampled on. It is one thing to say that Cadbury and Rowntree might be well placed under foreign ownership, but it is quite another for there to be swathes of activities that are removed from the UK altogether. There is no reason for foreign companies to be worried about the balance between different kinds of activity in the UK, between services, managerial and manufacturing functions for example. And an entirely free market may not deliver the balance that suits the domestic environment. That has to be watched and I'll return to that later.

All in all, though, our long history as a trading nation and our consumerist instincts have made us relatively open to global integration. It has made us what we are today and there is no going back.

PART 2

MANUFACTURING

4

The Psychology of Manufacturing

In 1972 my parents bought a book called *Know Britain: The Heritage and Institutions of an Offshore Island*. The cover showed a picture of Concorde, a gold sovereign, the QE2, a coal mine and a London pub. Everything you could possibly need to know was in that book – from the counties and their populations to the order of succession right down to number 36 (Benedikte Ferner, daughter of Princess Astrid of Norway) to an inventory of the RAF's aircraft. I often referred to *Know Britain* and kept it in my bedroom because in the days before Wikipedia it was a mine of useful information. Those were the days when facts didn't become out-of-date quite so quickly. You could refer to it years after publication without quibbling with the data.

By the late eighties, however, I realised the book really was past its prime, but I hung on to it anyway. I thought that it would one day enjoy an afterlife as a useful historical archive and, I'm pleased to say, *Know Britain*'s moment has come.

I have been looking at it again recently, in particular its chapter entitled 'Economy, Industry and Trade'. It tells us that Britain is ninth in the world in terms of national income per capita and provides 8 per cent of the world's exports of manufactured products. It doesn't just talk about Britain's manufacturing. It is noted that Britain is one of the world's major banking nations and is the 'financial centre of the sterling area, an economic grouping which includes about one quarter of the population of the world'. But it is the physical production that seems to matter most: 'This clear commitment to a manufacturing economy is borne out by the fact that no other developed country has such a small proportion of the working population engaged in agriculture.' To back up the assertion, the book tells us that Britain at the end of 1970 had seventy-one blast furnaces and 756,000 people employed in textiles.

How things change.

These days, we have seven blast furnaces and just over 100,000 people work in textiles. Few would say that we have 'a clear commitment to a manufacturing economy'. Our market share of the world's manufactured exports has halved. No wonder we have a sense of our nation as in manufacturing decline.

Is this really a decline? The answer is both yes and no. Yes, manufacturing has become a far smaller share of our economy. From about a third of everything we produced when *Know Britain* was put together to about an eighth today. But this is in the context of a country that is far richer and more successful than it was in past decades. In 2007, before the financial crisis hit, our manufactured output was 28 per cent higher than it was in 1970. In fact, our manufacturing output hit its all-time peak in February 2008.

This does not stop people worrying that we don't make enough. Or, that if we do we are somehow in a slow lane with others overtaking us. I noticed a recent article in the *Guardian* headlined 'UK economy in 2050: stuck in the past and trailing Vietnam'. Little in the article justified the claim. In fact, the

The visually stunning British pavilion at the Shanghai Expo, 2010.

The Derwent Valley, home of Arkwright's original mill, was the birthplace of the Industrial Revolution.

© AA World Travel Library/TopFoto

Cotton mills in Union Street, Manchester, 1835. Lancashire became the centre of the cotton textiles industry in the early nineteenth century.

Mary Evans Picture Library

Power looms in a cotton mill, 1800s.

© 2001 Credit: Topham/Fotomas

The British car industry in the seventies: union members showing their support for striking British Leyland workers, 1970. Getty Images

The British car industry today: Nissan workers in action on its production line in Sunderland. © PA Photos/TopFoto

I'm Backing Britain: the five Surbiton secretaries whose actions started the 1968 campaign.
© Credit: TopFoto

Despite this gentleman's enthusiasm for 'I'm Backing Britain', the hoped-for bounce in economic activity failed to materialise.
Photo by Bill Zygmant/Rex Features

Punch cartoon from 1845, depicting Free Trade campaigner Richard Cobden hurrying Prime Minister Robert Peel along the Free Trade path.

World History Archive/TopFoto

A hat designed by London hatter W. Marriott in support of the abolition of the Corn Laws.

World History Archive/TopFoto

Joseph Chamberlain campaigning against Free Trade at Bingley Hall, Birmingham, 1903.

© 1999 Credit: Topham Picturepoint

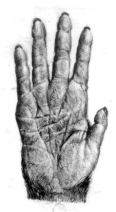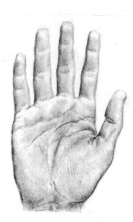

The hands of a gibbon, chimpanzee and *Homo sapiens*. Is there a link between our pleasure in making things and the evolution of the human hand?
© 2003 Credit: Topham Picturepoint

The Acheulean hand axe. This basic design was used and made by man for the best part of a million years. Mary Evans Picture Library

Made in Britain: the
McLaren MP4-12C
sports car . . .

. . . the Eurofighter
Typhoon . . .

. . . and the Brompton
folding bicycle.

The Thanet Offshore Wind Farm, the largest of its kind in the world.
TopFoto

The Burgar Hill Orkney wind turbine. Britain missed an opportunity to become a world leader in wind technology in the eighties.
© orkneypics/Alamy

table accompanying the piece showed that Vietnam would still be trailing the UK in 2050, even if it succeeded in going through decades of rapid economic development. But you will not be unfamiliar with the kind of insecurity such articles engender.

When we consider what Britain does and how it will continue to pay its way in the world, the single most important task is to get manufacturing in perspective. To put it in its rightful place. Neither elevated to a special status above all other sectors of the economy nor looked down upon as old and outmoded. Unfortunately, the debate over manufacturing is polarised. Some people think manufacturing is a bit grubby and that financial services are what all modern economies get up to these days. But a far larger number, in my experience, think manufacturing should be seen as part of a special higher class of activity. It seems that, deep down, we are instinctively programmed to think of physical production as the most useful activity.

This is quite natural. Everywhere I went in the filming of the *Made in Britain* television series, I asked people involved in manufacturing if it gave them an innate sense of satisfaction. The answer was invariably 'yes'. One of the clearest responses came from an engineer, Felina Merrifield, who works on building the Typhoon aircraft at a BAE plant. Felina joined the company in September 1997, immediately after finishing school. She had always been interested in engineering and saw herself as a 'hands on' person. She was fortunate that her school had fostered links with British Aerospace, and applied for a craft apprenticeship with the company.

What interested me in particular was the enthusiasm that Felina clearly had for her job. She described her satisfaction in creating products, turning them from an idea on a piece of paper into something tangible. Felina enjoyed the sense of responsibility that came with her work, and the ultimate reward is the finished product: she is very proud of what she helps to produce, and describes her sense of fulfilment whenever she sees a Typhoon flying over her home town of Preston. With people pointing up at the sky, excited by the sight of the plane, Felina enjoys the satisfaction of thinking, I made that. She had spent a period of work experience for a graphic design company but never found it very satisfying.

Felina's obvious pride in her work could not be in starker contrast to Mitch Robbins, the character that Billy Crystal played in the 1991 film *City Slickers*. Robbins works in radio advertising, more specifically selling the time slots in commercial breaks – 'selling air', as it is known. In the film, he is invited to speak at his son's school as part of a programme of parents explaining the world of work to the children. The father speaking before Robbins is a construction worker, and finishes to huge applause. Mitch Robbins's son, played by a very young Jake Gyllenhaal, is so embarrassed by what his father does that he claims he works on a submarine. When Mitch Robbins eventually explains to the class what he does do, the response is bewilderment and indifference.

Both Felina Merrifield's experience and the Billy Crystal character in *City Slickers* touch on what is a fascinating subject for economists and psychologists alike. In terms of monetary value, being an aircraft engineer and an advertising salesman are each well rewarded. Yet at the same time there seems to be a fundamental difference between making an aircraft and 'selling air': the contrasting response of people in Preston to seeing a Typhoon and the classroom in *City Slickers* hints at something that the remuneration of the labour market does not reflect. Is there something intrinsic to the process of making things that is innately satisfying? If so, where does this come from? And in a modern, developed economy, does this matter?

The value of making things has long been acknowledged. In

The Craftsman, Richard Sennett cites the example of Hephaestus, Greek god of fire and craftsmen. Hephaestus is lavishly praised by Homer in *The Iliad* as 'a bringer of peace and maker of civilisation'. Early Christian thinking made much of the fact that Jesus was the son of a carpenter – a humble yet practical and worthwhile profession that one could learn from. In medieval society, meanwhile, the importance of the craftsman was clear in the growing political and economic power of the guilds.

One writer who has attempted to make sense of this question is Matthew Crawford, the author of *The Case for Working with Your Hands*, which is illuminatingly subtitled 'Why Office Work is Bad for Us and Fixing Things Feels Good'. Crawford worked as a director of a political think tank before quitting to open a bike shop. He not only found the experience of fixing and fine-tuning motorbikes a more rewarding experience, but to his surprise also found it more intellectually stimulating: 'the wad of cash in my pants feels different to the checks I cashed in my previous job ... [I] could not see the rationale for my being paid at all – what tangible goods or useful services was I providing to anyone? This sense of uselessness was dispiriting.' The contrast with his new career could not be clearer: 'I feel I have a place in society. Whereas "think tank" is an answer that, at best, buys you a few seconds when someone asks what you do and try to figure what it is than you in fact do, with "motorcycle mechanic" I get immediate recognition.'

One of the things, then, that Matthew Crawford and Felina Merrifield have in common, and that Billy Crystal's *City Slickers* character lacks, is recognition. It is rewarding for Felina to see people's reaction to the aircraft that she helped to build; it feels rewarding for Matthew Crawford that people instantly understand what it is that he does. There is no reason why this satisfaction needs to be linked to occupations that involve making things, but there is something about a physical end product that anyone and everyone can immediately understand and respond to.

Another attribute of making things is the ability for the creator to put his or her stamp on the work. Greek potters inscribed their name on their work – 'Exekias made me'; Roman builders would mark their work both to denote where they were from and also to say, as slaves, 'I exist'. The Yorkshire craftsman Robert Thompson was renowned for marking his furniture with a mouse carved into the wood. At the factory in Brentford, west London, that makes Brompton bikes, which I visited in the making of the *Made in Britain* programmes, I was shown the personal signature of a brazer on one of the parts he had created. His personal sign was not dissimilar to the famous mark of Zorro, the Z slashed out by the fictional hero.

This urge to leave a signature is something that philosophers call the 'politics of presence'; Crawford describes it as 'a kind of communion, between others and the future'. The maker is putting something of themselves into their creation, which has the potential for subsequent generations to admire and appreciate. Once more, this sense of pride and ownership isn't necessarily unique to the making of physical things but again feels more straightforwardly linked.

This personal pride in physical work leads on to the idea that working with other people to produce something feels rewarding and worthwhile. This sense of community is something that again takes us all the way back to early societies. In his book *The Hand* Frank R. Wilson describes the process of 'heterotechnic co-operation' as distinguishing man from other creatures: from the very beginning, man would divide up the task of making tools, with different people working on different parts of the process. Studies of Australian aborigines show that they 'are not simply jacks-of-all-trades with crude stone tools. In deceptively primitive working conditions they actually demonstrate all of the basic principles of modern manufacturing ... Silicon Valley designers and engineers conceptualise, design, test and perfect electronic machines in a process that is indistinguishable from that seen in Aborigines in stone tool manufacture.'

I don't find it particularly surprising that so many of us have such an affinity with physical production. The ability to use tools is one of the fundamentals of human evolution. Man isn't the only creature to do so – chimpanzees, for example, are also capable of creating basic items – but what singles out the evolution of man is the development of the hand: the importance of the thumb and the ability to grip in different ways allowed early man the possibility to create and make tools well beyond, if you'll excuse the pun, a chimpanzee's grasp. The ancestors of *Homo erectus* made tools that were essentially lumps of rock bashed to create an edge. *Homo erectus*, in contrast, made the more familiar shape of the Acheulean hand axe, and this basic design was used by early man for the best part of a million years.

This might all help explain where Felina Merrifield's pride in contributing to the production of a Typhoon comes from. But I wonder whether we overstate our love of the physical? The hands do not, after all, work separately from the mind: a good physical job is as much a mental as a manual process, a process of creativity and problem-solving, a combination of not just thinking or doing but thinking *and* doing. A skilled manufacturing job has all of these attributes as, for Matthew Crawford, does the fixing of motorbikes. The work might seem physical at first glance (an idea reinforced by the end result), but it is the stimulation of having to think things through that makes the work rewarding. Such reward can be found – or found wanting – as much in an office as on a factory floor.

If the pleasure of making things taps into something in our evolution, we need to be wary of placing too much emphasis on it. According to the science writer Matt Ridley, there is a mismatch between what we do now and what evolution has prepared us for. So, for example, our bodies have been designed to crave sugar; this came about because of the difficulty of finding fruit to eat in the past. But while this craving helped early man to survive, our predilection for sugar leads to a present day fondness for sugary foods and drinks, with negative consequences for our health in modern times.

Could it be that we cling to our longing for tool-making when our economy should be evolving beyond such activity? Maybe our yearning for manufacturing is simply a failure to appreciate the value of non-physical labour. To clarify some of the issues, let's look at an example in some detail. I'll call it the case of the fancy towel boutique.

The question is this: which contributes more to life, a manufacturer mass producing relatively plain towels that fetch a wholesale price of £10? Or a fancy towel boutique that puts the mediocre mass-produced towels on a tastefully designed shelf, gives them a homey kind of brand name and wraps them in nice paper (replete with rustling sheets of soft tissue between the folds of the towel) when satisfied customers buy them for £25?

The towel factory operates out of town and employs people in blue-collar outfits. The workers get the usual satisfaction from the physical experience of seeing the towels piled up in cartons as they leave the plant. The shop, on other hand, is in a prime location and employs people in fashionable clothes who take the time to make the customers feel special when they come in to the store. They discuss bathroom décor, colour combinations and fluffiness. They appear to be interested in the towelling needs of those they talk to and they choose background music which it is pleasurable to buy towels to. They also keep track of trends in towel-buying, which are reflected in the orders they place with the factory.

Compare the two economic activities. The towel factory creates £10 of value. The shop, on the other hand, creates £15 –

the £25 at which it sells the towel minus the £10 it had to pay for the towel. Instinctively, I think most of us would think the towel maker is more important to this particular supply chain than the shop. And most of us would hold on to that instinct notwithstanding the fact that I have constructed the example to make the shop's contribution to the £25 price paid by the consumer bigger than that of the towel factory.

So why do most of us think this way? First, the shop couldn't survive if no one was out there making the towels for the shop to sell. The shop needs the towel-maker for its existence. And, if this particular shop had not sold the towel for £25 a supermarket might have sold it straight out of the carton for £18. The consumer would have got the same towel and would have been £7 richer. Moreover, the towel lasts for years, while the customer's experience in the pleasant surroundings of the store is ephemeral. Once the fancy packaging has been thrown away you are left with the same old towel. It is almost as if there is something phony about the shop, as though it is trying to dress up mutton as lamb.

These are all natural reactions to the softer side of our economy. But let me now make the case for the towel boutique. In the real world, market stalls and supermarkets sell towels at knockdown prices but some people still prefer to spend more money to buy them in more voluptuous conditions. If enough consumers are happy to do so to justify the existence of the fancy towel boutiques, who are we to say that those consumers are wasting their money? And while it is of course true that any towel shop needs a towel-maker to sustain its existence, is it not also true that towel-makers need places that sell towels? If you argue that the towel-maker would find an alternative place to sell its towels, can I not retort with the claim that the shop would find other things to sell in the absence of the towel?

It is true that the towel lives on when the satisfaction

provided to the customer by the towel shop has expired. But if the shop directs the customer to a towel of the right colour and texture, the effect is not entirely short-lived. And even if it is, what does that matter?

I think that when people draw a distinction between the manufacturer and the retailer they are retreating to their evolutionary instincts and thinking about the issue as if we live in a subsistence economy with barely enough to keep ourselves alive. If we had almost nothing and had to make a choice between a towel and a fancy boutique selling towels we would surely go for the towel. But we do not live in such an economy. The choice isn't a towel or no towel; it is a choice between yet another towel or a nicer retail experience. Is it really obvious which is the more desirable?

My suspicion is that if you are reading this book you are more likely to be a manufacturing enthusiast than a manufacturing sceptic. If you are, the economist John Kay rather disparagingly refers to you as a 'manufacturing fetishist'. I don't want to put you off your fetish entirely. I share your view that manufacturing is important. But, for me, lots of other sectors are as well, and each is worth what it is worth. No more, no less.

There are huge differences between a subsistence economy, a poor industrial economy and a modern affluent one. It is best to tailor your instincts to the one you actually live in rather than one left behind centuries ago.

So the most important thing to do in thinking about the modern British economy is to ignore our subsistence-economy instincts and place ourselves firmly in the present. How far should we be worrying about manufacturing today and the decline in the number of blast furnaces and textile workers? The answer is we do need to worry – and we'll consider why in Chapter 6. But before we get to that we have to understand why we don't have to worry nearly much as most people do.

The main reason for this assertion is that, far from decaying, manufacturing is one of the most dynamic sectors of our economy, and is one that improves its performance most quickly year by year. Ironically, it is that success which gives people an entirely false perception about the state of our factories. As they get more productive their costs tend to fall (or at least rise more slowly than elsewhere) and the prices of manufactured goods follow.

The paradox is that this success in manufacturing makes you feel it is in more of a decline than it is. As it takes fewer people to produce the same amount each year, there is a tendency for manufacturing jobs to be lost. We end up with smaller numbers working in factories but more goods coming out of them. You can call that decline, but do at least be aware of what kind of decline it is.

The crucial feature of manufacturing is that we tend to improve our ability to produce things in that sector more quickly than we do in other parts of the economy, for example in personal services or the arts. This was a point made back in the sixties by one of the greatest economists never to win a Nobel Prize, the American William Baumol. In 1965 he produced a paper, co-authored by William Bowen, called 'On the Performing Arts: The anatomy of their economic problems', and then his own 'Macroeconomics of Unbalanced Growth: The anatomy of urban crisis' in 1967

In the latter, he found a good example: 'A half-hour horn quintet calls for the expenditure of two-and-a-half man hours in its performance, and any attempt to increase productivity here is likely to be viewed with concern by critics and audience alike.' In other words, it takes the same number of people to play a quintet as it did in Mozart's day.

What a contrast to the output of motor cars. Nissan says that in 2000 it took a total of over ten man hours to produce a car. It is fewer than eight hours today. The workers have been equipped with machines that have made production far easier and we have designed far better cars. And, in contrast to the horn quintet, it is also possible to ask the workers to work faster. In short, we have got far better at making cars and no better at playing horn quintets. In fact, we have got better at making most physical things but not at delivering most human services. We are able to farm with fewer people but we still need as many staff to wait on tables at a posh restaurant as ever. We can manufacture buses more efficiently but each bus still needs at least one driver.

The consequence of these simple observations is that, over time, the price of manufactured goods tends to fall in comparison to everything else as production costs come down. If you want to buy a bus it gets cheaper, but if you want to ride on one it does not. Food gets cheaper but restaurant meals do not as the most important component of the cost is labour.

The phenomenon is evident in the inflation figures produced by the Office for National Statistics. You are probably used to seeing headlines about the different measures of inflation that are published each month: the Retail Prices Index (RPI), which has been used for many decades as a broad indicator of inflation; CPI, the measure targeted by the Bank of England; and the one that *used* to be targeted by the Bank of England, RPIX.

Often more interesting than overall inflation are the many detailed statistics that are produced at the same time, giving individual inflation rates for different items or groups of items. In particular, the statisticians produce an inflation rate for 'goods' (mostly manufactured items) and one for 'services'. Services inflation typically runs ahead of goods inflation, which is a reflection of us getting better at making things faster than servicing them.

In fact, imagine we live in a curious world where we consume nothing other than cars and horn quintets. What will happen after a decade or two, during which time car production gets more and more efficient?

First, more and more cars will be churned out of the factory each year, but the availability of horn-quintet recitals will not rise as the same number of musicians resolutely stick to the tempos the composers intended. If we keep the factory going unabated people will eventually have cars coming out of their ears, so the relative price of quintets will rise and the price of cars will fall. That price change sends a signal to the producers of cars and to orchestras. As car manufacture is less profitable at low prices, it tells the car factory to slow down. And it tells the orchestras to expand. The implication is that the car factory will make workers redundant and orchestras will be hiring.

All that is happening in this society is that the capacity to make cars is growing more quickly than the desire to consume them. People want more cars, but they also want more quintets, so resources have to transfer out of the fast-improving sector to the less dynamic one. This is, of course, a rather stylised example, but it emphasises the key point that the most dynamic sectors of an economy can be the ones that generate the negative headlines.

But there is even more to this paradox.

Underpinning this transfer of resources out of a dynamic manufacturing sector is the observed taste of consumers for services. You would think that as manufactured goods become relatively cheaper we would want to buy relatively more of them. But when you look at the data it seems that is not the case. We want more services year by year, despite their fast-rising prices.

The things we want more are the things going up in price. If only we could force ourselves to love manufactured goods more we could be so easily satisfied. But we can't help our tastes and if it is services we want, do not be too surprised if a well-functioning economy delivers more services. The appeal of services is often overlooked, but it is documented by the statisticians who record which items we actually buy. They track in enormous detail the spending patterns of many different consumers to fill a typical household shopping basket. That is useful in compiling inflation figures, because it tells them what weight to attach to each of the hundreds of items whose prices are monitored.

After the Second World War, wild rabbits, mangles and corsets were in the shopping basket. Sadly they now have no place there and so the rising (or probably falling) price of corsets is no longer reflected in our monthly inflation data.

But most important to my argument is the diminishing weight of 'goods' as opposed to 'services' in household spending. As the prices of manufactured goods have fallen, so has their corresponding share of the typical household's spending. In 1987 goods accounted for 62 per cent of the shopping basket; by 1997 that had fallen to 56 per cent. And in 2007 it dipped below half for the first time, to 48 per cent. So the car–quintet economy in fact captures quite a lot of what has actually happened over the decades in the UK. The hourly output of our manufacturing activities has risen far more quickly than the hourly output of our service operations. The prices of those services have risen far more quickly than those of manufactured goods. Hence people have moved from working in factories to producing services, although we still tend to manufacture more year by year.

Some of this basic data is in Table 4.1, which represents the evolution of our economy over the decade up to 1997. I picked that period because after that things started changing very rapidly with the rise of China. (In the next chapter you can see what happened after China came along, but this table is designed to tell you about the natural development of our economy without those special circumstances exaggerating the effect.) In 1997 we were manufacturing more than in 1987, but it comprised a smaller share of our total output and fewer people were employed. Manufactured goods prices rose less quickly than those of services over the decade so, relative to services, goods became cheap. At

4.1 Manufacturing and Services
How the two sectors have evolved

	1987	1997
Typical shopping basket		
Percentage of spending on 'goods'	62	56
Percentage of spending on 'services'	30	35
Consumer price inflation		
Average 'good' priced at £1 in 1987	1.00	1.48
Average 'service' priced at £1 in 1987	1.00	1.76
Employment (millions)		
Manufacturing	4.87	4.28
Non-manufacturing	22.18	24.3
Output		
Manufacturing (billions of pounds, 1987 prices)	89.6	104.8
Manufacturing share of output (%)	23.3	20.3

Source: ONS, RPI, workforce jobs and *Blue Book* gross value added data

the same time our consumption – the contents of the typical shopping basket – became more heavily weighted towards services rather than manufactured goods.

What all this shows is that we cannot attribute all the unfortunate loss of manufacturing jobs to the fact that we don't value factories properly or we can't make things any more. The loss is not a sign that the government failed us or the Department of Trade and Industry didn't do its job. It is simply the outcome of those 'big forces' – mentioned in Chapter 2 – which guide an economy and make certain developments almost inevitable. As our tastes and technology change, so does our economic orientation. That is a sign of success, not of failure.

Indeed, you could read the table as telling us that we got so much better at making things that we didn't need to work so hard at it because we didn't want all the extra manufactured goods that we were able to produce. The service sector is the slow learner, and thus needs more help. By one means or another we have found ourselves transferring people over there.

Manufacturing is in decline. Long live manufacturing.

If you find this account too theoretical, and read it as simply a sophisticated way of justifying the callous destruction of everything that was good about our economy, let me try to persuade you of its relevance with an argument from history. We saw in the last chapter that the Corn Laws were designed to protect our farmers, just as some people would like to protect our manufacturers today. Certainly farming and food were understandably rather important to people in the eighteenth century.

But did farming really need such protection? In 1750 the population of England was about six million, and just under half of that number was working in agriculture. The country was a net exporter of food. Over the subsequent hundred years – a period usually referred to as encompassing an industrial revolution – agriculture enjoyed some momentous changes. We got considerably better at it. It was, in fact, a very dynamic sector of the economy.

This was, for example, because the turnip came along. That was quite a breakthrough. It allowed farmers to reduce the amount of fallow land in their possession considerably. (Turnips can be weeded using a hoe while they are in the ground. Previously, farmers had left ground fallow to weed it with a plough.) Wheat and barley became more prevalent, replacing low-yield crops such as rye. And then there was the reclamation of the fens, which allowed high-intensity arable farming to replace lower-value activities, like fishing and fowling, there.

Something else occurred over the same century. The population of England trebled. That would be staggering on its own, but only a tenth of those extra eleven million people ended up working on farms. The proportion of the population working in agriculture dropped from just under half to just under a quarter. In fact, by 1850, we had a smaller proportion of our workforce on farms than anywhere in the world.

This represented quite an economic achievement. Usually, when a population grew food would become short and prices would rise. Not this time. The agricultural historian Mark Overton writes of the period:

> For the first time in English history, there was no longer a direct relationship between population and food prices ... For the first time, growth in population did not lead to a rise in prices that would eventually check that growth.

Although there were occasions when prices did go up, thanks to factors such as war and poor harvests, overall the extra output of our farms – achieved with relatively few extra people – kept prices down notwithstanding the surge in population.

By 1850, England was a net importer of food. But by then it was an exporter of other things. The growing population could do things other than farm, and so in that century we graduated to other, more valuable, activities. What would our modern media have said about those trends if it had been around at the time?

It would have worried about the declining importance of farms as factories spread across the land. It would have worried about the food trade deficit. It would have given voice to the farm fetishists who argued that farming was a 'real' activity, in comparison to the trivial manufactured items that did little to sustain life. And it certainly would have been anxious about the loss of job opportunities on farms and the small proportion of the population in agriculture.

Nonetheless, it would have been wrong. Our economy found its way to activities more valuable than farming. That was not because farming was a dead business; it was because it had truly come alive. It wasn't because we failed to understand how important food was that we let more of our workers move into the cities. It was just that we now had enough food and could turn our thoughts elsewhere. Having created the productive capacity to make other things, we could afford to import food on a sizeable scale.

If it was silly two centuries ago to attempt to keep more workers in the countryside, it would be silly now to carry on producing more and more manufactured goods simply because we can. It is inevitable that a responsive and dynamic economy will transfer resources to the activities we value most highly. The story of farming back then explains why we should not be overly concerned about manufacturing now. Of course the comparison should not be stretched too far. Our population has not trebled in the last two decades so demand for manufactured goods has not risen as fast as for food back then. But the basic long-run observation that strong productivity growth in one sector can lead to a sense of decline is the same, it's just that in the twentieth century it was not the turnip that was important, but the silicon chip.

These long-run trends are both fascinating and disorientating. How can one sector be dynamic and growing and in relative decline all at the same time? But that is the long-run trend of manufacturing in the UK, certainly in the decades up to 1997. Even then we were thinking that we didn't 'make' very much in this country. Clearly a great deal of that sentiment was driven by a failure to appreciate the way in which our economy would naturally have to evolve. This is not to say that everything is perfect in UK manufacturing – we will get to the downsides in Chapter 6. But it is to say that before worrying about things you need to separate the good effects from the bad.

In the decade after 1997, however, things changed very rapidly. As we all know, something else came along to disrupt our manufacturing on top of the long-run trends: China. Suddenly it wasn't the usual, slow evolution of a modern economy, it was a scramble to send factories off shore. Britain's deindustrialisation accelerated as we relied more than ever on imported consumer goods.

What possible good could that have been doing us, and what is there left for us to make? That's where we'll go now, and just as this chapter has alerted you to the fact that some deindustrialisation is inevitable, the next one will also paint a picture that is more positive for Britain than you would imagine.

5

What We've Lost and What We've Gained

It was at the turn of the millennium that I really started to notice that something funny was happening.

Manufactured goods were becoming cheap. One couldn't help but notice it at electronics stores or DIY sheds, at clothes shops and gift boutiques. Prices seemed very low. It was around then that I was planning to get an old duvet dry-cleaned. My partner casually mentioned that it was in fact cheaper to buy a new one. He was right. Argos sold new duvets – albeit synthetic ones – for not much more than a tenner. Getting one dry-cleaned in London cost more like £25.

Then a newspaper ran an article on a decrease in the number of burglaries in the UK. It was not attributed to any increase in the number of police, but instead to the falling price of consumer durables. What sort of burglar would bother to nick a second-hand DVD player when you can buy a new, legal one for £20?

On a walk down the King's Road with a friend, I noticed a shop selling a pair of shoes for £5. It seemed exceptionally cheap at the time, more so considering that we then went to

Starbucks a few doors away and spent almost that much on a pair of coffees. Somehow it seemed ridiculous that there could be a one-to-one rate of exchange between a shoe and a coffee. But soon I noticed that the shoes were part of a trend, with Asda selling jeans for £5.

That Christmas my brother commented that his children were getting a huge number of presents, not because he was trying to be generous but because toys had become so cheap he could buy much more than he was used to on his budget. At about the same time, I wondered whether the burgeoning sprawl of Christmas lights also reflected the amazingly cheap prices at which the lights were now available.

In the last chapter we saw that there's a long-run trend towards relatively cheaper manufactured goods prices over the years. But this was far more extreme. Something was clearly going on. And it was not just a phenomenon supported by anec-dote; it was visible in the detailed inflation figures. The prices of certain manufactured goods began to fall, clothes and footwear in particular. They fell in price in 1996, then rose again in 1997, then fell again in 1998. They carried on falling year after year right up to 2010. Consumer durables too started to drop in price in 1998, again continuing down until 2010.

In the decade 1987 to 1997 the prices of goods rose somewhat more slowly than prices overall, but in the decade after 1997 the divergence in inflation rates picked up markedly. And on services throughout the period, the data could not be more clear: they were getting relatively more expensive. That explains why it was getting more pricey to buy services such as coffee-making or the dry-cleaning of duvets, and less pricey to buy new duvets and shoes.

You might feel that the story of the relative prices of duvets and dry-cleaning tells you rather little about the direction of the UK economy. But this is a misconception. Up until 1997, the divergence between goods and services prices is just yet more evidence for the Baumol effect outlined in Chapter 4.

But the acceleration of price divergence after 1997 reflects something else: the opportunity to assemble things at a low cost elsewhere in the world. In the late nineties in particular, it was in China. That has driven down the global price of manufactured goods, which has in turn made it less attractive to make them in the expensive countries of the West.

As a result, many of the trends that were apparent before China came along suddenly became exaggerated. You can see them in Table 5.1, which is simply an extension of Table 4.1 from the last chapter. In particular, you will see the loss of manufacturing jobs

5.1 Manufacturing and Services
How the two sectors have evolved

	1997	2007
Typical shopping basket		
Percentage of spending on 'goods'	56	48
Percentage of spending on 'services'	35	38
Consumer price inflation		
Average 'good' priced at £1 in 1997	1.00	1.07
Average 'service' priced at £1 in 1997	1.00	1.47
Employment (millions)		
Manufacturing	4.28	2.97
Non-manufacturing	24.3	28.58
Output		
Manufacturing (billions of pounds, 1987 prices)	104.8	109.1
Manufacturing share of output (%)	20.3	12.4

Source: ONS, RPI, workforce jobs and *Blue Book* gross value added data

and the fall in the manufacturing share of the economy. Both would have been unimaginable back in 1997.

The statistics did at least show a rise in manufacturing output: the same old pattern was evident. Growth and decline at the same time. But, interestingly, in this decade there was some reason to think that the figures perhaps flattered the role of our indigenous manufacturing sector. Companies that move their factory from the UK to China still count as manufacturing companies, even if they don't do any manufacturing here at all. That means that their UK staff – employed, for example, in management and selling – still count as manufacturing employees and their desk work counts as manufacturing.

Amazingly, with the equivalent of ten thousand factory jobs lost every month for ten years, UK unemployment remained modest over most of this period. In fact, the economy sucked in foreign workers and found jobs for them on a scale that no one would ever have thought possible. It was truly an astonishing period for Britain, one of incredible and rapid change. And, like all periods of change, it generated concern. With the emergence of China as the world's default location for manufacturing, what on earth would be left for the rest of us to do? If there had been concern about our role in the world before 2007, it was multiplied several times over after that, when the financial crisis made it apparent that the lifestyle to which we had become accustomed was not sustainable. Although the British were less specifically worried by China's rise than were the citizens of most other nations, the shift of economic power from west to east undoubtedly affected everyone in Europe and the US, denting our sense of economic and cultural superiority. So it is time to take stock of manufacturing's eastward drift.

Just as people have tended to worry too much about our de-industrialisation before China came along, they worried too much about our deindustrialisation afterwards. To a large extent, we did not export our factories to them because they are better than us, but because they are so far behind us economically and have few other things to do. Thus freed, we can get on with more valuable activities.

Let me elaborate the argument, because it is easy to be daunted by the progress China has made. In 1983, at the start of its industrial revolution, the average Chinese income was at about the same level as the average British income in 1700, just before our own industrial revolution. What is astounding about China's performance is that in the two decades after 1983 it made the same economic progress that Britain took two centuries to make. In other words, its industrialisation proceeded at ten times the pace of ours.

Is this because China is better at economics than us? Has it found some magic formula for manufacturing that has eluded the rest of the world? No, of course not. China has enjoyed one insuperable advantage over eighteenth-century Britain when it comes to industrialising: it didn't have to invent the concept of industrialisation, it just had to import it.

China's business model has been relatively simple. It has engaged in a process of learning by producing. It produces goods for Western customers; and in return it gets the chance to learn how Western companies produce. The product designs are imported, as is (or at least was) the capital equipment. Once China has successfully made things for the West it can adapt the formula to make them for itself.

Looking at the Chinese success from the outside, it is easy to feel inferior. There are many historic parallels to the fears of Chinese economy domination. Think back to America's anxieties about Japan in the eighties, for example. Or the British fear of German industrialisation in the nineteenth century. But it's particularly easy to become anxious about countries like China, whose economies grow remarkably quickly. Most of us seem to have a habit of extrapolating recent trends: we see China's output grow at about 10 per cent a year for the decade after 1997 and hence assume that the country will continue indefinitely on that trajectory.

It is quite understandable that we might think that way, and when we do we get some striking results. For example, imagine China started from now, with a per capita output about one seventh of ours, and suppose it did succeed in getting its economy to grow at ten per cent a year for the foreseeable future. Chinese per capita incomes would overtake ours after twenty-five years, and would be five times ours within another twenty-five.

The arithmetic of extrapolation – whether it is set out numerically or is just a vague mental picture – often produces stunning results. Extrapolate the growth of a tadpole and it doesn't take long for it to turn into a whale. But, in practice, extrapolation is often misleading. While it is true that an exceptional trend may run and run, it is more often the case that an exceptional trend turns out have been exceptional. It is either an unsustainable spurt that soon reverses or a one-off adjustment that soon peters out. (That is, incidentally, why you should never buy a house on the basis that you have observed a remarkable rise in house prices over a few years.)

We can safely say that China will not continue to grow at anything like 10 per cent – or even 8 per cent – a year indefinitely, because the closer it gets to Western standards of living, the harder it is to grow; the more it has to invent its own progress rather than lift it off the shelf from those who have already invented it. Once it becomes as rich as us, China will undoubtedly innovate and invent as well as we do now, but that is a painstaking business compared with what the country can do now. It is therefore best to think of China's recent growth as simply reflecting its weak starting position. When its per capita incomes match ours it will undoubtedly face similar problems to us.

That all being said, there is a specific worry about the exodus of British factory jobs to China: surely we would be better off if we stopped buying things from China and made them ourselves? This is an appealing line of argument, so it is crucial to understand when it is true and when it is not. To illustrate the point, let's take a visit to the Shandong Province in eastern China.

It only takes an hour and a half to fly from Shanghai to Yantai, a city with a population equivalent to that of London, but which most of us have never heard of. From the airport, there is a ninety-minute drive west along a new toll motorway. It is unlikely that you will see many cars on it as China has built its infrastructure in anticipation that demand for it will follow. You will then arrive in Longkou City. Longkou is well down the pecking order of cities. It has a population of a mere 630,000 (making it somewhat bigger than Manchester, excluding the conurbation around it). A power station and aluminium smelting plant dominate the skyline. But it doesn't have the feel of a dirty industrial town: the roads are wide, the landscaping pristine. It boasts a big tourist attraction in the form of a giant Buddha up on the hillside. (I assumed it was hundreds of years old when I first saw it but was told it was in fact built just a decade ago. Along with the international convention centre, the golf course and the hotel.)

For all this modernity, Longkou is out in the sticks. Although the hotel is vast, when the *Made in Britain* team visited we appeared to be among only a handful of guests. Moreover, we didn't have to drive more than a couple of kilometres to hit the point at which the broad highway suddenly turned into a coarse country road. For Western catering, we were proudly introduced to the local KFC. Frustratingly, our Chinese hosts assumed it was what we ate all the time back home and would drop us there for lunch while they went to get something more to their taste.

We went to Longkou for one reason: to see a factory that typifies the transfer of activity and jobs from the UK to the Far East. It is a joint venture between the local conglomerate Nanshan, which owns the Buddha and the aluminium plant, and the biggest British suit-maker, Berwin & Berwin. It produces almost half a million men's suits for the British market each year.

Berwin & Berwin is used to making suits. The business was started in 1920 by Barnett Berwin, a Belorussian tailor who had arrived in Leeds thirteen years earlier. Barnett brought his sons on board and the business has remained in the family ever since. Today, Barnett's grandson Malcolm is president of the company, and the current managing director is his son, Simon Berwin. For most of its life, the company's manufacturing has been based in Leeds. The city had enjoyed its role as clothier to Europe, and the place where John Barran invented the band-knife machine that could cut multiple layers of cloth in one go, an innovation that more or less created the concept of ready-to-wear clothes. As recently as 1971, the Berwins combined their three factories in the city into one facility on the Roseville Road, but by the nineties, the company watched as other textile and clothing companies around the city closed their doors.

By the end of the decade the Berwins realised they could not carry on making suits in the city as their costs were simply too high to be commercially viable. So, in 2000, they picked up half a million pounds of machinery and moved production to Hungary, with the loss of hundreds of jobs in Britain. Simon Berwin was not at all happy with this, not least as the company had a reputation of looking after its staff.

But, as if to show just how fast things move, it wasn't long before Hungary was getting too expensive. 'I was probably the last to turn out the light in Britain but I won't be the last to turn out the light in Hungary,' Simon Berwin said in 2003. By 2006 he was ready for his company to move on. Having found a joint-venture partner in China, his company helped open the plant in Longkou. Four hundred jobs were lost in Hungary as a result, although a substantial production facility remains there.

So what should we make of the Longkou operation? In September 2010 I walked into the factory and was immediately impressed. I find myself dividing the production facilities that I visit into those that look white and clean and those that look more black and grimy. The Longkou suit factory is more white; spaced across nineteen thousand square metres, it employs thirteen hundred people. The equipment is state-of-the-art German, American and Chinese. In fact, a British factory doing this job would look very similar to this one.

It is hardly a Dickensian sweatshop, although I don't want to pretend the jobs are not arduous. Workers are often paid on a piece rate basis and are there six days a week. One of our biggest struggles is to ascertain what the staff actually earn. We were told they can get about 2500 yuan a month, which works out at an average of £250, or approximately £1.20 an hour. A figure of about £1.50 an hour was also quoted. But that does not necessarily mean all workers get that. I spoke to one or two individuals, and they seemed to be on less. My guess is that people earn from about 80p to £1.50. That is a huge saving on the UK minimum wage of about £6 an hour.

In fairness, the Chinese joint venture has invested in its workers. Many are migrants from other parts of China, who typically live in dormitories. The accommodation is subsidised and appears to be rather like the most basic student housing with four people to a room. Many have TVs and computers.

There are few Westerners at the factory or in the city, but we met one of them – Jon Fleming, who is one of Berwin's on-site managers. Trained as an engineer in the kind of equipment used in clothes manufacture, he has often found himself working abroad. He says the joint venture is going well. Berwin & Berwin own a quarter of the operation and it finds the customers, which are mostly familiar British brands who wish to outsource their suit production. So, while you may not be very familiar with the Berwin label itself, you will certainly have heard of Berwin's clients. In the factory we saw suits with Austin Reed labels, Next labels and I particularly noted a lot of Ted Baker suits too. You will not find a better example of an operation that has turned the British from people who produce things into those who consume them, than this Berwin & Berwin–Nanshan joint venture.

The important question is what we should think of the export of these suit-manufacturing jobs to China, via Hungary. This is not a simple matter. Is it good for the Chinese? For the British suit buyer? The shareholders in Berwin & Berwin? Or those who had worked at the now-defunct UK factory?

The first point is that the move is almost certainly beneficial to the people of Shandong Province. Factory jobs may be hard work and they may pay little, but they sure beat the daily grind of toiling in a remote field on a subsistence income. And be in no doubt, that is a realistic alternative. What would represent exploitation in the West looks more like luxury to the 150 million Chinese living on an income of less than £1 a day. Of course, you might criticise Western-led manufacturers for paying low wages to their Chinese workers. You might say they are exploiting Chinese labour desperate for jobs, and suggest they should offer something closer to Western-level wages. These are all perfectly reasonable ideas. But they don't detract from the fact that Western companies that employ in China do more good than harm to the people they employ. And anyway, if you think companies should pay more than they have to, you might ask why that should only apply to those companies that have already helped China by investing there. Why not ask those who have decided their most profitable strategy is not to invest there to help a bit?

Personally, I am convinced that when Western companies invest in China, particularly on the terms imposed by the authorities there, they create jobs that push up wage levels to the benefit of the population at large. Indeed, by moving into the business of manufacture and assembly China is simply following the familiar rule that countries specialise in activities which use their most abundant resources. China has large numbers of people fit, willing and ready to work in factories. But also remember China gets an additional benefit from the business. In line with the learning by producing approach, the Chinese partners pick up skills that allow them to benefit their own people. The Longkou plant is a nice example of this. When there I couldn't help but notice a large number of suits bearing the Paul Betenly label. Who on earth is Paul Betenly?

It turns out that Berwin's Chinese partners have opened a production line in the same factory, which makes suits for their own market. The suits have labels designed to appeal locally. The name of that non-existent English gentleman Paul Betenly looks suspiciously like an attempt to associate the suits with the Bentley car. It wouldn't work in Europe but it might out there. Forget the branding. Think of the time and effort required to design a production line from scratch. Working out which equipment to buy and how to configure the task performed at each station to the world's best suit-making standards takes years of experience. The Chinese are picking all that up in next to no time. If making greater numbers of consumer goods more easily brings a benefit to a society, then the Chinese have benefited from Berwin & Berwin in ways that the mathematics of rising wages fail to capture.

So much for China. They accept the work that we give them, so consider themselves to be benefiting from it. But what about us? What do we get out of exporting jobs and importing items instead?

Well, some arithmetic is useful here. The suit plant has a complicated production line that means probably up to three hundred pairs of hands take part in the manufacture of each suit. But the completion of each suit requires a total of only about two or three hours of labour. That part of the cost is thus only about £3. If the work had been done in the UK, Berwin & Berwin reckon there is little reason to think that it would be done any quicker or significantly better. At the minimum wage, it would thus cost about £15 per suit, making the saving on tailoring per Chinese suit about £12 (but remember these figures are very approximate).

Of course, there is an extra transport cost to be taken into account. The cost of shipping a suit back to the UK is about £2. So the overall saving per suit is of the order of about £10. When you are making four hundred thousand suits a year, that works out at a saving of £4 million – or more than the total cost of making the suit in China. And that is just on the tailoring of the suit. On top of that is another saving of an equal magnitude, which Berwin & Berwin can enjoy by sourcing the fabric for the suit in China. It is striking how little money China makes out of a typical suit. You pay £200 at a high-street store, but China's income from that suit is probably no more than a fifth of the total. Most of the rest covers the costs of Berwin & Berwin and the retailer.

Now, if there is a saving of at least £4 million, it is important to determine who gets that. Is it a benefit to the UK that is delivered in the form of higher profits to the company (which goes to its shareholders), or is it a benefit that is delivered to customers in the form of lower prices?

It's not easy to answer that question exactly. On the one hand, if Berwin & Berwin faced no competition at all and was alone in moving to China, the benefit would go to the company. On the other hand, and more realistically, there is competition in the UK market for suits and more than one company has tapped into the availability of low-cost labour in China. That competition should drive prices down and, as a result, one would expect the profits of Berwin & Berwin not to rise, but the price of its suits to have come down. In that case, it is the customers who see the benefit of the £4 million saving, in the form of lower prices. Simon Berwin is clear that it is not his company that gets the benefit: it is the customers, who have enjoyed lower prices. And it is a plausible contention, given the price data we looked at earlier, which did appear to indicate that a good deal of benefit has gone to retail customers in the form of cheaper goods.

So far we have seen China is better off; the Berwin & Berwin shareholders and its customers probably too, having split a £4 million gain between them. Is it too good to be true? Not quite. There is one more factor to take into account: the loss of income of the British workers whose jobs were taken away from them. Remember that, in the UK, workers would be getting wages of about £15 per suit, rather than the £3 of the Chinese workers. That £15 wage adds up to a total income of £6 million a year for British suit workers, which has been wiped out by the export of jobs. As far as the UK is concerned, there is really nothing to dance with joy about in uncovering a technique of generating extra profits or lower prices worth £4 million by taking £6 million of wages away from hard-working families. That sounds like the overall effect is minus £2 million.

However, the argument isn't over. Suppose the displaced workers succeed in getting new jobs that pay them exactly the same as the jobs they have lost? Then we really do have a £4 million gain. The workers barely suffer, but the customers and shareholders get the cheap prices and profits.

In reality, the likelihood is that most of the workers will get jobs, but ones that are not as good as those they have lost. The overall calculation would suggest that, at worst, the country is £2 million down, if none of them work at all; at best, we are £4 million up, if they get jobs as good as before. For there to be an overall benefit to the UK we need the workers to get jobs paying a total of £2 million. That would leave the country as rich as before, but it would still involve a big redistribution. The workers are well down, the customers and shareholders of Berwin & Berwin better off.

This may seem a laborious calculation, but it is important to think about what the back-of-envelope maths tells us about the loss of manufacturing jobs. It suggests that even if the British workers at Berwin & Berwin end up getting jobs only half as well paid as their previous ones, the nation overall is richer sending the work to China. At that level the benefits to the customers and shareholders more than outweigh the losses of the workers. This kind of arithmetic can be applied to most of the manufacturing that moved off shore in the last ten years. Cheap foreign labour brought lower prices and higher profits, which were partially offset by lower wages (or no job at all) for some British employees. Overall, I suspect the benefits to the country did indeed outweigh the costs, in particular because consumers enjoyed the benefits in the form of those lower prices.

It is easy for me to say. My job was not shipped off shore. These calculations are callous because we are weighing up benefits and losses without regard to who enjoys or suffers them. I am not an unfeeling person and I take it as read that if a society chooses to make itself more affluent through decisions that leave a significant number of relatively hard-working and low-paid people worse off, then some thought would be given to the welfare of those individuals and their families. But while we must remember those manual workers whose earning power has been undermined by the export of jobs to the Far East, we must not overlook the many low-income households whose spending power has been enhanced by the lower prices at which things are sold. From mobile phones to microwave ovens, an array of items that were previously unattainable has now fallen within their reach. That may not have been the case had production costs not been lowered by off-shoring.

The point is that when we think about what businesses our country should be in, we must not just think of ourselves as producers; we must think of ourselves as consumers too. The calculation of benefits and costs must not ignore the workers, but nor should it only consider them. We have already had a lesson in the futility of trying to keep everything on shore in the experience of Marks & Spencer. The short-term pain of engaging with China is considerable but the long-term gain to the nation as a whole is considerable too.

I need to add an important rider here. The world does not stand still. The disinflation documented at the start of this chapter can't continue for ever and it has already shown every sign of ending. Perhaps all the off-shoring to China that can occur has occurred, so bringing an end to the exceptional downward pressure on UK goods prices that was seen in the noughties. Indeed, we might see the price falls go into reverse because China will not remain as cheap as it has been. Just as Japan grew from being an economy associated with cheap, low-quality items to the most advanced manufacturing nation on the planet, so too China will develop into an economy that looks more and more like ours.

It may be worth moving some production away from China (Vietnam has plenty of room for expansion, one textile industry source told me) and it may even be worth moving some production back home. That will not tell us it was a mistake to move to China; it will remind us that constant adaptation is quite normal. On top of the potential for the 'China effect' to unwind, there is also the issue of more expensive raw materials created by China's industrial revolution. You can't have a billion extra people living a developed-economy lifestyle without some consequence. Higher raw-material costs, however, are best seen not as a result of our decision to export factories to China but more as an inevitable product of China becoming a richer nation. Sure, we could have attempted to thwart China's ambitions to move out of the eighteenth century, and we could have refused to hand over the secrets of industrialisation. Undoubtedly we could have slowed the country's progress and by doing so kept oil prices lower. But I think most people would agree that would not have been very generous.

All in all, I am probably sounding rather complacent about what might appear to be the wholesale off-shoring of British production. So let me give another reason why I am not as worried as many other people by our apparent deindustrialisation: when we dispatched machines, factories and jobs abroad, we kept the best bits here. There is still manufacturing in the UK, and it tends to be of a variety that is higher-value and more remunerative. It is pretty clear that, far from losing the ability to make things, we've still got it. We stopped doing many of the things that are easy and decided to keep the more challenging physical production on shore. We have every reason to be proud of what we can do.

Here are three examples of modern manufacturing that an affluent country like ours should be engaging in: high-end aerospace engineering, led in Britain by BAE Systems; a niche product in a specialist area, exemplified by Brompton Bicycles Ltd, and the canny combination of the two in McLaren cars. It is worth looking at what these companies do in order to show how much manufacturing did *not* go to China in the last decade.

If there is any industry in which Britain can claim to be a major player, it is aerospace. Most of us are brought up learning about our impressive heritage in the skies, and we can be pleased that our nation has been responsible for two of the most famous aircraft – the Spitfire and Concorde. Add the Harrier and the first commercial jet airliner, the Comet and you can see we have plenty to be proud of, notwithstanding the failures that have beset the industry through the years. I feel particularly lucky to have flown in a Spitfire as part of the media coverage of the seventieth anniversary of the Battle of Britain. And what a pleasure it was too. Having been warned that I could expect to be sick (the rule is, 'whoever brings it up, cleans it out') I was relieved to find that I felt no nausea at all. For all the barrel rolls and twists that my pilot, John Romain, executed, perhaps the most impressive thing about the plane was that he got it down to a speed as low as sixty-five miles per hour without the engine stalling. I hadn't realised that man-made objects could stay airborne at that kind of speed.

But the history we are familiar with; it is the significance of our current industry that people may overlook. Britain has fifteen companies in the 2010 *Flight International* league table of the Top 100 aerospace manufacturers – more than France, Germany, Italy, Spain and the Netherlands combined. Of course, these companies are global and much (if not most) of their work occurs outside the UK. But be in no doubt that we are second only to the United States in this sector.

BAE Systems is Britain's biggest aerospace company, and it is also our largest manufacturing company. It was formed in 1999 when British Aerospace and GEC's defence electronics and shipbuilding company, Marconi, merged in a £7.7 billion deal. It should be stressed that, as a result of its mergers, BAE Systems is a large shipbuilder as well as an aerospace company and it quite reasonably gets very touchy when people continue to refer to it by its old name of British Aerospace. The company has about 107,000 employees, of which about 40,000 are employed in the UK. BAE Systems has customers in over 100 countries worldwide, and in 2009 reported sales of £22.4 billion. It is the largest defence contractor in Europe, and vies with Lockheed Martin and Boeing to be the biggest in the world.

So how did this modern economic giant come about? Every company has to begin somewhere, and for BAE Systems its origins can be traced back to the start of the twentieth century, and the beginnings of flight. Perhaps the starting point was on 8 June 1908, when Alliot Verdon-Roe became the first Englishman to achieve powered flight, at the Brooklands motor racing circuit in Surrey. Two years later Verdon-Roe joined forces with his brother to build aeroplanes at Bromfield Mill in Manchester, and in January 1913 registered AV Roe and Co as a public company.

Verdon-Roe's company was one of many small firms springing up in this fledgling industry: there was the De Havilland Aircraft Company, the Sopwith Aviation Company, the Bristol Aeroplane Company, and many others with equally evocative names. One of the most important was John Davenport Siddeley's Siddeley Autocar Company, which started out making four-cylinder cars before moving across into aircraft design. What gave the aerospace industry its crucial kick start was the First World War: in the first ten months of the war 530 aircraft were built in the UK; in the last ten months, that number was 26,685. While the Great War had a devastating effect on so many industries, for British aviation companies it accelerated progress in a way that would never have happened in peacetime.

What followed was a story of consolidation and merger as these many small companies became fewer and larger. The invention of the gas turbine engine was a key event, paving the way for the jet engine, and with the dawn of commercial flights British companies found themselves facing competition from American companies such as Boeing and Douglas. There was no doubting the technical excellence of the British planes, but for all our vision and skill they lacked the capacity of their US counterparts. The result was the formation of the British Aircraft Corporation in 1960, and an ongoing government strategy to consolidate the industry in order to help it survive on the international stage.

The result was a string of success stories, such as the development of the Vickers VC10, the Harrier and the Nimrod in the sixties. There was also the Aérospatiale–BAC collaboration that launched Concorde, perhaps the most beautiful plane ever made, but which never really made the commercial impact that had been hoped. Then, in 1977, the government decided the way forward was to merge all the British aircraft companies into one state-owned outfit: British Aerospace. This was floated on the stock exchange in 1981 and fully privatised in 1985. Two years later it was Europe's largest aerospace company, and has continued to grow and prosper ever since.

The contrast between the sort of products that BAE Systems make and those of, say, the textiles industry couldn't be starker. Aircraft design is a high-end, high-skilled industry: out of the 40,000 or so workers that BAE employ in the UK, about 18,000 are engineers. These workers are not necessarily graduates, but each has completed the company's four-year apprenticeship course that teaches them the physics and engineering required for the job. This is the very opposite of low-wage, low-skilled work, and cannot easily be transferred elsewhere to cut costs. The majority of the BAE Systems workforce outside the UK is in America and Australia – similarly developed economies with the requisite pool of well-educated, skilled workers.

One only has to look at BAE Systems' facilities to get a sense of the huge and complex investment involved. Their plant at Samlesbury in Lancashire, where 5000 people work, is, to use that well-worn phrase, the size of 197 football pitches. I visited a brand-new 'milling and drilling' plant there, which was housed in an enormous hangar about as far removed from the noisy, oily and labour-intensive facilities one might normally associate with 'milling' and 'drilling' as you could get. Titanium casings come in to be polished and have holes drilled into them to a 50µm (micron) tolerance (to give you some idea of the sensitivity, a human hair is 20 µm). Because titanium is so hard, the carbide cutting tools in the machine need to be replaced every thirty minutes, at a cost of £12 million a year. But it is worth it. It is barely an exaggeration to say that the casings enter the machine worth about £100,000 and leave it worth double that figure. The facility is manufacturing Joint Strike Fighter components for the US government.

The work of BAE Systems is specialised and is super high value. It builds on something we are good at, our years of accumulated experience, knowledge and investment. It is globally integrated too – working closely with partners on projects such as the Typhoon and with developed export markets around the world.

I spoke to Nigel Whitehead, who has responsibility for BAE Systems' UK business. I asked why it was that the company had sold its stake in Airbus and moved out of civil aircraft altogether to focus exclusively on defence. In one of the best examples of a company engaging in a strategy of constant adaptation to position itself in the highest-value sectors possible, he told me that the civil aircraft are too easy to make. Other countries can do that (Brazil's Embraer, for example). BAE Systems did not want to overstretch itself or its capital, and thus had to specialise in the things that others couldn't do: the much more challenging defence aircraft.

Many, of course, feel uncomfortable that such a prominent manufacturer is in the defence sector, and that it has been the subject of a high-profile Serious Fraud Office corruption investigation. But whatever one feels about the sector – critics call it 'arms', supporters call it 'defence' – the company is at least an answer to the question, 'Do we make anything these days?' Yes, some very expensive things that foreigners want to buy. There is, however, a significant commercial downside to the fact that it is defence in which we flourish: exports are to some extent limited. China might like to buy Typhoons, but the European suppliers are not allowed to sell them to the country.

The company is aware that any kind of competitive advantage is temporary and so is always looking for the next big thing. As high spec and high tech as the Typhoon is, its shelf life is nonetheless limited. The future for the company comes in creating new products that make the most of the ever-changing technology. One such area of development is UCAVs – Unmanned Combat Air Vehicles – and in July 2010, the company unveiled the Taranis, an unpiloted aircraft with both stealth technology and artificial intelligence that can be controlled via satellite from anywhere in the world. Once again, investment isn't cheap: the trial aircraft alone cost £143 million to make, but this is what it takes to remain ahead of the game.

It's not just high-end engineering that Britain excels at. Another area in which we are successful is in niche manufacturing. Rather than competing with foreign companies in the production of mass-market products, there are a host of British companies that thrive on carving out a specialist segment of a particular industry. One great example of this is in the manufacture of bicycles.

But who is the biggest bike manufacturer in the UK? Your first answer to this question might be to go for someone like Raleigh, and indeed, in the past, this was by far our biggest manufacturer. In the fifties, the company produced over a million bikes a year, selling them not just in the UK (where the company boasted a remarkable 75 per cent market share) but also exporting them around the world. By the eighties, however, things were very much in reverse: the British market was full of imports from France and Taiwan, and although Raleigh invested in new technology they made the mistake of not using lighter and cheaper aluminium frames, as other manufacturers were doing. A few years before Britain's noughties cycling renaissance, the company stopped production at its Nottingham factory altogether and these days is active only as a trader, not a manufacturer, of bikes.

The answer to who makes the most bicycles in Britain today is the company that Andrew Ritchie began back in the mid-seventies. Ritchie left university with an engineering degree but was working as a landscape gardener when he came up with an idea for a folding bicycle. The folding bicycle in itself wasn't new; what Andrew Ritchie came up with was a new way of folding the bicycle. While other models folded in half lengthways, Ritchie's design saw the bike fold in on itself, which made the end product smaller and far more practical for commuters. Ritchie worked on the prototypes in his bedroom in South Kensington, overlooking the Brompton Oratory school, from which he took the name for his creation: the Brompton folding bicycle.

There followed a struggle familiar to entrepreneurs everywhere, as Ritchie attempted to secure the funding to turn his vision into reality. After several hard years production proper began in the late eighties. Two decades later, the company makes 25,000 folding bikes a year at its factory in West London. Even that is not enough to satisfy demand: there remains a waiting time of two to three months for a bike. These eager customers are not just British, who in fact account for only 30 per cent of the company's sales. Brompton does brisk business in countries such as Germany, Austria, France, Norway, Sweden, Denmark, South Korea, the Netherlands and Spain. In 1996 the Allgemeiner Deutscher Fahrrad-Club (ADFC, German Cycling Federation) voted the Brompton its Bike of the Year.

The Brompton bicycle might not be high tech in the way a BAE Systems Typhoon is, but it is in its own way an engineering masterpiece. Each bicycle is made up of 1200 components, of which about 900 are unique to the Brompton. The importance of attention to detail was shown when a deal was signed for a Taiwanese firm to make the bikes under licence in the Far East in the early nineties: as quality control issues arose, it quickly became clear that the bike wasn't something that could be made and manufactured in a mass-market way.

The relatively high price of the Brompton compared to other bicycles (they retail at £600 to £1,500) hasn't put off potential buyers. If anything, their relative scarcity and desirability only serve to increase people's interests – exactly what capturing a market niche is all about. Brompton might not be as big as BAE Systems, but its current managing director, Will Butler-Adams, is nonetheless keen to invest in new models. As well as continuing to fine-tune and improve their basic bicycle design, the company's future plans lie in the building of an electric version, which they hope will transform the market all over again and continue to keep them one pedal-revolution ahead of their rivals.

Another company for whom staying in front of the competition is ingrained in their DNA is McLaren. I have long been aware of the impressive track record of its Formula One team: only Ferrari can lay claim to a longer racing history, and over the years, McLaren can boast twelve drivers' championships (including victories for the likes of James Hunt, Alain Prost, Ayrton Senna and Lewis Hamilton). I have also been aware that Formula One is a big business, and one that is primarily located in Britain. With the notable exceptions of BMW Sauber, Ferrari and a couple of smaller teams, all of the constructors have their headquarters in the UK. This cluster of companies is sometimes called 'Motorsport Valley', spreading out through Oxfordshire and beyond, with huge benefit to the British economy as Formula One revenues are generated internationally. I have also heard the statistics – that, for example, UK Motorsport supports almost 40,000 jobs, of which 25,000 are for qualified engineers.

What was interesting to find out was that McLaren is quite a lot more than a Formula One constructor. Most notably, it is trying to capitalise on its track success to sell road cars. Not just any old cars, I should hasten to add: combining the high-tech engineering of BAE Systems and the niche appeal of Brompton bikes, the market McLaren have decided to explore is that of the supercar. The company has had some experience of manufacturing up-market cars, such as the SLR, which was built in conjunction with Mercedes. But the MP4-12C, set to be launched in 2011, will be McLaren through and through. The company is building a dedicated factory at its technology centre in Woking. Ron Dennis, the obsessively perfectionist executive chairman of McLaren, explains the company philosophy thus:

It's a mindset thing ... we clean people's feet as they come in by going down different surface finishes, and ... we try to do it with their minds as well, we try to get them into a tranquil mindset, which is consistent with what we want to achieve in our building. I'm not a great believer in lots of personal effects around your desk ... we forbid people to eat and drink at their workplace, because this is their workplace ... we are focused on trying to be the best, and therefore you've got to have a certain mindset, a certain buy-in to the McLaren DNA.

Remember the general rule is to specialise in the things you do best. The Formula One connection automatically provides McLaren with the marketing, but the company had to come up some brilliant and innovative engineering too. What it succeeded in making was a car with a carbon-fibre chassis at a price half that of the nearest competitor. The aim is to build a thousand cars a year to begin with, expanding to four to five thousand cars by the end of the decade.

BAE Systems, Brompton and McLaren aren't the only success stories in British engineering; we've already heard about GKN, and we could have visited many other successful companies that you may well have never heard of, such as Cobham or Meggitt, each boasting a global turnover of over a billion pounds. It is evident that each company understands the importance of invention and design, of research and development, and of continually moving forwards and coming up with new products. The high-value sectors are as much about excellence in creating intellectual property as in manufacturing physical property, and as intellectual property is so important for our economy this will be explored in later chapters.

But before we get to that, there is more to say about manufacturing. And, following this mini-tour of UK triumphs, we need to look at some things that have not gone so well.

6

Room for Improvement

So far, this has been a rather Panglossian account of UK manufacturing. It is dynamic and productive; we were probably right to let a lot of it go to China; and we still manage to produce about as much as we ever have because we held on to all the best and high-value bits. What on earth could there be to worry about? Well, I suspect that many of you have a nagging sense of discomfort with this argument. And here's where I confess that I do too.

Let me give an example. On 23 September 2010, the then world's largest off-shore wind farm opened off the Kent coast. Thanet OffShore Wind Farm comprises a hundred turbines which should generate 300 megawatts of power (the equivalent of enough power for about 200,000 households). Put aside the arguments over whether we need green energy and whether wind – off-shore wind in particular – is the right shade of green for the UK: many countries have decided to invest in this technology and the global business is worth tens of billions of pounds. And, like it or not, Britain has decided that wind should provide a substantial portion of its energy.

The UK lies far behind the US, Germany, China and India in the amount of power generated from wind. In fact, we lag behind France, Italy and Spain too. But when it comes to off-shore wind power (which is the top-end, technically challenging, expensive kind) we have installed more than any other country and are the world's biggest producer.

If we have the biggest market, one might expect that we would therefore be a world leader in the production of off-shore wind technology; that we would be exporting high-value turbines to the rest of the world as they try to keep up with us in this fast-growing sector. That is the usual pattern: companies develop a specialism on the back of a dynamic home market and then use their expertise to conquer the rest of the world. But it is not what one observes in the UK industry. The Thanet Offshore Wind Farm is an impressive achievement, which cost £780 million pounds. But only 20 to 30 per cent of the capital expenditure on the project went to UK contractors. The plant belongs to Vattenfall, a Swedish state-owned company. As the company gets the income that derives from Thanet's power, Britain has in effect ended up importing its own wind energy from Sweden. That is not to decry the Swedes, nor is it to say we were wrong to let them get involved. If Vattenfall is better at building a wind farm, there is no point in doing it ourselves. But it is still somewhat disappointing that we don't have a strong industry of our own.

It is particularly sad given that back in the eighties, when the technology was in its infancy, a Glasgow engineering company, Howden, did appear to have something of a lead in the industry. It built the world's largest wind farm at Altamont Pass in California in 1984. But the operation suffered repeated mechanical problems and the company withdrew from the sector. Essentially, Howden were over-ambitious in their design: while most turbines of the time were about nineteen or twenty metres in height, Howden, despite little prior experience in building wind turbines, opted to jump from its similar-sized prototype to a final design of thirty-one metres. Despite its size, it was unreliable and outperformed by other, smaller models.

Howden's interest in wind turbines stalled in the late eighties, which was understandable given the lack of demand at the time. In Britain, the old Central Electricity Generating Board had toyed with research into different turbines but by the late eighties, the power industry was more interested in nuclear and gas. This meant that when, decades later, interest in wind-turbine technology finally did surface in Britain, the Scandinavians already had the industry sewn up.

The story of UK wind farms can be filed with those of the tilting train and the EMI CT scanner – those lost opportunities in which Britain managed to turn itself from a potential leader into an also-ran. These cases frustrate us sufficiently to ask whether there is some pattern to them. Is there something that we are doing wrong?

In investigating the outcomes of these various cases, there are factors specific to each of them – simple bad luck, or poor business decisions that turned out to be critical. These make it hard to draw general lessons. But to paraphrase the old saying, the less you practice, the unluckier you get. In any individual instance there will always be specific problems. We should never use that as an excuse for repeated failures. Instead, we must ask whether we have in some way stacked the odds against ourselves, making unfavourable outcomes more likely than they need be. And this is where we have to face some bad news.

For all the good that exists in British industry, the manufacturing enthusiasts' instincts that our economy is not perfect are not entirely off the mark. Britain has historically been marked out by the interesting characteristic that, as a nation, we have a strong consumer culture but, perhaps as a result of that, we have tended to save and invest rather little compared to some of our counterparts. This has almost certainly had consequences for the structure of our economy and may well have caused us to have too little manufacturing. No one can say that is why we have not invested in our own wind farm at Thanet, but it is reasonable to assume that the less a nation saves and invests, the more likely it is that others will end up investing for us. And the more likely it is that a setback in an industry (like a mechanical failure at an innovative California wind farm) will prove fatal rather than fleeting. So what is the problem?

We have already noted two important things about Britain's balance of payments in the post-war period. First, we saw in Chapter 1 that the deficit can be seen less as a reflection of our skill at exporting and more as evidence of an inclination to spend too much relative to income. Secondly, we have seen that Britain has been running a deficit in most years. That implies our outgoings exceed our income with respect to the rest of the world. To put it more bluntly, we spend more than we earn as a nation which means that we consistently borrow from foreigners or sell a few assets each year to pay for our imports. It must be stressed that the numbers are not huge. The average deficit in the last three decades has been 1.5 per cent of national income. Some small ongoing deficit is nothing to worry about, but 1.5 per cent is bigger than we should be comfortable with.

So here's the question: if all was going well, would we not do a little more saving and a little more investing? A little less importing, a little more exporting and hence a little more manufacturing? The answer to all these is yes, we probably would. As with so many questions in economics, though, the answers are not definitive: it is hard, for example, to say what the 'right' level of savings is. But the interesting contention is that if anything has been wrong over the last few decades, it has *not* been Britain's ability to make products that people of other nations want to buy. It has been the economy more generally: the supply of capital for investment; the level of the exchange rate (which is affected by the level of savings); the obstacles and difficulties that have constrained company decisions and which have nurtured a lack of ambition among British producers outside a rather narrow industrial base.

If this account is correct, the companies themselves are not to blame. Nor are the Bank of England or the Treasury or the government department responsible for business. The problem is down to us. Our collective behaviour has made life difficult for manufacturers, not someone else's. So let's explore the argument that it is time for us all to hang our heads in shame. Start by looking at the two tables overleaf. The first shows Britain's place among the seven big advanced industrial nations in terms of saving. They are ranked according to the percentage of household income that is not consumed. The second shows Britain's place as a nation that invests in physical capital: that is, how much we spend on everything from new houses to roads, to factories. The stuff that adds to our productive capacity. In this table countries are ranked by the proportion of our national income we spend this way. Each table takes an average going back more than a decade. (The dates covered have been selected to reflect the availability of a consistent series of data.)

It will not take you long to notice that we lie at the bottom of both tables, and saving and investment can be seen as two sides of the same coin. The money households put aside by saving can be taken by companies to pay for the building of new factories, for example. How might one interpret these tables?

It appears that we, the public, save very little. We thus don't

6.1 How Much We Save

Percentage of household
disposable income that is saved
Average 1995–2008

	percentage
France	12.2
Italy	11.3
Germany	10.2
Japan	6.9
Canada	4.5
United States	3.5
United Kingdom	0.7

Source: *OECD Factbook 2010*. Author's
calculations based on household net
savings rate data

6.2 How Much We Invest

Percentage of national income
invested in fixed capital
Average 1970–2008

	percentage of national income
China	31.3
Korea	29.5
Japan	29.1
Italy	22.2
Germany	21.9
Canada	21.1
France	20.8
United States	18.8
United Kingdom	18.1

Source: *OECD Factbook 2010*. Author's
calculations based on gross fixed capital
formation data

put much money into savings accounts or into pension funds or
life insurance. As a result, when financial institutions go about
their business of lending money or buying shares they have to
be rather fussy about where they put their money as they don't
have much of it to put: the amount we save has a direct impact
on the financial institutions' behaviour.

In this vastly simplified account our low savings rate leads
to a low investment rate. That has an important consequence.
Remember the rule I set out earlier: countries will usually end
up specialising in activities that use the resources they have.
If Britain has few funds available for investment, it will develop
industries that don't need much capital. That would mean steering away from manufacturing, with its hunger for big factories

and expensive equipment, towards things like office work, where all you need are desks and computers.

As a result, the decisions taken by each of us in terms of how much to spend determines the structure of our economy. The argument is strengthened by the figures mentioned back in Chapter 1 that showed our capital stock per worker compared to that of France and Germany. We were bottom there too. (For those bewildered by the array of different figures that all sound like they measure the same thing, I should point out that the stock of capital is closely related to the level of investment but is not identical. It is a measure of the total amount of capital we have accumulated, while investment looks at the amount we accumulate each year. The capital stock counts, for example, the number of computers we have; the investment figure counts the number we are buying.)

The picture seems pretty clear cut. But it is vastly simplified. In reality, while there is a link between the decisions that we each make about how much to save and the amount that the country manufactures, it is less direct and more complicated. Our economy does not just consist of households and businesses. There is a government too, and we trade with other countries, which means that not all the money we save goes to industry. We can invest it in foreign companies as well as British ones, or we can lend it to governments in the bond market or to house buyers in the mortgage market. Equally, not all the money for British industrial investment comes from British household savings. Much of it is from the profits that companies themselves earn. It can also come from savers overseas, or indeed from the government itself. So the connections between the amount a nation saves, the amount it invests and the amount it manufactures do not make it inevitable that a low level of household savings will destroy the manufacturing sector, nor that a high level of savings will build it. But one can say that a high level of saving and investment certainly helps. No amount of complexity should be allowed to obscure the general rule: countries that consume too much tend to have a smaller manufacturing sector than they otherwise would.

The relationship holds partly because a smaller supply of savings can reduce the funds available for investment, as I've already described. But it works in other ways as well. Apart from the need for savings to support the capital-intensive sectors of the economy, the level of domestic consumption will affect business decisions about where the biggest profits are to be made, whether from serving local people or selling abroad. And the flows of savings affect the exchange rate, which is important in determining how favourable it is to export.

To get a taste of the panoply of indirect ways in which our decisions affect the fate of the economy, just imagine a small cosmopolitan country where factories operate successfully; where the population saves plenty and invests it both at home and abroad; and where industry draws its funds both from its home base and from abroad. The country maintains a high level of investment. Imagine too that there is no trade deficit or trade surplus. The population is not borrowing from the rest of the world to finance its spending, nor lending to it. In short, everything is in balance.

Now suppose this hypothetical economy is given a nudge. All of a sudden, the population decides to save only half as much as did before, and to go on a spending binge. What happens next? Of course, a lot happens. Hairdressers, taxis, construction workers and restaurants will do well. These are businesses that really only exist to serve the local market, and with a local boom they will enjoy the biggest proportional growth in their sales. Profits will soar and soon these businesses will be looking to expand in order to keep up with demand.

Manufacturers typically exist in both the local market and

the export one. They too will enjoy an uplift in sales, but it will be an unbalanced uplift. They will notice that it has become easier to sell things at home, but it will be no easier to sell them abroad on the global market. So only half the overall market the manufacturers sell into has taken off. For typical manufacturers, the relative attractiveness of domestic and export activities will shift in favour of the domestic-facing, with resources allocated accordingly.

Suddenly the nation's business orientation has moved away from exporting towards the local market. The profit opportunities appear be to at home and so corporate decisions will be tilted that way. But there is more. We have to think about the exchange rate.

The supply of savings has dried up, and so fewer savings will flow out of the country. Fewer locals are buying foreign currency to invest overseas. And because there is a domestic boom, there will also very likely be more foreign money flowing in. The gap left by domestic savers has left the door open for foreigners to finance domestic investment.

What happens when money stops flowing out and instead starts flowing in? The exchange rate will tend to rise as foreigners buy the local currency and savers stop buying foreign ones. Yes, with the boom comes the feelgood factor of a strong currency. Everybody will undoubtedly say how well the economy is doing and how confident foreigners are in its future. The government will win the subsequent election.

Alas, the boom in restaurants, retailers and construction will hide the fact that the export sector – dominated by manufacturing firms – is failing to keep up with the surge in imports. The balance of payments slips ever further into the red. It is hard for manufacturers to compete in an economy bursting at the seams with spending. How can they even attract good workers when there are so many other well-paid jobs in domestic-facing sectors? And how can manufacturers gain markets overseas when hamstrung by an exchange rate so high as to be uncompetitive? All in all, the effect of the fall in savings is a re-orientation of the economy away from exports and factories towards locally provided services.

This account is designed to demonstrate the links between trade, exchange rates and savings only very briefly. The simplest way to visualise it is that nations normally put most of their savings to use in two different ways: either they invest in physical capital for use at home or they invest in some form abroad. Take away the former use of savings, and the capital-intensive sector suffers. Take away the latter and the export sector is affected.

None of this would matter for the odd year or two. Keep up a low level of saving for a sustained period and the economy naturally adapts to the conditions it finds itself in. Manufacturing's problem is that it is typically over-represented in the export and capital-intensive sectors. So a long-term deficiency of saving tends to hit hardest there.

It cannot simply be a coincidence that the two manufacturing leaders in the affluent world are both nations which have traditionally had very high levels of investment and savings: Japan and Germany. Nor is it chance that two other nations with notably high savings rates are the other two global manufacturing leaders, South Korea and China.

Britain, on the other hand, has been different. Our attempts to maintain a certain lifestyle through the decades has conspired to make life difficult for manufacturers. It hasn't always been down to a low level of household savings, but we have certainly seen periods of exceptionally low saving in two recent cycles: in the late eighties and the more recent years of the noughties. These were classic consumer-led booms associated with very low levels of savings and high levels of borrowing. Exactly as outlined in the hypothetical case above, low savings meant a strong pound, a large balance of payments deficit and a re-orientation of the economy towards domestic industries.

Nowhere was this scenario better encapsulated than in a television advertisement for the NatWest bank in the early noughties. In the advert, an old woman turns up to the local branch of her (rival) bank to discover it has changed: 'Oh dear,' she says, 'my bank is now a trendy wine bar.' This shift in the building's purpose portrayed exactly what Britain was doing – no longer going into the bank to save, but going out to spend their money instead.

I'm not sure whether any of JD Wetherspoon's premises have ever been called a 'trendy wine bar', but the pub chain is just one of the many businesses that profited enormously from such spending behaviour in this period. A classic domestic-facing business whose success mirrored the decades of strong consumer spending, the chain was started by Timothy Martin in London in 1979: his first pub was not a converted bank, but a former betting shop; his second, opened two years later, was originally a car showroom. By the end of the eighties the company had grown to a chain of forty pubs. But it was in the late nineties and the noughties that the chain really took off: in 1996, there were 150 pubs; two years later this number had doubled. By the end of 2009 JD Wetherspoon boasted 743 pubs, and has become a classic example of the reorienting of our economy towards domestic things.

In fact, as a nation, we have managed to uncover a variety of ways of inflicting pain on our manufacturing sector through the decades. In the seventies, it was less the household savings rate that led to problems than industrial strife and an upward spiral of prices and wages that represented a disagreement between workers and employers over the balance between wages and profit in the economy. Workers wanted to maintain their spending power while companies tried to prevent them from doing so. It was an argument over living standards; a nation whose citizens were between them trying to consume somewhat more than the total the country could afford.

It was a costly way of resolving the issue of who should get what, and it resulted in higher inflation than that of most other comparative economies. Apart from the economic circumstances not being particularly propitious for industry, the disputes themselves distracted management from doing much in the way of developing good products and efficient processes.

In the early eighties it was North Sea Oil that did for manufacturing. Once we had it on tap at a point when the price of oil was high, the pound became very strong. The oil revenues allowed the nation to consume more than it previously had expected; we didn't have to buy so much imported oil so the pound rose and the orientation of the economy again focused on domestic consumption rather than overseas export. It was the end of a huge swathe of our manufacturing base.

The only way to have subverted this effect would be to have followed the example of Norway by saving the oil money and investing it off shore. That would have kept the exchange rate low (as the country would have bought foreign currency to invest overseas) and allowed manufacturing to carry on regardless of the oil gain.

You get the picture. Decade after decade we have struggled to maintain consumption; the more we carry on consuming the more import dependent the economy becomes and the more resources switch from export industries to the domestic. And it is also important to point out the role of elected governments in this kind of problem. They have at times been less than fiscally cautious, so while households might have saved the Treasury has chosen to borrow, using up savings that might have gone into private investment.

More controversially, some argue that governments have crowded out industrial investment and exports not by borrowing, but by simply spending money. The more they tax and spend, the argument goes, the more workers will expect to be paid and the less profit there will be in the economy, hurting the level of corporate savings to finance investment and pricing British goods out of export markets. The government has also been accused of under-investing in the national infrastructure, in order to keep taxes down or public service spending up. Again, it is all part of a pattern. There are many ways in which a nation can squeeze its exporting sector, but they pretty well amount to the same thing: an attempt to prop up current spending.

I eschew simple economic rules, but you might interpret all this as conjecture that, other things being equal, the more you produce and the less you consume, the more likely it is that your production will be exported, that it will be capital intensive and thus the more likely it is that it will be manufactured. It is a pretty poor rule as other things rarely are equal. But it is not a bad thought to carry around. And, as Britain has not elected to make things easy for its capital-intensive sectors and its exporters, perhaps we shouldn't be surprised that we have had a balance of payments deficit and a low investment rate in recent history.

While I hope I have made a point, my argument is not complete. What I have not yet done is establish that we do have a problem. Just because someone has a few drinks doesn't mean they are an alcoholic, and just because a nation likes to shop doesn't mean it has saved too little. It may be that we have good reason not to save and invest. Perhaps it is the Germans and Japanese who have a problem. Maybe it is they who consume too little rather than us who consume too much. This is no small detail. Contrary to the instinct that so many of us have, saving is not always a virtue. It can go too far. We can be abstemious to the point of stupidity. We can, for example, invest in technology that is not cost-effective. So yes, of course we need to worry about the future, but not if it involves a disproportionate sacrifice for those living in the present.

In my view, we should not save and invest more in order to help manufacturing industry. Manufacturing is not an end in itself. Instead, we should save and invest a sensible amount and be happy with the manufacturing that results. Take it this way round, and in order to justify the claim that we have too little manufacturing we have to find grounds for asserting that we save too little.

Well, as it happens, I do have grounds for suspicion. They come from looking at the saving for pensions that I observe people putting aside relative to the pensions expectations of those doing the saving. I'm not alone in thinking that people have been saving inadequately. Indeed, my anxiety has been so widely shared, particularly since companies have scaled back the saving they do for us in staff pension schemes, that Britain is embarking on a policy designed to raise pension saving considerably, by automatically enrolling all employees in a modest pension scheme.

To make this less anecdotal, let me defer to a higher authority, one who has looked at the issue more systematically. Martin Weale ran the National Institute of Economic and Social Research from 1995 until he was appointed to the Monetary Policy Committee of the Bank of England in July 2010. He has studied the levels of saving and capital in Britain and several other European nations.

And his conclusion in a 2008 paper about the levels of consumption in those countries?

The findings of this study are fairly clear. In none of the four countries studied is the current pattern of consumption by old people affordable for young people.

The fact is that none of the four countries studied can afford to carry on as they are; in France and Spain it is only the youngest people who need to adjust while in Italy and the United Kingdom the whole population needs to. The adjustment may be planned or unplanned but it needs to happen.

Of course, when we get to retirement age and find that we are poorer than we'd like to be, we will undoubtedly just continue working to make up for the lack of savings. But Weale and his co-author think we are saving too little, even if we intend to work an extra five years.

It all seems quite clear. We are not saving enough. When we do, our economy will change. The long talked about 'rebalancing', away from borrowing towards saving; away from financial services towards manufacturing; and away from importing towards exporting, will occur.

There is a complementary account of how we have let our industry down. It's not uncommon to hear people say it is all down to our being obsessed with home ownership.

Putting aside the fact that we are not uniquely obsessed with home ownership (Spain, Italy and Ireland all have higher levels than us, and Canada and the US are very close behind), why would houses hurt industry? At its most basic, you hear that as we put all our money into housing there is none left to invest in industry. This is a seductive argument but it is a mistaken one. I don't know about you, but the last time I bought a property someone else sold it to me. Hence all the money I invested in it was disinvested by the seller. The housing market sees money going round in circles rather than going up in smoke.

People seem to get very confused by this. Some think we can make ourselves poor by shuffling houses around between ourselves in this way, while others appear to think that we can all make ourselves rich buying into property. My own view is that a society can't do either. Buying and selling homes is simply a distraction, albeit sometimes a rather costly one if we end up with too many estate agents.

It is true that there is one significant way in which the housing market can consume real resources. We do more than shuffle them around when we build new homes or improve existing ones, and that really does take away funds that could be used in constructing factories. Bricks, mortar and labour are scarce, and any day they are devoted to residential investment is a day they are not devoted to industrial investment. But to believe that housing has killed British industry in this way you really have to follow the consequence of the argument and assert that we have built too many homes. I rarely hear people argue this.

However, I don't want to exonerate the housing market altogether. It quite probably has caused trouble for British business, and so it is worth setting out how. This account draws less on the idea that it has used up scarce resources that could have been devoted to building an export-led economy and instead focuses on the fact that our economy has been relatively volatile. We have suffered (or maybe enjoyed, I'm sometimes not so sure) housing-led booms and busts. In these stop-go cycles we seem to eschew the grown-up approach of jogging steadily and instead sprint until we are exhausted, then collapse in a heap on the ground to have a rest before getting up and sprinting again.

We are hardly alone in enduring major ups and downs, but we have been somewhat more prone to them than other well-performing nations. They are annoying for anyone in business but they make life particularly difficult for companies facing overseas competition, most often manufacturers. It is far better to have an even 2 per cent growth for two years than to have 6 per cent one year and -2 the next, even though the two come out at the same total. We have seen how a sustained period of high consumer spending hits British manufacturers with a rise in the exchange rate and a shift of the economy towards spending rather than producing. But just as bad is a short-lived consumer boom followed by a rapid bust. The downturn ironically hits manufacturers just as the consumer boom does, as they are disproportionately reliant on the British market. Any kind of domestic lull represents a significant dip in sales and is thus hard to endure.

It is a fascinating feature of the economic cycle that when the economy overall suffers, manufacturing production tends to suffer far more. After the financial crisis of 2008, the economy sank but manufacturing dived. In 2008 and 2009, two years of deep economic contraction, the economy shrank by five per cent but manufacturing output dropped by 13 per cent.

In general, volatility that is most extreme in Britain is bound to have far less impact on foreign producers, for whom the UK is just a small corner of the world. A violent lurch in sales in our economy just feels like a gentle swing to them. So while the foreign companies can meet demand in the booms and comfortably survive our busts, British companies struggle at both ends of the curve.

Another effect of volatility is that it reduces the quantity and quality of investment. On average, an unstable economy is an unattractive one to invest in. But, just as significantly, in an unstable economy people constantly make bad investment decisions. At the height of a boom even the most stupid ideas look plausible, and too much money is wasted on ideas that have no hope of surviving the inevitable downturn (like unsellable inner-city flats). At the bottom of the slump it is hard to get any investment at all as credit is hard to come by. For a sector such as manufacturing, which relies on long-term investment, these are all real problems.

Why do we have a volatile economy? I am unlikely to fully explain that issue here, just as Gordon Brown failed to solve it despite investing enormous political capital in trying to do so. Many would probably blame the authorities and it is tempting to argue that the Bank of England and the Treasury have between them exacerbated the economic cycle with undisciplined fiscal policy and interest-rate setting. But personally I am sceptical of any account of UK economic weakness that is based on the premise that Britain has been uniquely disadvantaged in having authorities that are incompetent.

No, the best suggestion I have heard as to why we have been more cyclically accident prone than most others is down to our housing market.

The problems that arise from the volatility of the property market are not just that we own houses in large numbers. They come from the dangerously self-reinforcing nature of housing cycles. What would happen in most ordinary well-functioning markets is that rising prices would dampen demand. Why buy more of something that is expensive? The problem is that when it comes to housing logic is rather topsy-turvy. When prices rise, people want more homes on the basis that if they don't buy they will be left out of the gold rush, or will never get a foot in the door. So house prices don't rise a little and then fall back a little. They tend to gain a momentum of their own, rising until they are ridiculous and only then falling back.

In addition to amateur speculators and panic buyers entering the market just as house prices are getting high, we also have an unusually competitive mortgage market which itself exaggerates the cycle. The more available are mortgages, the greater the demand for homes. So it is not untypical to find that when mortgage credit expands and house prices go up, lenders feel more confident about loaning against the value of homes and sell yet more mortgages, thus fuelling even more price rises. In fact, it is at the height of the boom that competition for mortgage business is at its most intense as lenders' margins shrink, making it cheaper for borrowers to get a mortgage and they then bid house prices up and up. The reverse happens when house prices are in decline: mortgage lenders withdraw credit, escalating the fall in house prices.

On top of that, Britain is unusual in having a mortgage market with such a preponderance of variable rate products on offer. Long-term fixed rates (ten or twenty years) are quite a rarity. This itself can be destabilising if home buyers (wrongly) assume the current variable interest rate represents the long-term cost of their mortgage. When variable rates are low, people become too optimistic about the affordability of housing and thus tend to bid house prices up to unsustainable highs.

Potentially, another way in which this self-reinforcing cycle is amplified is through media coverage of house prices. I feel I have a little bit of responsibility here as the BBC's economics editor during the last housing boom. I couldn't help but feel a little anxious at the frequency of our reports on rising prices. There are a lot of regularly published measures of house prices (much of which comes from parties with an interest in the market such as lenders Halifax and Nationwide, and websites like Rightmove) so quite often it seemed that one month's rise in prices might be reported up to four different times. This would create the feeling that house prices were rising not just the once, but every week, again exacerbating the sense of 'buy now while stocks last' and relentlessly driving prices up. Of course, since house prices have been heading in the opposite direction the accusations against the media have also swung 180 degrees. Instead of being accused of talking the market up, now journalists are criticised by estate agents for scaremongering and spreading gloom.

The media has other effects too, taking a legitimate form of investment and creating a fashion out of it. Inspired by a glut of property programmes – *Property Ladder, Location Location Location, House Doctor, Grand Designs* and so on – we cast ourselves as would-be property developers, doing up houses and selling them on for a handsome reward. So influential did these housing programmes become, that one stockbroker, Durlacher, created a 'TV Index' to monitor them and used it to predict fluctuations in house prices.

These house-price booms tend to ripple through the economy and create more general economic booms as the rising house prices make people feel rich and thus keen to spend more – quite irrationally, as on average we are no richer at all when house prices rise; the gains of some are more or less offset by the losses of others. It is important to remember, too, that with a surge in the buying and selling of houses comes a boom in a host of associated industries, whose fortunes echo and then exaggerate the cyclical nature of the housing market. The most obvious of these is the DIY trade, with people either working on houses to sell or decorating them afresh once they've moved in. With the purchase of a new house often comes the buying of additional goods: appliances for the kitchen, perhaps, or a flat-screen TV for the living room. The housing market again inspires a consumer boom, which flatters the performance of the economy and makes people feel rich, thus justifying the spending that created the boom.

I could go on and on identifying myriad ways in which the market behaves badly. This is not to say it is easy to improve. The basic point is simply that because we have a high level of home ownership, the housing market in the UK matters.

You will notice that this housing market account of what is wrong with our economy is built on the premise that people are a bit silly. Surely if buyers knew what they were doing they wouldn't buy more homes as they got more expensive; lenders wouldn't lend more carelessly when house prices were high; people wouldn't confuse a housing-market inspired consumer boom with a permanent improvement in the economic outlook; and the media wouldn't get excited about house prices and housing. And so on. As it happens, I'm uncomfortable with any account of economic life that is based on a premise that people behave in such crazy ways; we usually make sensible judgments rather than stupid ones. Unfortunately, this account of housing market dysfunction is one that I find all too plausible given what I know about my own feelings towards housing. I bought my first flat in September 1988, which was just about the peak of that decade's boom. The mistakes that I have outlined are hard to resist.

If you believe that irrationality can drive the housing market, and the housing market can drive the economy, then you should inevitably believe we have a volatility problem in Britain and it is one that probably hurts some industries more than others. Who knows whether this really explains our cycle? The good news is that during the latest boom–bust, our growth performance has not been outlandish relative to that of other countries.

It remains true that in some small measure through volatility, and in larger measure through the exchange rate, saving and investment, the UK has had macroeconomics problems with real effects on the balance of our activity. We have allowed others to build our wind farms and have left a gap in our balance of payments that needs to be addressed. Hopefully when we do address it, as we inevitably shall, we will do so sustainably, rather than enjoying another five steady years before accelerating into consumption mode again.

Over the last few chapters, we have looked in detail at British manufacturing in a way that I hope both illustrates our current strengths and weaknesses, and illuminates how these have come about. There is not so much an elephant as a dragon in the room when it comes to British industry, but I have attempted to show that China is not so much a threat as an opportunity. It has allowed us to let go of certain sectors of manufacturing, to the benefit of the British consumer, and to focus on the more sophisticated, high-end products that a forward-looking economy should be basing its manufacturing sector around.

There is little wrong with many of the products we make as a country: what we need to do is to produce more of them, and to extend out our manufacturing base. The problem here, however, is that the success of these industries is dependent on investment and that is where we fall down. Our levels of saving have been low in recent years, and so the banks have had less to lend – the result is that the economy more naturally leans towards other industries where capital requirements are lower. Our obsession with housing, and the volatility in the economy that stems from it, also has a negative effect on investment: it leads to people wasting money on bad ideas in boom times, and being refused credit when times are harder.

I have also looked at some of the commonly held misperceptions we have when thinking about manufacturing. What at first glance might seem to be evidence of a sector in decline is, on closer inspection, revealed to be an increasingly efficient sector. I have looked, too, at the psychology behind making things, and the question of whether there is anything intrinsic in manufacturing that differs from activity in other parts of the economy. One conclusion is that it is not so much that there is anything special about manufacturing, but that we lack understanding of other, less tangible sectors of the economy to make a proper comparison. In order to help with this understanding, it is time we looked in detail at these other parts of the economy: first, the group of industries that are collectively known as the 'knowledge economy'.

PART 3

INTELLECTUAL PROPERTY

7

The Science Bit

For many years, *The Economist* ran a succinct and highly recognisable advertising campaign of sharp slogans in white type on a red background. Phrases such as 'Great minds like a think' and 'What exactly is the benefit of the doubt?' were emblazoned across billboards to underline the newspaper's image of being a thoughtful, intelligent and challenging read.

Of the many advertisements that the newspaper has run over the years, one that has always stuck in my mind was run on posters at train stations. No one, the advertisement knowingly told passengers staring out of the train window, ever became a success by staring out of the train window. It's a clever line and, in a strange kind of way, one that touches on the subject matter of the three chapters in this section: intellectual property.

When considering how Britain earns a living, it quickly becomes apparent that more and more of what we make is invisible and intangible. It is everything from the clever advertising of *The Economist* to the well-written content of the newspaper to the innovative design of products that feature in some of its pages. This is all intellectual property, a vast category that covers anything from a branded chocolate bar to a piece of accountancy software to a poem to a complicated industrial process. Although these seem very distinct, they do have certain features in common.

Broadly, the next chapter will look at the strength of British companies in the fields of advertising and branding. *The Economist*'s campaign is a great example of this. The contention of the chapter is that marketing really does add value to a product, and so we have no reason to be worried about devoting so many resources to it. This chapter, however, examines the science bit: research and development, or R&D. I hope that these chapters will demonstrate that Britain is a leading performer in the world of intellectual property, and that we have made ourselves rich from so being.

One person in particular who became rich in this way is J. K. Rowling: ironically, her success was contrary to the claim of *The Economist*'s advertising as it was on a train journey from Manchester to London at the start of the nineties that she came up with the idea for Harry Potter. In Chapter 9, we look at the implications of building a 'Harry Potter economy' – one that relies on the wizardry of creativity and brain power to earn a living rather than physical labour.

But let us begin our journey into the world of intellectual property not staring out of the train window but with the window itself. The manufacture of glass might well be something to which you have never given much thought, particularly in the context of ideas and high-value manufacturing. Yet whether it is the windows of the skyscrapers that make up Canary Wharf and the City of London, or the windscreens in vehicles from Sunderland's Nissans to McLaren's supercar, the vast majority of the world's flat-glass production – 90 per cent, according to one industry expert – is made using a technique created and developed in Britain.

*

Glass has long had a symbolic value in the development of the British economy. In 1851 the Great Exhibition – the forerunner of today's Expo fairs, such as the one I visited in Shanghai – was held in London's Hyde Park. While officially titled the Great Exhibition of the Works of Industry of All Nations, the phenomenal success of the Industrial Revolution meant that the success of British companies and ideas dominated the event. The exhibition was housed in the Crystal Palace, an enormous pavilion structure designed by Joseph Paxton. Paxton's palace was made out of a then cutting-edge design of cast iron and glass to symbolise the best of British industry: it is estimated that just under 300,000 panes were used in its construction. The glass was made by the Chance Brothers of Birmingham, the leading British glass manufacturers of the age; they also supplied the glass for the Houses of Parliament and the clock tower that houses Big Ben (they were the only company capable of making the opal glass used in the clock face).

What with these hundreds of thousands of glass panes to produce, the Chance Brothers probably didn't take much notice of a small Lancashire glassworks. Pilkington Brothers had started life as the St Helens Crown Glass Company, which was founded in 1826 by a group of local entrepreneurs. William Pilkington, a wine and spirit merchant, was one of these businessmen and in 1849 he and his brother Richard bought out the other partners and renamed the company Pilkington Brothers. It was the Pilkingtons rather than the Chance brothers who would ultimately dominate the British glass industry: a century later, the Birmingham firm was bought out by their Lancashire rivals.

But for Pilkington that was just the beginning. The mid twentieth century saw the company transform itself from a vibrant national company into a world leader. The company achieved this through their innovation in making glass. Before this period, glass manufacturing was done in one of two ways: first, there was plate glass, a technique that produced perfect results but was both slow and expensive owing to substantial labour and machine costs. Sheet glass, by contrast, was relatively quick and inexpensive to produce, but with a noticeable difference in quality. For all glass manufacturers the goal was to come up with a technique that could deliver plate-glass quality at sheet-glass prices. The burgeoning motor trade, in particular, was demanding such a product: the quality of sheet glass was only good enough for side lights and headlights; windscreens needed better-quality glass, but at a competitive price for mass production.

Pilkington Glass had a long history of innovation. In the twenties it had come up with a continuous grinding and polishing process, which it then licensed out to other plate-glass producers. In 1935 the company developed its 'twin' machine: this allowed the plate glass to be polished on both sides at the same time. Creating and developing new systems, then, was something that the company had both the experience of and a reputation for. In the fifties, however, the stakes were substantially higher. Pilkington knew that other leading glass manufacturers – St Gobain of Belgium, the Pittsburgh Plate Glass Company, Asahi Glass and Ford Motors itself – were all experimenting with new production techniques. Whoever succeeded in a creating a system to produce good-quality, inexpensive glass would dominate the industry in the years ahead.

In the summer of 1949 Pilkington set up two development teams, one of which was headed up by Alastair Pilkington. In an ironic twist, particularly given his subsequent importance in the company's history, Alastair Pilkington was not actually a member of the immediate family that owned the company. A few years earlier there had been a company project to trace the Pilkington family tree. In the course of this, the researcher had tracked down Alastair Pilkington's father, who was distantly related. Alastair's father suggested that his son could do a job for the company, a recommendation that was to turn out to be gold-plated.

Alastair Pilkington's research team was based at the company's Cowley Hill plant in St Helens. They began by looking at a glass-making system that was in development in the US. The Bowes process smoothed the hot glass as it came out from the rollers and was still soft. The difficulty was in how to move the glass along the production line while it was still cooling and thus liable to mark. Ken Bickerstaff, an engineer on Pilkington's team, came up with the idea of using a liquid metal as a means of transporting the glass. Experiments using molten tin began at the company's Doncaster plant: in theory, molten tin and molten glass would not mix or have an adverse reaction when put together.

In 1952 came the two breakthroughs that built on Bickerstaff's original suggestion. Alastair Pilkington realised that the molten tin would help in smoothing the glass direct from the rollers, removing the cost and expense of the Bowes process. He also came up with the idea of 'freefall'. Pouring a liquid on to a flat surface will naturally form a pool, and it turned out that molten glass poured on to molten tin naturally flows until it is a quarter of an inch thick – exactly the thickness required in the manufacturing process.

This is the basic theory on which the float glass procedure is based. But coming up with the idea was just the beginning. It would take seven years, and a lot of research and investment, before Pilkington was ready to go public. It is estimated that the company spent £7 million – £80 million in today's money – developing the process, and the work was fraught with difficulties. With costs running at £100,000 a month (£1.14 million today), the Pilkington board met repeatedly to discuss whether to go on funding the research. But continue funding they did, and fine-tuning continued right up to the end. It wasn't until September 1959 that the Cowley Hill plant was consistently producing high-quality glass by the new float process.

The research and development of the float glass process was by no means straightforward, but the rewards were immense. Pilkington had been careful to make sure that the key inventions in the process had been patented in as many countries as possible before they announced their breakthrough. But it wasn't just the inventions themselves that were important. Over the years of research, the Pilkington engineers had accumulated a wealth of minutiae about the float process: the small details and sensitivities that were required to produce perfect glass. These were recorded in a collection of manuals and detailed engineering drawings, and everyone who had been involved in the research was bound by a confidentiality agreement. In other words, Pilkington's control over its idea was more than just a legal one: without access to the company's files, the system was unworkable. To give an idea of the level of detail involved and its importance, in 1973 a Portuguese syndicate were caught attempting to steal a set of key drawings; the drawings alone, which were intercepted at customs, weighed in at 27 kilograms.

Pilkington believed that the float process would become the dominant way of manufacturing glass, and so it proved. It wasn't long before Pilkington's major rivals all bought licenses from the company to use their system: Pittsburgh Plate Glass were first, swiftly followed by Luffy Owens Ford and the Ford Motor Company. Long after the original patents had expired, Pilkington was still able to legitimately enforce protection of its technology and obtain licence fees for it. By the time of Alastair Pilkington's death in the mid-nineties, the process had been licensed to forty-two manufacturers in thirty countries. It is difficult to place a precise figure on the amount Pilkington has earned from the licensing of its invention, but as an indication, a US court case in the early nineties suggested that the figure at that point was in the region of $4–5 billion (about £3 billion at the then exchange rate, or about £4 billion today, and that sum excludes any subsequent licensing deals).

At the time Pilkington announced its innovation, the company was the fifth-largest glass manufacturer in the world. In the subsequent decades, the company's reach grew dramatically: in 1967, a plant was built in Canada, and was followed by other factories in Australia, South Africa and Sweden. In 1979 Pilkington acquired the German float and safety glass operations from BSN, giving the firm access to the thriving German automobile industry. In America, Pilkington acquired its former competitor Luffy Owens Ford, and with it their lucrative relationship with General Motors. With these two acquisitions, the company became the biggest glassmaker in the world. Today, Pilkington is owned by NSG of Japan. Even so, the float glass story remains a great British success; a classic example of the rewards that high-value manufacturing, innovation and R&D can bring.

Pilkington is just one example of how research can ultimately make more money than manufacturing per se. When we talk about high-value manufacturing, we are really talking about a combination of the two. But wouldn't all countries prefer to be high-value? Who wouldn't rather be making sizeable returns from inventing and making complex pharmaceuticals than earning mediocre profits engaging in more straightforward production, such as baking bread? So why are these high-value products the preserve of some nations and not others?

For the answer, we go back to the three basic rules or principles that all economies tend to follow, which were outlined in Chapter 2. These were that, first, a country will build its economy around the resources it has available. Second, a nation will deploy these resources in the highest-value activities that they can find. The third guiding principle is that as things change, nations adapt. These rules are the perfect explanation of why Britain has let its economy evolve in the intellectual direction it has followed: we have moved up-market because we can, because others can't and because it's well paid if you do.

Take pharmaceuticals and bread as examples. It takes massive amounts of research to invent or discover the drugs, but little work to design a loaf of bread. Because the high-level research skills to invent the drug are scarce, only a very limited number of players are in the business, while almost anyone can make bread. Because not many people can compete in the pharmaceuticals market (especially given the existence of patent laws) you can get away with charging more for drugs than for bread.

These are the secrets of being a high-value producer. One might summarise the journey that Britain's economy has taken over the decades as moving from being a country that makes bread to one that makes drugs. To reiterate an earlier point, the importance of manufacturing production will almost inevitably diminish as an economy advances. Just think about why. The wholesale price of a loaf of bread is substantially accounted for by the direct cost of producing each loaf: the flour, the depreciation of the equipment needed, the labour involved and so on. When it comes to bread, it's all about the baking. But that is not true of the cost of a drug. The production cost of each pill is relatively trivial. Instead, the cost of the pill is incurred upfront in research bills that are run up whether you make one pill, or a hundred tonnes of them. When it comes to drugs, it's all about invention and discovery.

To give an example of this, let's compare the 2009 annual

reports of two of Britain's top companies, the pharmaceutical giant GlaxoSmithKline (Glaxo to its friends) and the food company Premier Foods, which makes a number of branded items (including Hovis) and some unbranded foods as well. In the accounts, each company has a measure of the direct production costs of their output, the so-called 'cost of sales'.

For Premier Foods, that cost of sales is the vast bulk of its overall turnover (70 per cent), implying that most of what Premier Foods does is spend its money on making stuff. Not so Glaxo. Its production costs are only a quarter of its turnover, indicating that the company is primarily not about producing pills. It does, however, have an annual £4 billion R&D bill, amounting to 15 per cent of Glaxo's turnover, and for which there is no Premier Foods equivalent.

The two sets of accounts demonstrate that a difference between a pill and a loaf of bread is that the costs of the former are mostly overhead while the costs of the latter are mostly production. Don't be surprised therefore, that as our economy has advanced our manufacturing has evolved so that there are relatively smaller production costs and relatively bigger overheads including, in large part, what one might call 'applied intelligence', or the fixed costs of innovation. These overheads mean producers have to apply high mark ups to their output, but because the products that they make are valuable and scarce, they can get away with charging higher prices.

Another good example of the principle is Apple's iPod. On the back it says 'Designed by Apple in California; assembled in China'. One study looked at the how the $300 retail price of a particular iPod broke down. It turns out to be rather interesting: for the design, R&D and marketing, Apple gets $80. For the assembly, the Chinese get less than $5. Of the rest, $75 goes to the retailer and wholesaler and $140 goes to the suppliers of the components that go into the iPod. It would be nice to say how much of the final $300 price is spent on manu-facturing the iPod or its components. That is hard to do precisely, but it is probably a little over a third of the price. The rest of the money goes to activities in the production process that are not manufacturing but add value in some other way.

It is the intellect, ingenuity and dexterity of those undertaking these activities that make them high value. At the extreme end of the higher-end products are the cultural and creative ones. The work of art is many times more valuable than the cost of the paint and the canvas; the book is far more than the bound pages. And only an idiot would measure the value of a movie by the length of film it fills. The physical material is just not where the action is.

Top-end activities form a large part of British trade and there is evidence we are good at them. The people in these fields are rarely working on the factory floor and, in fact, they typically don't even have to be located in the same country as the factory itself. But no factory can work without them.

We are not alone in trying to survive and thrive this way. It is what most affluent societies do. In fact, most modern developed economies follow a very established pattern, one that Britain has followed perfectly (if not actually led). First, we are clever so we become rich. We apply our technological and business skills well, and quickly become more affluent as we find ways to produce things more effectively than we used to. Then, once we are rich we remain clever, because affluent societies can afford to invest in education and research. I suspect most people don't realise it, but Britain is generally regarded as having one of the most tech-nologically advanced manufacturing sectors in the world. Let's explore this in detail by looking at two hugely important British companies: one of our biggest British manufacturers, the afore-mentioned GlaxoSmithKline, and a company that leaves the making entirely to other people – ARM Holdings.

*

The story of GlaxoSmithKline is one that mirrors this bread–drugs transition in the British economy, though in this instance the transformation was from powdered milk to complex pharmaceuticals. The company started out as a general store in Wellington, New Zealand, in the mid nineteenth century. The store sold everything from clothes to crockery, ironmongery to spirits, but it was their line of Glaxo dried milk that really did the business. By the turn of the twentieth century the product was being exported to the UK, and a dedicated Glaxo department was created. The company became best known for its infant foods and its slogan 'Glaxo Builds Bonnie Babies'. In 1924 the company entered the pharmaceutical market with Ostelin, a Vitamin D product. The growing importance of the division, and its continuing research and diversification was recognised in the creation of a new subsidiary, Glaxo Laboratories, and the building of a modern factory and offices in Greenford, West London, in the thirties.

In the same way as the First World War had a transforming effect on the fledgling UK aviation industry, so the outbreak of the Second World War was to have a similar impact on Glaxo's fortunes. One of the most important tasks in the war was to find a way of manufacturing penicillin. Everyone was aware of how useful it could be on the battlefield in saving lives. But it had been over a decade since Alexander Fleming's original discovery and producing it in a form that could be used therapeutically had proved extremely difficult. Some progress had been made, however: Howard Florey and Ernst Chain, working at Oxford University, had been carrying out tests and by 1941 felt that they were finally ready to begin trials on humans.

Glaxo's Greenford laboratory was one of those supplied with nine strains of penicillin and by October 1942 it was producing the drug in small amounts. The following month the government formed the General Penicillin Committee to coordinate supply.

As the war continued, and tests showed the drug's enormous potential as a life-saver, pressure mounted on Glaxo to increase production. In July 1943 the company was approached by the Medical Research Council and asked to increase its production fivefold. With the help of the Board of Trade, Glaxo requisitioned part of a rubber factory in Watford to help in the production of flasks to hold the penicillin. These came on to the production line in February 1944, which at its peak was producing 300,000 flasks every twenty-four hours.

In autumn 1943 penicillin was supplied to hospitals in North Africa, specifically for use on soldiers in the Sicilian campaign. The drug was by now a 'designated' project – the highest level of government priority. By this point in the war, with Hitler stalled and ultimately to be defeated at Stalingrad, Allied planning was turning towards the invasion of mainland Europe. The risk of casualties from this attack was clear, and the supply of penicillin vital.

For Glaxo, all this concentrated effort and focus produced remarkable results. In late 1943 new innovations were discovered. This was just as well, because the Ministry of Supply wanted the company's output to be increased still further. The government gave extra facilities and factories to the company in order to achieve these targets. All in all, it is estimated that the number of staff working on Glaxo's production of penicillin increased twenty-fold in the period from 1941 to 1946.

But this endeavour was to reap its reward, both for the war effort and ultimately for Glaxo itself. On 6 June 1944 Allied troops landed on the Normandy beaches as D-Day got underway. The planning of the campaign had been meticulous, and the manufacture of penicillin just one small, but crucial, component. Out of the 160,000 troops who landed, it is estimated that there were about 10,000 casualties, out of which about 2500 soldiers died. How many more would have done so without the availability of penicillin is impossible to say, but that the drug reduced the death toll by treating infected wounds is undeniable. The efforts of the Glaxo scientists were largely responsible for the lives that were saved: about 80 per cent of the penicillin made in the UK and used during the Normandy landings was produced in Glaxo's factories.

All this ultimately led Glaxo to shift its focus towards pharmaceuticals. This was a decision helped by the creation of the National Health Service: suddenly there was a captive market for drug companies, and from its modest beginnings in the field just a few years earlier, Glaxo were in prime position to capitalise on this.

That is not the end of the Glaxo story, of course. It became one of the world's most profitable firms after the discovery of another drug, Ranitidine (marketed as Zantac), three decades later. We will come to that story in Chapter 9, but since becoming a specialist in pharmaceuticals it has never really looked back. In 2000 Glaxo merged with SmithKline Beecham to become GlaxoSmithKline, or GSK. The firm is one of the largest pharmaceutical companies in the world, with a 7 per cent market share; in 2009 it achieved sales of £28.4 billion and a profit of some £8.5 billion, and it spends more money on R&D than any other company in the UK. But it is a hit and miss business; the chief executive Andrew Witty told me that:

Of 10,000 new molecules that we might synthesise, so that we might create 10,000 possible new drugs, probably one will be a drug. If I go all the way forward now fifteen years in the development programme ... of thirty big programmes in advance development ... maybe we'll get 60 per cent of those across the finish line. So even at the very end, you still almost have a one in two probability of failing.

GSK is a global company, of course. It has about 99,000 employees in over 100 countries worldwide, of whom 16,000 are in the UK. But Britain's apparent skill in pharmaceuticals goes well beyond GlaxoSmithKline. With AstraZeneca, the country has two of the world's top ten pharmaceutical providers and we have research establishments in the UK that belong to foreign companies. For example, Viagra was developed at American firm Pfizer's facility at Sandwich in Kent. Britain has thus been in the forefront of developing some of the world's most talked-about treatments. This is not to say that the British pharmaceutical industry has it easy. Pfizer closed its facility in Sandwich and emerging economies are finding they can do pharmaceutical research too. The cycle by which we all strive to move up market never stops.

I could have put the story of Glaxo into the section of this book concerned with manufacturing. It is, after all, a manufacturer of the medications it sells. But as I have said, manufacturing is not where the action is. Getting a successful therapy invented and ready for production typically costs half a billion pounds. Once the production line is ready each pill costs a few pence. So the crucial thing is that the production process is front-loaded, but nonetheless we cannot disregard the importance of physical production altogether as it can be extremely complicated to effect, involving minute doses of chemical compounds being mixed in precise quantities. Andrew Witty described the process of making one particular drug at their Ware plant: 'Raw material that's been manufactured in Singapore comes over to the UK, [and] we micronise it. What that means is we make ... absolutely microscopic particles that you can't see with your eye.' Witty explained that there has been a tremendous increase in the potency of drugs over the last few decades, a scientific advance that has led to a number of production issues: 'That [progress] creates all sorts of new manufacturing challenges. How do you deal with products where you literally can't see it? And maybe your whole year's supply of raw material is 50 kilograms?'

But you might wonder how far the intellectual-property model can be pushed: is it possible for a company to be successful by focusing just on the R&D part of the process without bothering with the manufacturing at all? The answer is yes. The Cambridge-based firm ARM Holdings is one such example. ARM concentrates purely on the creation and design of a product. It does not actually make anything, but instead generates income by licensing out its designs to manufacturers.

Even if you haven't heard of ARM Holdings, the chances are that you own several products that include its technology. ARM designs microprocessors that can be found in all sorts of modern electronics, but particularly in mobile phones: it is estimated that ARM designs can be found in 95 per cent of all mobile phones and 25 per cent of all electronic devices. In the next three years, some 2.5 billion smartphones will probably be produced with ARM-based chips; and the smarter the smartphone, the more ARM chips it is likely to rely on. Just as Pilkington successfully licensed its float glass process to other companies, so ARM's licensing deals for its intellectual property have been both extensive and lucrative: the company has done more than 700 processor licensing deals with about 250 different semiconductor companies. It does the brainy bit and leaves the physical work to someone else.

Mighty oaks, so the saying goes, from little acorns grow. The acorn in ARM's case was a computer. In today's world of iPads and laptops, a world without personal computers feels like a different age, but it is only thirty odd years ago that such devices were first widely available. In the United States companies like Apple, Commodore and Tandy were at the forefront, while in the UK the leading lights were two Cambridge start-ups: Sinclair and Acorn.

Acorn's early success was assured when it did a deal to design the BBC Microcomputer – a machine that was to be used both in schools and as part of the *BBC Computer Literacy Project*, a public computer-education series on television. It was not, it has to be said, the most attractive computer in the world – a large and rather cumbersome cream box with a dark brown keyboard casing and red function keys – and its memory was what now seems a mind-bogglingly small 32 kilobytes (though if you think that was tiny, there was an Acorn with an even smaller memory, the 16Kb Electron). But in the early eighties the BBC Micro was a powerful home computer and a testament to British inventiveness.

The BBC Micro was, like other computers of the time such as the Apple II, based around an 8-bit chip or processor. In order to create a more powerful machine the next generation of computers would need to be driven by a 16- or 32-bit processor. There were such processors available on the market – it was at this time that Intel was starting its growth towards its pre-eminent position in the manufacture of microprocessors – but the Acorn team felt that none of them was quite what they looking for and so the company decided to build their own.

Acorn set up a secret team to develop the processor, and the work was codenamed Project A. Resources were limited, which meant that the device couldn't be too large and complex; it needed to be small so that it could be designed and tested easily, and inexpensive to produce. After eighteen months the team had created the Advanced RISC Machine, or ARM for short (the RISC, if you're technically minded, stands for Reduced Instruction Set Computing). The team's success in designing the chip did not, however, translate into sales: the processor was first used in Acorn's Archimedes computer, which struggled in a market now dominated by the IBM personal computer. By the end of the eighties it was becoming increasingly clear that Acorn was not large enough to sustain its own in-house processor design team.

In 1990, with investment from Acorn, Apple and VSLI Technology, an American integrated-circuit manufacturer, a new company was created around the skills of the ARM development team. Moving out of Acorn's Cambridge headquarters to a converted barn in the Fenland village of Swaffham Bulbeck, the aim of Advanced RISC Machine Ltd (subsequently ARM Holdings) was to continue the development of its processor, and to generate revenue through licensing designs rather than making them.

The technological developments of the nineties and noughties played perfectly into ARM's hands. As computers became more mobile, and mobile phones became more like mini-computers, so the demand for smaller and smarter processors to drive them has increased. When ARM had originally developed such devices back in the eighties, the cost restrictions in developing anything more complex might have felt like a hindrance. Now, though, their designs were perfectly sized to drive an ever more mobile electronic economy.

Whether it is clock radios or fuel injection systems for cars, digital cameras or credit cards, microprocessors make the modern world go round. ARM only gets a few pennies for each one of its designs that is installed in a device, but with so many being installed that added up to £400 million of revenue in 2010.

Is the company worried that, in choosing not to have any role in the manufacturing, it is rather like an entity from science fiction, a brain without a body? Not at all. 'I prefer to think of us as the heart ... inseparable, embodied in these devices,' ARM president Tudor Brown told me, explaining the company's philosophy. 'Fundamentally, we don't want to manufacture. If you go into the business of manufacturing you have to build a factory that costs you $5 billion. Before you start, it's a hugely expensive game. We have no expertise in that ... We're damn good at what we do here and that's what we want to keep going.'

The stories of float glass, penicillin and ARM's processors are just three examples of British innovation and success. There are plenty more. Britain is one of a few big players in this arena as global spending on corporate R&D is highly concentrated. Over 80 per cent of it occurs in just six countries: the US, Japan, Germany, France, Switzerland and the UK. Of course, it is hard to judge exactly how inventive a nation we are; interestingly, statistics compiled globally do in fact show that we devote a smaller share of our national income to R&D than the other top research nations. And we have a relatively low rate of registering patents internationally compared to them too. This would seem to imply that we rank at the bottom end of the high-tech elite. But there are forms of investment in knowledge that are not categorised as R&D, and on broader measures of investment in intangible assets Britain scores higher. The message re-emerges: we have plenty of which we can be proud, but little to be arrogant about. What we can say, though, is that the British economy has moved towards producing higher-value goods over time and our exports (although there are too few of them) are generally rated as being unusually skewed towards high-value sectors.

Obvious questions raised by this account are why it is the UK has evidently succeeded in developing some kind of competitive advantage in certain knowledge-intensive industries, and why do the older established industrial countries maintain such a lead in these industries?

The answers lie in history. Ideas and innovations take time and money to develop so countries earlier into the arena of industrial production are more likely to have progressed further down the track. We industrialised first, we established universities relatively early and we have enjoyed the benefits of extended education for longer than emerging economies. It should not, therefore, be surprising that we have been better endowed with resources for research and study than many other nations.

But there is an even more striking feature of brain-powered industries that explains why older economies hold the lead in them. The people who work in them prefer to work near other people who work in them too, which means there is a very pronounced tendency towards clustering. Rather than science-based firms being evenly spaced out around the country, such companies tend to be clustered together in the same geographical location.

This is not new – in the Industrial Revolution, it was first the Derwent Valley and then Lancashire that were very much at the heart of events. With the computer-based industries prevalent today, Silicon Valley in Northern California represents the cluster that everyone else in the world wants to emulate, hence the corny proliferation of 'Silicon' monikers attached to modest-sized clusters of electronic firms, from Silicon Hills in Austin, Texas, to Silicon Glen between Edinburgh and Dundee and Silicon Alley in Manhattan.

Britain's most successful such cluster is Silicon Fen, the area in and around Cambridge where many of our leading high tech companies are based, including ARM Holdings. It is estimated that there are over 1400 high-tech ventures within a 25-mile radius of Cambridge, employing around 43,000 people. These areas suck in huge amounts of investment: in 2004 Silicon Fen companies accounted for 24 per cent of all UK venture-capital investment, while one third of such American money goes into Silicon Valley.

It is not just in science-based industries that this phenomenon can be observed. From Hollywood to the Square Mile of the City of London to the linoleum cluster in Kirkcaldy (yes, by 1877, the town was the world's largest producer of the floor covering), industries that are built on specialist skills have tended to follow the pattern.

Why does such clustering occur? There are different reasons in different industries, but the short answer is that in high-tech areas clustering breeds creativity. A compact geographical huddle of similar companies fosters an environment of both cooperation and competition that is highly conducive to the development of ideas. The competition provides a spur, and the cooperation means no insight goes to waste or is left unexploited. In short, whereas physical items are made in factories, knowledge is expanded through networks of skilled people.

In his book *Where Good Ideas Come From*, Steven Johnson describes the 'superlinear scaling' that occurs between cities and creativities: 'a city that was ten times larger than its neighbour wasn't ten times more innovative; it was seventeen times more innovative ... the average resident of a metropolis with a population of five million people was almost three times more creative than the average resident of a town of a hundred thousand'. The close proximity of high-tech firms is part of the same naturally occurring phenomenon: it is no different, Johnson argues, from the rich variety of life that is found on coral reefs, which make up 0.1 per cent of the earth's surface, but are home to 25 per cent of its marine life.

This explanation of clusters tells you that you might expect to find them where the seeds of knowledge networks are planted: near universities. It is Stanford in Palo Alto that explains the rise of Silicon Valley in California, and the presence of the university explains why we have Silicon Fen near Cambridge but no Silicon Scilly Isles. Cambridge University set the whole ball rolling, in fact. It has long boasted a highly regarded computer science facility; in 1970 Trinity College helped set up the Cambridge Science Park, which is often credited with being the starting point of the 'Cambridge phenomenon' – this proliferation of high-tech companies in the area. Out of the 1400 high-tech industries that operate in Silicon Fen, about 200 are direct university spin-outs. And all that's without mentioning the talented pool of Cambridge graduates that such firms are able to draw on.

The factors that make clustering worthwhile can be seen not just between companies, but within them as well. So much so that GlaxoSmithKline have thought long and hard about the physical layout of their labs and have promoted the idea of multidisciplinary teams to help engender communication still further. A lot of research has to rely on serendipity – but serendipitous discovery is made far more likely by, for example, fostering conversations over water coolers. Casual asides can lead to big insights. GSK also promotes the trading of information between the company's scientists and its manufacturers to refine processes that are necessary in the company's factories. It is reminiscent of the Industrial Revolution relationships that were forged between academics and industrialists in groups such as the Lunar Society. That openness and shared interest in scientific ideas was vital for the development of early British manufacturing: it is fascinating to see a modern echo of that.

For Britain, there are two pieces of good news in support of the idea that, once these networks are established, they are to some extent self-sustaining. The first is that they are hard to lift up and take away. Whereas a country like China can come across to Britain and buy an old factory (like the Rover plant at Longbridge), ship it back home and very quickly replicate what had been produced in the UK, it is not as easy to buy up a complex and ill-defined network of academics and company scientists. From the outside, it is hard to know what to buy.

The second piece of good news is that once a cluster has been established, talented people from elsewhere want to join it. The existence of talent attracts more talent, which attracts yet more. This implies that Britain enjoys the privilege of being a country with an inherited advantage in hosting high-end activity.

That explains why our historic skills in science and innovation remain strong, even though we are just a medium-sized country with about 1 per cent of the world's population. Most of us know that Britain boasts more winners of the Nobel Prize than any other country apart from the US, but this is not just an area in which we are living off our past reputation. We score well right up to the present, though not necessarily with indigenous British scientists. We earn a living by attracting good scientists to come here and then by making them productive once they arrive.

I should qualify all this by saying that new clusters are formed all the time and old ones fade. And emerging economies are creating them too – Bangalore is the most notable high-tech cluster outside the West. There is no reason why a country such as China could not achieve a dominant position in such industries in the long term. But to build world-class universities and to have talented graduates on tap is not something that can be achieved very quickly. For the near future at least, Britain's comparative advantage in such industries is assured. The challenge for the years ahead is to ensure the UK economy uses its historic privileges well.

8

Branding and Advertising

Under the heading 'A Retrospect', a 1900s magazine advert portrayed an image of how life in Britain used to be: a disgruntled husband looking despondently at what was (or rather wasn't) for supper; his wife sweating and scurrying away in the kitchen. The advert explained what was causing this terrible state of affairs: 'One day in seven, the house was filled with the odour of nauseating suds. Odd scraps served for meals, the housewife looked weary & worried, the inmates fretful ... It was wash day!'

It's one of those things that we don't really think about now, but back before the advent of white goods, the week's washing could be a major and time-consuming event: servants were known to start wash day as early as one o'clock in the morning, and work all the way through until early evening. Add in drying and ironing, and the process could take two or three days. The most basic method of washing was 'beetling', which involved beating the clothes with a bat or 'beetle' against a wooden washing block. Another method was to soak the clothes in lant – stale urine – the ammonia from which would do the cleaning.

Using soap was obviously preferable, but for many years this had been an expensive option. Soap could either be made with train oil (whale blubber), which was a difficult process and produced a coarse and odourless finished product, or with olive oil or tallow. There were concerns that using tallow to make soap would not leave enough left for the nation's candle production. To ensure resources weren't depleted, soap was subsequently heavily taxed and became a luxury good. It wasn't until 1853 that William Gladstone repealed the tax, and the British soap industry began to flourish: no more so than through the brilliance of one particular man.

William Lever was born in Bolton in 1851. His father ran a grocery store, and one of the ways that William would help out in the shop was cutting the soap. At the time, soap was sold like cheese from a deli counter: there would be a large block from which the required amount would be sliced and then wrapped. After initially going into the family grocery business, William Lever decided to turn his attentions to making soap. In the mid-1880s he acquired a chemical works in Warrington, and with his brother James came up with his own recipe for soap: a mixture of palm oil, cottonseed oil, resin and tallow. So far, so cleansing. But Lever's genius was not so much in the creation of his soap but in the way he sold it. Rather than being made in long chunks to be sliced up in store, Lever sold his yellow soap in small, individually wrapped bars, and gave his product a name which was printed on the packaging: Sunlight.

Lever's product, according to the 1900s advert, altered the nature of clothes washing itself: 'Sunlight Soap has changed all that! An ordinary washing is done in much less time! Wash day is the same as other days with Sunlight Soap. You merely rub the soap well on the clothes, roll them up for a couple of hours & rinse them out. Sunlight Soap requires no toiling!' All of which was, presumably, good news for both the hard-pressed housewife and her hungry-looking husband.

Whether or not Sunlight 'changed all that' in terms of washing, Lever's soap and the way he sold it did revolutionise the marketing of products. Sunlight Soap is one of the first examples of what we would call a brand today. Instantly recognisable, Sunlight Soap was a huge success: in 1886 Lever's factory was producing 20 tons of soap a week; two years later, it was producing 450; and by the mid-1890s the company was selling 40,000 tons of Sunlight Soap a year. The product was not just selling in Britain, but also in Belgium and Holland, and in parts of the British Empire such as Canada and South Africa. Even Queen Victoria used Sunlight, appointing Lever Brothers 'Soapmakers to Her Majesty'. Through their marketing innovation Sunlight Soap, both figuratively and literally, cleaned up.

Sunlight Soap was to prove the first of many successful products for Lever Brothers: in 1894 they launched Lifebuoy Soap, and 1899 Sunlight (later Lux) Soap Flakes. In 1930 the company merged with the Dutch firm Margarine Unie to become Unilever. Employing a quarter of a million people in Britain, the group was worth more than any other company in the UK. Today, the company remains one of our biggest firms, producing an array of well-known household products, from Flora to Marmite, Lux to Lynx, Persil to PG Tips. Sunlight Soap is now discontinued as a product in the UK, but the name lives on in many territories abroad – in Sri Lanka, for example, Sunlight laundry soap has a market share of over 75 per cent. More important, it lives on in its legacy as one of the world's first branded goods.

Things have never been the same since. We have become more and more conscious of brands, of packaging and advertising. Indeed, we are told we are obsessed with them. Almost everything is branded and enormous resources are devoted to the process of selling things rather than simply making them.

Many are unhappy at this turn of events. We are more trivial, they say, more materialistic, driven by consumerist values rather than anything deeper. I once heard a politician lament that we should spend more time reading poetry and less time destroying the planet trying to acquire the latest trainers. If that criticism is right, it surely applies to Britain as much as anywhere. When it comes to the arts of branding and advertising, this country is a world leader. We have been following a path of putting relatively more emphasis on selling things rather than making them for quite a while. And (my evidence is anecdotal) we do not spend very much time reading poetry to each other. When it comes to the culture of branded-good consumerism, we are as guilty as anyone else.

What I want to do in this chapter is persuade you to be less dismissive of the art of marketing, and to show that it adds value to manufactured goods. I want to persuade you that it is quite natural – indeed possibly inevitable – that our society has carried on in the direction upon which William Lever set it. And I'd like to demonstrate that we do make money from our skills in this area. I even want to persuade you that our preoccupation with brands is environmentally friendly. While most people don't read poems to each other, consumerism is an important form of modern cultural expression. All in all, I want to convince you not to be surprised at the way our economy has evolved in this direction, and not to be ashamed of it either. Branding creates a form of intellectual property, just as research and development does.

Just as magazine readers in 1900 could remember how tough life had been before Sunlight Soap, we can look back at how far we have come in the last few decades. Much of that is down to the scientists and engineers encountered in the last chapter.

I think back to a few examples from my childhood in a family that was well-to-do but not super-wealthy. I can remember our wonderful Ford Zephyr. It was our first car to have seatbelts and a radio, but it seemed to break down all the time, especially on holiday, and it was always rusting.

Since then of course, thanks to the brain work of the world's car makers and electronics firms we have cars that don't rust; we have airbags as well as seatbelts (every time you buy a car these days, you find that it has more airbags than the last one you bought); we have MP3 connections in the car and sat-nav too. These are all the result of innovation and improvement. Or take the telephone. My family was very lucky: we had two. One in the hall and one in the bedroom. In the early seventies only 42 per cent of the population had a phone. In this country, there are now more mobile phones than people. Economic progress of this kind has allowed most of us to live far more comfortably than in the past and, as a consequence we have, not surprisingly, allowed ourselves to devote more time and resources to education.

When I was growing up, my father was a reader in the Department of Electronic Engineering at the new University of Surrey. It was created in 1966 out of the Battersea College of Technology, which was in the process of expanding out of London to the present Guildford site. At the time, about 6 per cent of school leavers went to university. In fact, it was quite normal to leave school at fifteen. I was only nine years old when the law changed to ensure everyone stayed on to sixteen. My school acquired a new building – the RoSLA unit (RoSLA standing for Raising of School Leaving Age) – to accommodate the extra numbers of pupils involved.

These days, we assume most people will have some education or training up to the age of eighteen. In 2007–8, the numbers at university were 2.5 million instead of the 621,000 in 1970–1.

And the share of national income devoted to education has risen from 5.1 per cent in 1978–9 (the first year of such records) to 6.1 per cent in 2008–9.

It is our relative affluence which explains the RoSLA units and new universities. Of course there has also been a change in cultural attitudes that has seen us become less elitist about access to knowledge, but perhaps one reason for our change in attitude is that we could afford to do so. We may have become so accustomed to economic growth that we fail to register how much increasing affluence changes us. Since 1830 our economy has enjoyed growth averaging about 2 per cent a year. The population has increased over that time too, but per-capita incomes have grown at about 1.4 per cent a year since 1830. There have been good times when incomes have gone up much faster (such as the fifties), and bad times when they have gone up much more slowly (as in the last few years). But, on average, they have gone up at about 1.5 per cent. And at that pace, our incomes double about every fifty years. Or to put that another way, each generation can expect to be twice as rich as its grandparents.

As we have become more affluent and educated we have become more middle class, more white collar and more concerned with life's frivolities. We have the luxury of worrying about little things rather than big things. Our consumption patterns have changed. No longer are we interested in the mere basics of survival; we are interested in the more aesthetic aspects of products, which manifests itself in a greater interest in the brand name of an item or the fancy packaging around it. My father firmly asserted that you should never buy a car because of its looks. My mother would shop for the most functional items at the grocers rather than the top brands. I became familiar with the words, 'Don't pick that one, you're just paying for the fancy packaging.' These days, many of us go out of our way to buy fancy packaging. Three pounds for a paper gift bag for a bottle of wine, for example. We buy cars on the basis of their looks (although I suspect most people always did). And the basics of life comprise a far smaller portion of the average shopping basket. To paraphrase *The Hitchhiker's Guide to the Galaxy*, the three phases of human development can be summarised as: Will I eat? What will I eat? And where shall we do lunch? We are in the third of these phases.

The richer we are, the more important becomes form over function because our functional needs are increasingly satisfied. Companies therefore, and quite sensibly, orient their efforts towards satisfying our relatively frivolous tastes, putting inordinate amounts of effort into marketing, advertising and branding. Because we have moved a long way in this direction, Britain is sometimes accused of having a cappuccino economy: all froth no substance. There might be some truth in that, but we should be glad we produce frothy cappuccinos if that is what our population wants.

What we have overall is a picture of a country with hard skills in science and technology and soft skills in marketing and advertising. The former add value to products before they are made; the latter add value to them after they are made. When we saw in the last chapter that Apple makes $80 from each iPod it sells, it is hard for us to know whether that is predominantly a return for the quality of the product or for the effectiveness of the marketing. But, personally, I don't much care. Apple has succeeded in making a product that has an appeal greater than any other MP3 player. That is an achievement, regardless of the technical specification of the device.

There is a counter view. Some would argue that clever marketing by companies like Apple foists unnecessarily expensive items upon us and is thus value-destroying rather than value-adding. We could have bought a cheaper MP3 player of the same quality if only Apple hadn't put so much effort into making theirs look nicer. I understand this argument. There is evidence of consumers being duped into buying things they don't need and children being sucked by advertising into a futile competition to show off or be left out. I believe the people who say that supermarkets wastefully throw away good food simply because it doesn't look very appealing on the shelves of their stores. I don't doubt that some value destruction occurs in marketing. But I am also aware that it happens in lots of other professions too, including from time to time worthy professions such as education and journalism. The question is whether that is the appropriate way of looking at the bulk of what goes on. My own view is that it is not.

What appears to have occurred is that we now have a choice, a choice made by Western companies attempting to make money by satisfying the observed tastes of Western consumers over the decades. As we get more affluent, we don't just want more consumption, we want a more intense consumer experience. Rather than buying two MP3 players, we would rather have one MP3 player that costs twice as much and feels twice as nice. That is why Apple prevails in the market for MP3 players, and the generic manufacturers do not.

Let me take another example: biscuits. In 1998 the McKinsey Global Institute (a body attached to the consulting firm) published a report called 'Driving Productivity and Growth in the UK Economy'. It had many well-researched studies of different sectors of the UK economy that it thought were less efficient than they should have been. On the manufacture of biscuits in the UK, the report said the following: 'UK biscuits manufacturers produce 2.6 times as many products as those in the US ... this product proliferation reduces line downtime, wastes R&D and marketing resources and leads to lower productivity'. In other words, if we used our resources more efficiently to make a smaller range of biscuits we could make many more of them. We would then undoubtedly have cheaper biscuits.

I am no expert on the making or marketing of biscuits, but I wonder whether in the grand scheme of things we aren't better off having a bigger range of biscuits rather than bigger quantities. Visit a supermarket and behold the sheer number of biscuit-related items, each of which carries a certain appeal and meaning to a certain segment of the market. There are Pink Panther wafers and Happy Hippo biscuits for children; Oaties Hobnobs, everyone's favourite office biscuit; there's Cornish clotted cream shortbread, all-butter shortbread, shortbread fingers, choc chip shortbread rings – more varieties of shortbread than a society could possibly need. From bourbons to Jaffa Cakes, chocolate caramels to custard creams, there's no doubt that Britons love their biscuits! Yes, we pay more for biscuits as a result; all that packaging uses money that could have been directed at manufacturing. But do we not enjoy biscuits more as a result of the choice? And what damage would be done to the planet, were we to deploy more resources into biscuit factories to churn out ever greater quantities? If I was Mother Earth, I'd go for the option of employing more people using fewer raw materials, designing new forms of green energy any day.

A walk around a supermarket shows that in almost every category of product we have made an expensive decision to proliferate choice and to give pleasure through the aesthetic quality of the products we consume. Why else are there eighteen different dental floss-type items on a Tesco shelf, all of which do the same job of cleaning between your teeth?

It is not a choice that suits everyone. For those that can't afford the basic requirements of food to eat, it is unfortunate that we have devoted resources to marketing fancier items. Just as it is unfortunate that we have devoted some resources to yachts and diamond rings. But, all the same, it is a choice that our society has made as to how to spend some of the extra income at its disposal and it is one that has shaped the activity that our economy engages in.

Another telling example is that of Levi's jeans. They were extremely popular in the eighties and nineties, and were priced at something of a premium over some other brands. The margins were high and Levi's wanted to keep it that way. But supermarkets knew they could sell those jeans at lower margins in larger quantities if they could get hold of them. A long battle ensued between supermarkets getting hold of Levi's through back-door channels to pile them high and sell them cheap, and Levi's, who tried to keep them exclusive to more expensive and fashionable outlets. Who was right in this battle? Your answer depends on whether you think customers are buying a piece of cloth to cover their legs or a statement about themselves. Is it the denim that matters or the label? If it's the label, then putting it on a supermarket shelf degrades it, as an upmarket retail ambience is important to the cachet the product is designed to carry. If it's the denim, then the supermarkets are right to get it out to us at the cheapest price possible.

The answer ultimately has to be a bit of both, but probably it is the label that people really wanted. The evidence for this is simply that other cheaper jeans were available and could easily be sourced by supermarkets. If it was just the fabric people wanted, there was no need to go to so much effort to ensure the branded denim was the one on the shelf. Levi's were probably right to argue that supermarket positioning undermined the value of the jeans being sold. The expensive £50 Levi's 501 jeans were soon to be less fashionable as consumers graduated to £110 Diesel jeans and other even more premium brands not available at supermarkets. Meanwhile, for those not interested in making statements about themselves in the clothes they wear, it was possible to buy unbranded £5 supermarket pairs that were perfectly good at keeping you decent.

I haven't answered the question as to why people like to pay more for a branded product. There is much one could say about that. But I distinguish between those cases where people want to buy a particular product and look to the brand simply as a certificate that they are buying what they want. And the case of biscuit and jean manufacture, where the label and the design associated with it are an integral part of the appeal. In these cases our consumption of a brand signals something about us to others, and it also says something about us to ourselves. It allows us the luxury of enjoying a connection to a world that we like to identify with, or to express an aspiration that moves us. I see nothing pernicious about this and no reason to think someone is a victim of it any more than they are a victim when they watch television or read a book. It is just part of some people's vocabulary. It is not for everyone, but it works for some.

I don't know if there are still traces of William Lever's old Sunlight Soap in the British water supply, but the fact remains that when it comes to branding and advertising, we are up there among the world leaders. London is a global hub of advertising. The modern-day Mad Men of New York might have something to say about that, but the United States is big enough to make much of the business there American-based. As the British market is smaller in both scale and scope, our advertising firms look for work beyond the UK – outwards towards Europe, the US and beyond – and that is one of the reasons that our industries are both truly international and have truly global appeal.

There are many examples of great British branding and advertising campaigns that have been used around the world.

Back in 1982, when BBH co-founder John Hegarty visited an Audi factory as part of his research for a new campaign, he saw the phrase '*Vorsprung Durch Technik*' scrawled on the factory wall. Almost thirty years on, the slogan remains at the heart of Audi's advertising worldwide. Other British campaigns that have enjoyed international success include Cadbury's drumming gorilla (made by Fallon), which has been used in Canada, Australia and New Zealand; BBH's 'Flat Eric' campaign for Levi's; and Wolff Olins's branding of Orange, which France Telecom has used to rebrand its services around the world.

I mention London as being the main home of these advertising and branding firms, but in fact one can be even more specific than that. Advertising forms a creative cluster that makes Silicon Fen seem disparate in comparison. One could go on the advertising equivalent of a guided tour of W1 post-codes, to visit a whole host of world leaders: beginning in Charlotte Street with Saatchi & Saatchi (blue-chip clients include T-Mobile and Emirates airline); on to Marylebone Road to see Abbot Mead Vickers BBDO (creators of Guinness's award-winning 'white horses' advert), Rathbone Street for CHI & Partners (Pfizer and Samsung), to TBWA in Whitfield Street (clients including PlayStation), Fallon in Great Titchfield Street (who came up with the Skoda car cake), BBH in Kingly Street (the Boddingtons creatives), and WCRS in Great Portland Street (Sony and Santander). There is a second cluster in the Shoreditch area of East London, of whom perhaps Mother is the most well known: clients include such minor international firms as Ikea and Coca-Cola.

Our leading branding firms are more spread out across the capital, but with no less an impressive roster of clients: Interbrand's office in London came up with the name for the Ford Focus. Futurebrand's clients include GlaxoSmithKline and

Microsoft; Wolff Olins is the branding agency for Orange and the 2012 Olympics; Brand Union represents Vodafone.

The last chapter examined how Britain has used its competitive advantage garnered from its education system and science skills to good effect in R&D-led industries such as pharmaceuticals and technology. The strength of our creative industries gives us the same edge in branding and advertising. Just as we saw how firms such as ARM Holdings make money through their designs rather than actually making things themselves, so our branding and advertising firms generate revenue through the ideas they create. And they generate international revenues too, not just profits from UK consumers. So how precisely do they go about doing this?

It is rather hard to put precise figures on it. But there are of course the fees generated from the sale of services to foreign clients. Even if the value from a campaign is generated by staff working overseas for a UK-based company, the British parent earns some profit.

The second way that our skills in branding earn export revenues for the UK is by adding value to British products that are then exported abroad. A particularly good example is Lipton Tea, another hugely successful Unilever product. Like Sunlight Soap, Lipton's roots stretch back to the late nineteenth century. Born a year before William Lever, Thomas Lipton followed a similar early career path; with his parents also owning a small shop, this time in Glasgow, Lipton worked for the family firm before turning his hand to producing his own goods. He entered the tea trade in 1888 and Lipton Tea quickly established itself as a popular British brand.

Today, Unilever may no longer market Lipton Tea in the UK, but we're one of a small group of countries where it isn't for sale. With sales of about £2.5 billion a year, Lipton is the world's best-selling tea by quite some distance: its market share is three times larger than its nearest rival. The famous yellow-label brew is available in 110 countries worldwide, but nowhere is this story more remarkable than in the country that invented tea itself: China. One quarter of all tea comes from China, and the country is responsible for one sixth of all tea exports. Yet in a classic 'coals to Newcastle' case, Lipton is by far the biggest tea brand in the country, garnering a 30 per cent market share of the teabag market according to one survey.

So what do Lipton and Unilever bring to the table in order to sell so much tea back to its spiritual home? In some ways, the situation in China is not dissimilar to that of soap sales in the late nineteenth century: for blocks of unbranded soap then, read unbranded loose-leaf tea today. That is what the vast majority of tea China exports is, and as discussed earlier, the lack of brand leaves the tea traders competing on price alone. Lipton as a brand offers the consumer something different: a world-renowned name. The associated internationalism appeals to the younger Chinese generations, as does the convenience of the teabag: this is true both in making the tea itself and where to buy it from – the brand is readily available from supermarkets instead of traditional tea stores. For an increasingly aspirational and time-poor urban population, the appeal of the Lipton brand is understandable. For the British firm owning the brand, its worth is invaluable.

The third, and perhaps most controversial, way that we make money in this sector is by creating brand-led companies, which we then sell to foreign firms for a substantial profit. One example was the mobile phone service provider Orange. A brand created from scratch by Wolff Olins and a memorable advertising campaign – 'The future's bright, the future's Orange' – from WCRS was eventually bought by France Telecom, which decided to use the Orange name for all its internet services.

Another good example of Britain profiting from brand creation sold into the hands of foreigners was the takeover of Rowntree Mackintosh by Nestlé in 1988. Rowntree had been making chocolate in York since the 1860s. Indeed, York could be considered to have been something of a confectionery cluster, with Terry's and Cravens also based in the city: for many years, rail passengers arriving at York station were greeted by a Yorkie Bar hoarding: 'Welcome to York: Where the Men are Hunky and the Chocolate is Chunky!'

It wasn't just Nestlé who were interested in purchasing Rowntree in the late eighties: their Swiss rival Suchard also wanted to buy the firm. There followed a fierce battle between the two firms, played out against a backdrop of concerned locals and factory workers. Rowntree was one of the biggest employers in York: would the takeover lead to redundancies? Would decision-making be transferred from the company's British headquarters to Switzerland? Would production be shifted abroad?

In the event, the answer to these questions was predominantly no. The £2.55 billion that Nestlé spent in buying the company was spent because Nestlé wanted not just the household brands that Rowntree made – Kit Kat, Smarties, Fruit Pastilles, Polos – but also the know-how in making these brands a success. Rather than asset stripping, Nestlé actually invested money in improving the infrastructure: £15 million on replacing the building that had made Polos since 1948; £20 million on a new Kit Kat factory. Perhaps most importantly, the York research centre was doubled in size, given a £6 million makeover and boosted by scientists flown in from around the Nestlé empire. And though there were some job losses, these were broadly mitigated by an increase in productivity and output: around the same number of people were employed in making Kit Kats, for example, but producing double the amount.

What's more, Nestlé were able to boost Rowntree's international presence, selling its brands in territories that had been beyond its reach before. Kit Kat, which for so many years was the best-selling chocolate bar in Britain, at one point regularly outselling second-place Mars by 50 per cent, became a huge seller in India, China and Eastern Europe. By 2010, the seventy-fifth anniversary of the bar's launch, the Kit Kat was sold in more countries than any other chocolate bar, with 17.6 billion of the chocolate fingers produced every year! But, rather than production having been transferred abroad, the York factory was still making three million bars every day.

In many respects, the sale of Rowntree to Nestlé in 1988 was no different to the merger of Mackintosh with Rowntree in 1969: that earlier coming together was also to do with brands, in Mackintosh's case the likes of Quality Street, Rolo and Toffee Crisp. The reason we feel differently, of course, is because of the issue of foreign ownership. But the Rowntree experience shows that it is not necessarily a negative experience as businesses can grow and reach markets that they would not otherwise be able to. It is the British success with creating brands that made a firm like Rowntree such an attractive prospect; a company like Nestlé knows not to tamper with that, and understands how to maximise its potential – to everyone's benefit.

I hope I have made the point that we have skills in the area of branding and marketing, and that these skills have a value in the world. But I don't want to exaggerate British success in these industries. Other countries have strong branded goods too. The French and Italians hardly need lessons from us in selling expensive branded luxury goods; the Germans and Japanese have some wonderfully strong brands built upon their solid reputations as good manufacturers; and it would take too long to list all the successful American brands. But our economy has performed with the best in orienting itself towards this lucrative activity, which is perhaps not surprising given our recognised strengths in the creative industries. Before we leave the subject of intellectual property, however, we need to explore some of the implications of making a living in this area.

9

The Drawbacks of
Being Clever

We should probably celebrate the fact that our country is high in the global rankings of technology and science, that it is respected in the worlds of advertising and marketing, and that it is a world leader in the creative industries. These are good businesses to be in and are handsomely rewarded. But before we get carried away with the celebrations and before we develop an inflated sense of our nation's cool, it is worth noting that brainy nations are in some senses rather vulnerable ones. Frustrating as it may seem, we have to feed and clothe ourselves in the material world with all its wearisome constraints like the laws of physics. Making a car or growing wheat are very different from manufacturing an idea. Unlike physical objects, ideas are easy to share, easy to copy and annoyingly easy to steal. So in this chapter we shall take a short journey into the world of intellectual property and the implications for our companies, our economy and our society of our nation attempting to make its living by producing thoughts rather than things.

One might start by asking why do we not give ideas to people for Christmas instead of physical items? For an answer, you might like to try it on a small child to see what reaction you get. I doubt it would be very favourable. Children instinctively understand the difference between intellectual property and physical property. In the case of the former, the idea may be theirs once you have given it to them, but it is not theirs alone. And as a gift, which we might view as an expression of commitment or affection marked by the offering of a small sacrifice, the idea fails because I can happily give it to you and to several other people as well. A nice idea doesn't cut it at all: it is not a sacrifice as it costs me nothing to give it. The same is not true of a pair of socks.

Take another example. Which would you rather your teenage daughter confessed to, the theft of a bar of chocolate from a shop or the illegal downloading of a song? However hard the music industry tries to tell us that illegal downloads are theft, most of us can't help but see a difference between cases where the thief deprives someone else of a piece of property they own, and those in which the thief allows the owner to keep the property they already owned intact.

If intellectual and physical property are distinct when it comes to giving and taking, they are just as different when it comes to buying and selling. Imagine I try to sell you an idea. I do, of course, have to tell you what it is in order for you to know whether you want to buy it, but once I've told you what it is, you probably don't need to buy it because you now have the idea in your possession. Once given, an idea can't be taken away. These characteristics can make it hard to persuade people to pay for ideas in the way that they happily pay for real objects. What exactly are you paying for? And then, even if I do succeed in making you pay for an idea, it is very hard for me to stop you selling it on for a slice of the profit of my intellectual labour.

The fundamental problem is that it costs almost nothing to reproduce a thought once it has been articulated. Once an idea has been recorded, filmed, printed or explained all exclusivity is lost. When we use the word 'property' in the term 'intellectual property', we are really using it metaphorically. We try to make it similar to real property by creating patents, as well as copyright and trademark laws. That makes it easier to claim ownership than it would otherwise be, but it is still not very easy.

To understand the problem, take a good example of an area in which there is no recognised form of intellectual property protection: the joke. If someone creates a funny one it can spread like wildfire, giving a few pence worth of pleasure to huge numbers of people. The joke's creator, however, gets no financial reward and probably no credit either. Economists worry about this kind of thing: why would anyone bother to think of a joke if they can't be paid for it? Fortunately, their concern is misplaced. Amateur and professional comedians do still exist and they occasionally manage to be handsomely remunerated (though not as handsomely as they would be if we lived in a world where it was practical to charge people for re-telling their gags). I suspect that comedians exist because a good deal of wit lies in the way they tell it, rather than in the punchline, so they can still charge for their time. Even so, comedians who invent large numbers of jokes live in fear of their theft.

The comedians particularly at risk are those whose routines consist of quick one-liners rather than more story-based material. Tim Vine, for example, faced problems when a viral email was circulated consisting of a number of his gags, which had erroneously been credited to the late Tommy Cooper: as a result, he found himself repeatedly accused of plagiarism. In 2009 stand-up Dan Antopolski won the award for the funniest joke at that year's Edinburgh fringe with his one-liner, 'Hedgehogs – why can't they just share the hedge?' Within weeks, the joke was being repeated by numerous amateur stand-ups around the country as their own, and could be found emblazoned across T-shirts (with no credit, or royalties, to Antopolski).

It should be said that in terms of British comedy there has been a shift in attitudes towards joke ownership over the years, with a clear difference of opinion among 'mainstream' and 'alternative' comedians. In his book *How I Escaped My Certain Fate*, stand-up Stewart Lee explains that 'traditionally, mainstream acts aren't precious about material in the way that their Alternative Comedy cousins are. To them, jokes are just jokes, naturally occurring phenomena like wind or rain, resistant to the abstract notion of ownership.' Lee is one of a number of comedians who have used their skill in humour to exact revenge on such appropriation: so incensed was he with Joe Pasquale using a joke by fellow comedian Michael Redmond, that in his *'90s Comedian* show Lee discussed the incident at length, before delivering a carefully crafted joke that was impossible for Joe Pasquale to steal. The Mighty Boosh, riled by a Sugar Puffs advert they felt echoed part of their act, got their own back by killing a Honey Monster as part of their stage show.

In contrast to the weak protection afforded to comedians, it is sometimes the case that the safeguarding of intellectual property can be absurdly strong. The song 'Happy Birthday to You' is listed in the *Guinness Book of Records* as the most recognised song in the English language. The famous ditty started out in a Kentucky kindergarten at the end of the nineteenth century, when sisters Mildred J. Hill and Patty Smith Hill wrote 'Good Morning to All' as a way of welcoming children at the start of the day. In 1893, the song was published in a collection of children's songs, *Song Stories for the Kindergarten.*

Somewhere along the way, the words of the song were adapted to the 'Happy Birthday' lyrics. It remains hazy as to when this happened, or who first did it, but in 1935 the Clayton F. Summy Publishing Company of Chicago copyrighted 'Happy Birthday To You' with a third Hill sister, Jessica, who had successfully shown the similarity between the two songs in court. Summy was bought by Birch Tree Limited in the seventies, which in turn was bought by Warner Chappell in the nineties, and today the copyright resides in a division called Summy Birchard Music.

The copyright of the song is stringently enforced, bringing in an estimated $2 million in royalties a year. In the 2003 documentary film *The Corporation*, it was suggested that Warner Chappell charge $10,000 for use of the song in a film. Which probably explains why you seldom hear the song in a movie – directors tend to go for the copyright-free 'For He's A Jolly Good Fellow' instead. The good news for budding filmmakers, and anyone wanting to use the song, is that the copyright lease won't exist for ever: it is due to expire in Europe in 2016 (a hundred years after the death of Mildred Hill) and in 2030 in the United States.

'Happy Birthday' is an exception. The usual pattern is for those who toil at intellectual labour to struggle to maintain their property. Of course, in the real commercial world very few thoughts exist in isolation. Just as jokes are sometimes best told by the professional comedian, most clever ideas are best delivered in some physical form – a book or a record, a pill or a high-tech piece of equipment – all of which can be traded in conventional ways with the usual protection afforded to physical objects. But that protection is small relative to the value of the underlying cleverness, which is most of the value of the object.

If this all sounds a bit abstract, just think of those trying to sell newspapers, music, pharmaceuticals or high-fashion items. Protection of their intellectual property is an enormous preoc-cupation. It always has been, but never more so since digital reproduction cut the material component of a great deal of it to almost zero.

Dealing with the problems of piracy is nothing new for the music industry: back in the eighties, the rise of the blank cassette led to an industry campaign that claimed 'Home Taping is Killing Music'. Compared to the difficulties record companies now face with illegal downloads, home taping probably seems like a halcyon age. It has become as difficult to protect music as it is jokes. In 2010, Francis Keeling, vice-president of digital at Universal, the world's largest music company, admitted that the battle had effectively been lost: 'Are you going to stop piracy? No, you're not,' he told a music convention. 'We've got markets like Spain and Italy where [people say] "You buy music? What are you doing buying music when you can get it for free?"' For countries such as Spain, the effect on local music is potentially devastating. Between 2005 and 2010, album sales of Spanish artists fell by 65 per cent. The result is that record companies are investing in English-language artists, who have more inter-national appeal – turning countries like Spain, in the words of another music executive, into a 'cultural desert'.

With Amazon now selling more e-books than hardback and paperback books in the United States, digital piracy is a problem that book publishing has already had to face up to. Indeed, it is possible that you are reading a pirated edition of this book. (I'm tempted to condemn you for doing so, but I'll only extend my annoyance to those of you who would have bought it if you had had to; I suspect most piraters would not have bought it if they had to, so I'm not really losing any-thing by them reading it for free.) India is one potentially lucrative market where illegal versions of bestselling titles are

Mighty oaks from little acorns grow. From the BBC Microcomputer in the early eighties . . .

. . . to ARM Holdings, microprocessor designers of the modern world.

COULD there be more convincing proof that Glaxo not only "Builds Bonnie Babies" but lasting health and happiness in later childhood, than this photograph—a family of five sturdy children, happy, healthy and vigorous, all reared on Glaxo? Their father writes of one, the youngest:—"She is the bonniest of the lot— a lovely child. Needless to say, she has been reared on Glaxo."

Doctors and nurses themselves know that Glaxo amply fulfils all expectations. Not only do they recommend Glaxo when breast-milk fails, but they rear their own children on it.

Your Baby can grow into a happy, healthy youngster too, just as straight, well-knit, rosy-cheeked and good-spirited as ever you wished him to be—it is a question of either breast-milk or Glaxo. *Ask your Doctor!*

Glaxo
The Super-Milk
"Builds Bonnie Babies"

GLAXO (Dept. 31), GLAXO HOUSE, OSNABURGH STREET, LONDON N.W. 1.

Glaxo, forerunner of the modern pharmaceuticals giant GlaxoSmithKline, started out making dried milk.

Making penicillin in 1943. Glaxo's role in manufacturing the drug for the British war effort revolutionised the company.

Sir Alastair Pilkington, inventor of the 'float glass' procedure for making glass.

'Requires no toiling!' An advert for Sunlight Soap from the 1900s.

The proliferation of choice: a dazzling array of biscuit brands for the British consumer to choose from.

Having a break in Bhutan: the Kit Kat is a British brand with international appeal.

Levi's on sale at Tesco in Newcastle. Did the cheaper price cheapen the brand?
TopFoto

Li-Ning trainers. China is now developing its own brands to rival those
of the west. Getty Images

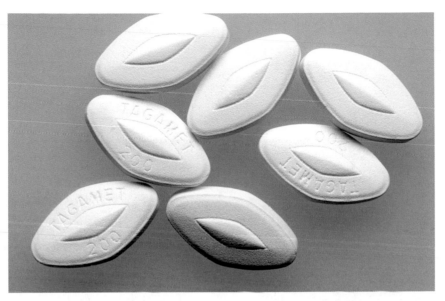

Tagamet was the highest-selling prescription drug of all time . . .

. . . until the arrival of
Glaxo's rival drug, Zantac.

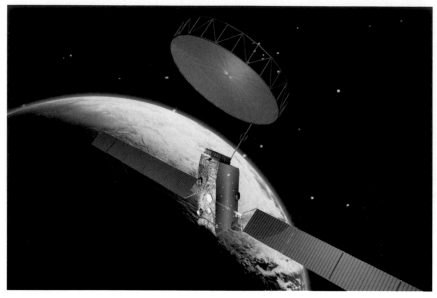

An artist's depiction of the Inmarsat I-4 satellite.

The Shard under construction.

An artist's impression of the
Shard at London Bridge.

Canary Wharf at dusk. Has our financial sector grown too big in recent years?
Gavin Hellier/Robert Harding

All my own work: George Brown with a copy of the Labour government's 'National Plan', 1965. Getty Images

readily available, to the detriment of publishers' sales (and authors' royalties). Some publishers do eventually succeed in getting these books removed from sale, but it inevitably takes time, money and lawyers to resolve the situation, resources that could have been used to promote its own publications.

An editor told me of his attempts a few years ago to acquire the rights to the autobiography of the cricketer Sachin Tendulkar. Tendulkar is one of the all-time cricketing greats and an Indian icon so his autobiography should be an enormous bestseller. But with India being the book's primary market, there would be difficulty in quantifying how many of the book's sales would be achieved via the publisher, and how many would be from pirated copies. As the estimated sales figures dropped, so did the size of the advance, to the point that the deal was no longer viable. The Tendulkar book that did eventually reach the market was one where his publisher found a somewhat unusual way around the piracy issue: with a print run of just ten copies, and a retail price of £49,000, the 852-page, 37-kilogram *Tendulkar Opus* features a signature page marked by drops of the cricketer's blood. As much as technology has improved, it is probably a few years yet before anyone is able to successfully pirate that.

There is another important fact of life for companies and countries producing and trading in the de-material world. When there is a flourishing market in physical objects – cars, for example – there will tend to be a wide range on sale. High-quality expensive ones will compete with lower-quality cheap ones. The market will naturally segment into different kinds of buyers with different budgets and different tastes, and producers will tailor their products accordingly. But what happens in a market of competing ideas? As the cost of reproducing thoughts is immaterial, there is a tendency for good ones to prevail over bad ones completely and absolutely. The winner takes all. It is easy to distribute the idea so the best can take 100 per cent of the market.

As dissemination costs are relatively low in the world of intellectual property, the market changes very quickly: market share can be gained or lost astonishingly fast. In the physical economy, it took decades for Toyota to displace General Motors. It took very little time for Google to overtake Yahoo! as the search engine of choice in the late nineties, or just a few years for J. K. Rowling to go from a struggling writer to one of the best-selling authors of all time.

Of course, it will rarely be quite this extreme, but at the very least the world of intellectual property is a capricious one. You can have a leading product (MySpace, for example) only to find it become a dismal runner-up within a couple of years when a better product (such as Facebook) arrives. Life in the world of intellectual property is never very secure.

To add to the challenge of sustaining a strong business position, there is the fact that other companies can see what you are doing, stumble upon a minor improvement and take your entire market. These are real business issues for those who inhabit the world of intellectual property. The story of Glaxo, Smith, Kline & French, Tagamet and Zantac is a telling one.

Tagamet is the trade name of the anti-ulcer drug Cimetidine, which was launched by Smith, Kline & French in 1976. It was based on a scientific breakthrough in the treatment of ulcers, and the drug's use vastly reduced the number of people who needed surgery to treat them. Within five years Tagamet had become the highest-selling prescription drug of all time. But by the early eighties, one of Smith, Kline & French's rivals, Glaxo, had developed Zantac, their own ulcer drug. The difference between Zantac and Tagamet was not on the same scale as the difference between Tagamet and previous anti-ulcer treatments: Zantac drew on the same scientific principles as Tagamet, but with an improvement in the end result. Glaxo's drug was slightly more potent, with trials suggesting an ulcer healing rate 6 per cent higher than Tagamet; there were also fewer side effects than from using Tagamet (though neither had many); the only other difference was that Zantac was more convenient for the patient, needing only to be taken twice a day, compared to four times for Tagamet.

None of these differences, then, was huge. As claims, they were not even incontrovertible: one report for the US Food and Drug Agency suggested that there was 'no adequate substantial data of which we are aware that shows Zantac is superior in overall effectiveness and/or safety'. Assuming that Zantac was the marginally more effective product, you might have expected it to achieve a slightly higher level of sales than Tagamet. But then, factoring in Tagamet's established track record and its lower price, you might have expected the advantage to have been removed, and sales of the two drugs to be identical. Instead, Zantac blew its rival out of the water.

Launched in the United States in 1983, Zantac achieved sales of $134 million in its first year: a record for a prescription product. This initial 8.9 per cent share of the market rose to 44 per cent by 1986; a year later it had captured 50 per cent of the market and was the biggest selling prescription drug in the United States. At the same time, the drug transformed the fortunes of Glaxo: its turnover increased fivefold in 1984, by 76 per cent in 1985, and 75 per cent in 1986. In doing so, it rose from being the twentieth-largest pharmaceutical company in the US to the ninth. Zantac became the first drug to achieve sales of $1 billion and earned itself a place in the *Guinness Book of Records*. Enough to give the makers of Tagamet an ulcer themselves!

Of course, Smith, Kline & French could have invented Zantac itself. Indeed, this is the way to make money consistently in the world of intellectual property: you ensure that as quickly as your rivals copy, tweak, or re-sell your old idea, you are on to the next thing. But the advice to stay one step ahead of your rivals is the sort of useless suggestion you find in business books, no more helpful than a training manual telling athletes to run faster than their competitors in order to win. Companies and countries with a strong lead in a product area are never unassailable. They can hardly build a long-term business plan on the assumption that they will remain cleverer than other people. Yes, they can exploit the natural advantage offered by their expertise to position themselves well for the next round of competition. But they are not definitely going to win that competition.

If a business faces particular challenges by choosing to operate in the world of intellectual property, so does a country. As an economy evolves away from manual labour, the distribution of economic power shifts and it does so in ways that tend to make a society less equal. To see the point, let's take a highly stylised example; a caricature, but nevertheless a revealing one. We'll examine the economics of J. K. Rowling.

She is British. Her output is popular, and is thus one of the world's greatest generators of intellectual property. She is also a great example of a beneficiary of globalisation. Instead of simply selling Harry Potter to her own nationals, or to English-speaking children around the world, she has sold over four hundred million books, many of them in China and India. The profits she has made from those two countries have only been attainable because their consumers have earned money selling things to us and thus are able to afford to buy things from us. There has been an additional benefit in that Harry Potter merchandise is cheaper to manufacture than it used to be, thanks to the low-cost production now available in places like China. So the opportunities for J. K. Rowling (or rather her publishers and licencees)

to exploit Harry Potter are vastly greater than they would otherwise have been.

The total revenue that has accrued from the creation of Harry
Potter is vast: the book royalties, the merchandise royalties, the
movie royalties, the income derived by Daniel Radcliffe, whose
career was made by the magic of Harry Potter, the studio and
location fees generated by the movie. It is all useful export
revenue for the UK. It is hard to attribute the costs to different
countries accurately, but the films have cost over a billion dollars
to make in total and they have grossed more than three-quarters
of a billion dollars each. Typically, less than a tenth of the market
has been in the UK, so over 90 per cent of the revenues have
derived from overseas. And with 400 million book sales it is
clear that Harry Potter has been a sizeable business. Much of the
movie revenue goes to local cinemas around the world, of
course; likewise, much of the profit goes to the international
movie studios and much of the book price goes to local bookshops, so we should be careful about exaggerating claims of
profit. But what is most interesting is the revenue that has gone
to J. K. Rowling herself.

She is said to have accumulated wealth of about half a billion
pounds (according to the 2010 *Sunday Times* Rich List, and this
is a perfectly realistic figure). That is roughly equivalent to £50
million a year for the decade she was churning out the books.
To get that in perspective, the manufacturing sector has an
output (measured in gross value added terms) of about £50,000
per employee per year. So Rowling was equivalent to a manufacturing business of about a thousand employees. Each could
have been paid a wage of £25,000 a year, with the company
making a very handsome profit on top.

That is the effect of the dissemination costs of intellectual
property. Unlike manufactured items, which have to be painfully
manufactured one at a time, a single Harry Potter can satisfy a

very large number of people almost simultaneously. One writer, one small boy, one huge contribution to mankind. And you don't need me to spell out an important consequence of the shift towards intellectual property. In the case of the small factory, the thousand employees had a claim to the income created. In the Harry Potter example, however, the money accrues to J. K. Rowling. In looking at the overall data for the UK, the thousand-person factory and J. K. Rowling might appear to be similar. The balance of payments will show a huge credit landing on the shores of the UK in either case. Fifty million pounds or so of exports pays for millions of those Berwin & Berwin suits manufactured in China. But that is little help if you can't afford those goods because you haven't written Harry Potter.

So it is an important contention about our economic journey up-market that the intellectual property economy is a rather unequal one. The winners tend to take all because they can conquer an entire market more easily than the victors in the battles that corporations fight in the material world. And anyway, it is quite possible that, as a nation, we are endowed with very unequal skills in creating intellectual property.

Fortunately, the enormous imbalance of winners and losers is not quite as bad as I suggest. J. K. Rowling needs to spend her money. She probably doesn't want a containerload of Chinese suits, but she might want a bit of help in the garden. As soon as she has spent some of her royalties on hiring workers, her employees have the opportunity to buy some of those imported goods. J. K. Rowling is also a very generous person, who has given her money away in large amounts. The people on whom it is spent or who are employed as a consequence of her philanthropy are benefiting from the resource trickle-through that her earnings create. Those people will, in turn, spend some of their money on domestically produced items and the author's wealth will thus move even further through the British labour market.

And we shouldn't forget that J. K. Rowling pays tax, by which her earnings become public property.

Moreover, as our society becomes more middle class it produces fewer factory workers and gardeners and more aspiring J. K. Rowlings. The vastly greater supply of children's novels will make it easier for publishers to secure contracts on favourable terms and harder for the J. K. Rowlings to earn megabucks, even when their novels do well. In the meantime, gardeners will become more and more expensive as you can't find one amid all the intellectuals trying to write books. That should offset the inegalitarian trend that has occurred in the Western world in recent decades. But whatever ameliorating effects there are to tame the winner-takes-all nature of the Harry Potter economy, the winner will still take a great deal. Not all the revenue earned will trickle down, and the amount that does trickle may not be sufficient to sustain the standard of living that workers in Britain expect. The lesson is simple: an economy built on intellectual property is a tough place for people with little intellectual property to sell.

There is something that makes the problem even more extreme. The J. K. Rowlings of the world are very attractive to all nations. If she is a one-person factory worth half a billion pounds, there is nowhere in the world that would not like to have her around, employing gardeners, giving away money and paying tax. So in order to attract the J. K. Rowlings, tax systems around the world are constrained from being too redistributive. With many attractive countries to choose from, the elite can secure a good deal when they shop around for a place in which to reside.

That is why immigration rules in many countries are more lenient for IT specialists and doctors than for unskilled manual workers. And it is why the most talented scientists are so much in demand at the universities of the world. Above all, that is why top tax rates are not higher. (We have all heard the argument that we will lose out if we try to take too big a proportion of the incomes of our most productive citizens as they will move off-shore.) That is also why the UK maintains the special tax status of 'non-doms' (people who are resident in the UK but who do not count as fully British and who thus – unlike the rest of us – only pay tax on their UK income, not on their worldwide income). It was particularly fascinating to see the Spanish introduce in 2005 a tax change designed to make Spain more attractive as a destination for rich foreigners. It was dubbed 'Beckham's law' as the English footballer was one of the first to take advantage of it when he joined Real Madrid.

David Beckham may not meet everybody's definition of a knowledge worker, but of course that is exactly what he is in the world of intellectual property. He is a brand, a marketing phenomenon and a creative talent who at his best could play ninety minutes of football and provide millions of spectators with hours of pleasure that they were happy to pay for. He is, in fact, rather similar to a Nobel physicist or an Indian steel magnate: all this top-flight talent is extremely mobile. Yes, of course Beckham's global migration has been constrained by his desire to settle where the best teams are located as that maximises the opportunities for him to flourish at his game. And yes, top academics want to settle at the best universities, so even they can't go wherever they want. But, unlike the rest of us, they are spoilt for choice in terms of locations. They can more or less dictate terms because the spin-off benefits to an economy of having a Beckham, a top academic or a J. K. Rowling are large and are thus worth paying for.

The idea of a Harry Potter economy is rather extreme, but it does illustrate some of the things that have been going on in our real economy over the last few decades as we have moved up the value chain and let other countries take on some of the work we used to do. All economic transitions are disorientating; they have winners and losers as new skills become more highly valued. In this instance, the bright have flourished; the unskilled have suffered. Brainy jobs have been well rewarded but physical labour has not. And there is also a remarkable effect in the middle. The huge increase in the size of the graduate middle class has made it slightly more difficult to stand out simply by being a member of the graduate middle class. The return on graduate incomes has gone down, as graduate numbers have gone up.

One might argue that the countries in which inequality has increased the most in recent decades – such as Britain – are the very ones which have been most successful in making the move towards high-end output. Few would doubt that we are right not to compete with the Chinese or Indians in low-value manufacturing; all Western countries are striving to be clever. But while we have had success, it comes at a price. Not only are companies in the sphere of intellectual property insecure, ever having to guard their intangible assets, but societies are affected too.

I do have some good news for people who feel the world has turned against them over the last decade or two. People who are not good at writing books, devising games, designing buildings or finding cures for cancer. People who have been told until they are weary that they must go to university in order to get a good job, or that there is no place for unskilled workers in the modern economy. The good news is that the world does not stand still. Just as China has made several million extra bodies available to the supply of manufacturing labour over the last ten years, it is following the path that we ourselves followed at breakneck speed. Don't think that the country hasn't noticed that we in Britain enjoy handsome remuneration from crafting high-value items while they toil away at the really hard work for a far lower reward. They want a piece of what we do so are now trying to move up the value chain. You can expect that, over the next ten years, the Chinese economy will converge on ours, implying that there will be a huge increase in the world supply of well-educated people. The laws of supply and demand suggest that trend should depress the price of people at the top, and rebalance things towards the bottom. The more clever people there are, the more competition between them and the less they get paid.

We will strive to stay one step ahead but, as I've already said, we cannot rely on that for ever. The emerging markets are catching up with us and the closer they get, the more they impact on the professional end of the economy: the engineers, the designers and the marketing professionals. It is inconceivable that they won't turn out to be just as good at many of the things we do better than them now. Just as China has gone from winning five gold medals at the 1988 summer Olympics to fifty-one at Beijing twenty years later, we won't have to wait long before China makes jet engines and pharmaceuticals. And just as we became preoccupied with brands and marketing once we had become relatively rich, so will China.

I saw evidence of that in Li-Ning, a sports brand I encountered in Shanghai. (If you Google the word 'lining', you'll find the first entry that comes up is not about the cloth that sits inside a suit; it is the company's website.) I had read a little about the brand, which models itself after Adidas or Nike, and when I went into the flagship store on the main shopping street in the city, I quickly saw just how fast the Chinese are picking up the skills to develop their own indigenous brands. The old Li-Ning logo was a curvy symbol rather derivative of the Nike swoosh. The old slogan was 'Anything is possible', which seemed like a feeble knock-off of the cooler Adidas phrase 'Impossible is nothing'. But Li-Ning is evolving fast. It has a new logo, a representation of the 'Li Ning Cross' posture invented by Li Ning himself, the Olympic gymnast who founded the company. There is a new slogan too: 'Make the Change'. The message is clear – you don't need an expensive western brand to get the values you aspire to. At first you copy, then you invent your own.

I met the marketing manager, Cindy Wu. She learned her marketing skills in the West and then brought them back to China. There was little anyone could teach her about brands today, and I was shocked to learn of the size of the company – turning over more than a billion dollars in 2009. While filming *Made in Britain*, we went to watch the making of a television commercial for Harbin beer, a regional product trying to boost its national appeal. The ad was a big-budget epic set on board a (fake) cruise ship. Any trace of my Western arrogance at the sophistication of our consumer culture and our ability to conjure up a magical brand out of a plain product evaporated that day. A Western advertising agency was involved, but the technique of 'learning by producing' that China has used in advancing manufacturing can be applied to other areas too. It won't be long before they will be churning out cutting-edge advertising without Western help.

This scares a lot of people. If other countries can eventually pick up the skills that we currently think we own – if China can make drugs, create top brands and design jet engines – what will we sell and how will we pay for anything? This does not worry me a great deal because I tend to assume that we will adapt as we always have done. When China makes jet engines, the world will be rather a different place. For one thing, I expect the price of jet engines will be lower. We would have to be a bit dim not to have noticed the trend and I hope we will have moved into a different, suitably profitable, niche. Perhaps we will even make suits again as, China having deserted that space, the price of suits goes rocketing up. Or maybe the economic balance of power will shift in favour of the arts; there will be so many engineers coming out of Chinese and Indian universities that the most profitable careers will be for artisan potters. All I can say is that the transition will be uncomfortable (they always are) but it is unlikely a talented and creative nation will sit twiddling its thumbs for very long. The lead we have acquired in the creation of intellectual property is commendable, just as our pioneering history in manufacturing was commendable too. But it doesn't mean we can stand still. All one can say is that whatever we do in the future, it will require us to be clever.

The intellectualisation of our economy is not the only trend that has been evident in the last thirty years. Britain has been among the front-runners of the large economies in developing its service industries. It is to this sector we now turn.

PART 4

SERVICES

10

The Upside of Services

It is the moment that any sailor hopes will never happen to him or her. On the night of 3 February 2011 a French yachtsman was in the middle of a solo Atlantic crossing from the Canary Islands to Guadeloupe when he discovered his boat was taking on water. His small yacht, the *Nacouda*, was no match for the 30mph winds and ten-metre waves. At a location of 1200 nautical miles east of Puerto Rico, the sailor took the decision to abandon his listing ship and launch his emergency life raft.

Fortunately, the French sailor had access to the services of a British company that could help him. Inmarsat is the world's leading provider of global satellite communications: its fleet of eleven satellites in nine orbital locations offers complete communications coverage – even in as isolated a spot as the middle of the Atlantic Ocean. In this instance, the sailor was able to make an emergency call that was relayed to the US coastguard in Virginia. The coastguard was able to locate the nearest ship to the life raft, a Filipino merchant ship called the MV *Sebring*

Express, which successfully picked up the stranded sailor six hours later. According to Rear Admiral Dean Lee of the US Coastguard, 'This man's Emergency Position Indicating Radio Beacon saved his life ... [it] allowed rescuers to quickly respond to his exact location, which is in large part why he was found, and found alive.'

I recount this story of a rescue at sea for one reason: to demonstrate that, contrary to the disdain so many people have for them, services really can be very important. Sure, there is no tangible product, but that doesn't mean they have little value, that we cannot export them or that they only generate ephemeral effects. For those of you who think services are for wimps, this chapter is designed to make you think again.

It is particularly unfortunate that this perception is so widespread, as the services sector happens to be one in which Britain is a global leader and we do not want to underestimate our national strengths. In Chapter 2 I outlined the rules followed by well-functioning economies: they use the resources they have to find the highest value activities possible to occupy themselves, and they constantly adapt to that end as the external environment changes. In Chapter 3 I explained that one of the distinguishing features of the British economy was its globally integrated nature. It has, for better or worse, been an open trading economy with a cosmopolitan edge. In this chapter, I'll set out how these two features have resulted in us becoming a nation strong in the trading of services. As I think our service economy is mostly the natural outcome of decisions taken in an economy that has been reasonably well-functioning, I am a defender of our niche as a service hub. But I used the word 'mostly' for a reason. In the next chapter I'll set out why some services might have grown too big for an economy of our size. But first, before I reveal my reservations, I want to disabuse you of any anti-service prejudices.

The satellite communications of Inmarsat are a rather good example of the kind of activity I have in mind when talking of services growing out of Britain's international role. The company was founded in 1979 as the International Maritime Satellite Organization (hence Inmarsat), a non-profit organisation created by the International Maritime Organization, a United Nations body. The company's shareholders were the UN member states until 1999, when it became the first intergovernmental organisation to be converted into a private company. The group was split into two: Inmarsat plc, and IMSO, a separate regulatory body; Inmarsat plc was listed on the London Stock Exchange in 2005 and has been a FTSE 100 company since 2008.

Inmarsat remains pre-eminent in maritime safety. It is the only provider of satellite services for the Global Maritime Distress and Safety System, and all large ships are legally required to have an Inmarsat system on board. But its mobile communications network is also used for less life-critical purposes, such as providing broadband services for ships, which allows the crew to browse Facebook while at sea. Satellite communication is used on land and in air too, when there is no reliable terrestrial network. This could be a usually well-covered area whose network is down, such as when Cyclone Yasi ripped into Australia's Queensland coast in February 2011. Or it could be a remote area with no coverage, such as the San José mine in Chile's Atacama region, where thirty-three miners were trapped in autumn 2010. This was one of the biggest news stories of the year, and Inmarsat's satellite technology allowed broadcasters to transmit the remarkable story of the miners' rescue live from where it was taking place.

Inmarsat doesn't make its phones, nor does it make its

satellites; it just sells the communication between them. That's why it is a service company. But keeping that communication going is a complicated matter that employs experts making a good living and earning large export revenues. Inmarsat achieved revenue of a billion dollars in 2009, although, of course, much of that value was earned outside the UK.

It is fair to say that in picking Inmarsat, I have chosen an atypically glamorous example of a service provider. But then it can also be said that there is no such thing as a typical service. The category is too broad to be useful in economic terms. It accounts for more than three-quarters of the British economy and covers everything from window-cleaning to international finance. Even in the manufacturing powerhouses of Germany and Japan, services account for over two-thirds of the economy. In distinguishing between our service economy and their manufacturing ones, as people often do, we are really making a great deal of a difference in less than one-tenth of our overall output. The term 'services' is thus little more than a default name for most things that most people do in most developed economies.

The statisticians whose job it is to categorise the various activities in the economy are the first to admit that it is increasingly hard to do so. The figures on British manufacturing include companies that make nothing in the UK, but are still defined as manufacturing entities because they make things overseas. But should we really call their UK activities manufacturing? Or should we more accurately think of it as the provision of management services? And even those firms that do manufacture in the UK generally employ plenty of service staff: they have marketing departments, legal staff, pay-roll departments and accountants. What proportion of the actual value generated is manufactured on the factory floor is hard to say when there is one output to which all the staff contribute a small amount.

If one wanted to draw some lines through the morass of services, one might distinguish between 'face-to-face' services, where the supplier and customer have to be located together – or nearly together – for the service to be delivered, and those where the two can be separated. A massage is perhaps the clearest-cut example of the face-to-face category. I would include all personal services; retail services (other than mail-order and online); restaurant and hotel services; transport; post and logistics; and most health and educational services in this group. The remaining services would largely be non location-specific: the bulk of financial services, law and accountancy, broadcasting and telecommunications. Of course these definitions are not very exact as many activities can be provided in one form or another, and technology is constantly moving the boundaries. But, looking at the broad headings under which UK production is categorised, face-to-face services account for about 45 per cent of our national output and non face-to-face services about 30 per cent.

The distinction between the two is important as the face-to-face services are self-evidently harder to trade internationally. No one has yet found a way to export massages, restaurant meals or haircuts in large quantities – you can't just pack them up in containers and ship them to the Americans or Chinese. That gets right to the heart of fears about our economy's orientation towards service output. If we need to export more – and, as explained in Chapter 6, I certainly believe we do – the big question is, can we rely on services to carry us through?

The answer is yes, up to a point. Britain, more than any other large developed country, has been a pioneering service exporter.

10.1 Service Exports
2009

	UK	France	Germany	US	UK rank in per capita terms
		Billions of dollars			
Transport	32	32	52	62	2nd
Travel	30	49	35	121	2nd
Communications	7	5	5	10	1st
Construction	3	7	13	1	3rd
Insurance	13	1	5	15	1st
Financial Services	53	2	12	55	1st
Computer and information services	11	2	14	13	2nd
Royalties and licence fees	12	9	14	90	2nd
Other business services	65	33	75	94	1st
Personal, cultural and recreational services	3	2	1	15	1st
Government services	3	1	5	22	3rd
Total services	231	143	230	498	1st
Total, excluding financial services	179	141	219	442	1st

Source: OECD EBOPS dataset

The above table looks at the service exports of Britain, the US and our two big European counterparts. It is rare to see Britain so high in a table of international standing: we lead Europe in the export of services (just!), and in per capita terms we are a far bigger exporter than any of the three other countries. It is pretty clear that, even excluding financial services from the total, we are a very substantial player.

Overall, we have recorded a surplus in services trade in every year since 1966. In 2011 the UK exported almost £190 billion of services, which is more than 10 per cent of our entire national income. Of course, we imported services – some £118 billion – but the surplus of about £70 billion a year went a long way to offsetting the deficit of almost £100 billion from trade in goods.

So how can items that you can't see or touch, and which often have to be delivered in the presence of a client, earn so much from customers who come from elsewhere in the world? The answer to this question comes in three parts. First and simplest, some services do not have to be delivered face-to-face and thus can generate a large overseas income while all the work is done at home in Britain. Insurance and financial services clearly fall into this category, and the table above demonstrates how much we earn from exporting those (although you might want to be wary of the extremely high figure for financial services as this might have perversely been flattered by the effects of the financial crisis).

But face-to-face services can still be exported. A second means of generating export revenue arises when British people or British-owned companies travel abroad to work. And the third, and most interesting, way is by foreigners spending money here.

To see the British in action overseas, I visited Dubai as part of the filming of *Made in Britain*. Dubai, one of the United Arab Emirates but with a strong British commercial presence, is a strange state and people understandably have different reactions to it. Some see it as dynamic and exciting (even if it did run out of money and have to be bailed out by Abu Dhabi). Others focus on the plight of its many migrant workers; you certainly hear dreadful stories of mistreatment. But Britain has not had any reservations about trade with Dubai, which absorbs most of Britain's £2 billion of service exports to the UAE each year.

It is not hard to see a basis for trade. Dubai is young place, with a population that has grown from tens of thousands in the early sixties to something approaching two million people now. With growth of that speed, it needs help. Britain has been a modern country for quite a while, and so the British have developed expertise in many different areas. Naturally, we can sell our expertise in that arena.

For example, a Dubai landmark is the Burj Al Arab hotel. As tall as the Eiffel Tower, the Burj is built on an artificial island that makes it easy to keep the curious non-paying public out. The architects who designed the Burj came from Atkins, an engineering and design consultancy based in Epsom in Surrey. The company is truly global, with 18,500 staff employed in twenty-eight countries and a revenue in 2010 of £1.4 billion. Atkins set up a regional headquarters in Dubai in 1979, and so was in a strong position to secure the contract when Dubai's ruler, Sheikh Mohammed bin Rashid Al Maktoum, decided he wanted to commission a grand architectural statement. The brief was to deliver an iconic tower that would be instantly recognisable among Dubai's many high-profile building projects: it was to reflect the growing prosperity of the city and also its seafaring history. It was a formidable project, taking three years just to reclaim from the sea the land on which the hotel was to be built. Forty-metre concrete piles were then driven into the sand to secure the foundations. The building itself, which boasts the tallest atrium in the world, contains over 70,000 cubic metres of concrete and 9000 tonnes of steel.

The Burj Al Arab is one of the most recognisable buildings in the world but is just one of Atkins's projects in the Gulf. The company was also employed to help install the new Dubai metro network. And then another British company, Serco, secured the twelve-year £500-million deal to operate the driverless system. Serco, described by one newspaper as 'probably the biggest company you've never heard of', is an 'international services company' that operates across a huge number of sectors. In transport, in addition to the Dubai Metro, they operate everything from London's Docklands Light Railway to the Copenhagen Metro; in aviation, they provide air traffic control services for, among others, Dubai and Bahrain and manage a total of 192,000 square miles of airspace; they run prisons in Britain, Australia and Germany; they provide maintenance services at CERN, home of the Large Hadron Collider, and manage education authorities and hospitals. They may employ seventy thousand staff worldwide, but they are based in Hook in Hampshire.

I mention all this just to give a small idea of the scale of this kind of international service activity. But here is the inevitable snag with services delivered abroad. For a country like Britain, which hopes to earn foreign currency on the back of service exports much as Germany earns export revenues from Volkswagen, the maths really do suggest that the potential is rather limited. Because so much value in service industries is generated from face-to-face delivery, most of the value of the work our companies do in Dubai ends up being created in Dubai. It isn't an export at all.

For example, suppose a British company designs a £100-million building in the Gulf. Most of that is paid out for the physical construction undertaken by the non-British workers on the site. When an Indian builder does a job in Dubai, the work does not generate any income for the UK economy. The building's architects may be British, but they might only expect to earn 1 or 2 per cent of the total building cost – a couple of million pounds. But much of that £2 million is spent on paying suppliers in the country where the building is constructed. Just as an Indian builder does not earn export revenues for the UK, nor does an Indian draftsman in the Dubai office of a British firm. So what money comes back to Britain? There are the (probably relatively modest) salaries of the British resident staff who flew out to Dubai to work on the project. And otherwise it is the profit that the British company makes on the £2 million earned. That may be 10 or 20 per cent of the total fee. In other words, we can marvel at a wonderful £100-million building designed by a British firm, but its value to the UK economy in terms of earnings might end up being just half a million dollars. It's better than a poke in the eye, but it is not really going to pay for many of our imports.

The reason that so little cash makes its way back to Britain is that the international services in Dubai are genuinely international, not British. The work Atkins or Serco do there is mostly done there – it could not be any other way. And those staff are not remitting funds to the UK. That inevitably means only the profits come home, not the entire value of the work done – the icing on the cake but not the cake itself. In services exports, the real money goes where the people are.

This brings us to the other way in which Britain exports face-to-face services. When an Indian draftsman works for a British company overseas, he contributes little to the UK economy. When the same person takes a holiday in Britain, almost everything he spends is now an export from Britain. The haircut, the restaurant meal or the massage, all now involve foreign money being earned by British workers. Indeed, if the Indian goes shopping in Oxford Street to buy British-made goods, the spending in the shop is an export, and even if he chooses to buy Chinese-made items, it is still the case that the gross retail margin of the store is now an export too. As Britain succeeds in paying its way in the world when foreigners end up giving their money to someone who works here, that happens in large measure when foreigners actually come here.

Just as we export services when foreigners come to the UK, we import services when the British go overseas. The evidence is that, in terms of tourism or other short visits, we tend to spend about twice as much abroad than foreigners spend in the UK. But not all foreign visits to Britain are short term.

Perhaps the best example of a service industry that exports billions of pounds within the confines of Britain's borders is education, and higher education in particular. We have seen in earlier chapters how high-end engineering firms such as BAE Systems, R&D-heavy industries such as pharmaceuticals, and high-tech innovators such as ARM all require a highly skilled workforce. They have been helped by UK universities. It remains the case that, whatever the failings of the UK school system, our university system is highly regarded. That, plus the English language, makes it unsurprising that students from other countries are eager to enrol at British institutions. Every time they do, the fees they pay – for a service we provide – bring money into the UK economy. While it might seem strange to think of universities as exporting businesses, the amount of money they pull in via international students runs into billions of pounds.

About 5 per cent of the UK student population comes from other EU countries, and 10 per cent – around a quarter of a million students – from outside the EU. These students bring money into the UK in two ways. First, through the fees that they pay for their courses: overseas fees broadly range from £4000 to £18,000 a year, depending on the course and the institution. For some subjects these fees can be even higher: an international medical student, for example, can expect to pay £12,000 in fees for the first two years, and £22,000 for the next three clinical years; that's £90,000 in total. For the academic year of 2007–08 international revenue for UK universities was £2.9 billion (out of a total turnover of £23.4 billion).

The students' contribution to the economy doesn't end with

the fees that they pay in order to study. There is the money that international students spend in the wider economy while they are here. For 2007–08, that was estimated at a further £2.3 billion, with their international visitors adding in another £135 million. In total, these quarter of a million students bring in about £5.3 billion to the UK economy.

The medical students are particularly interesting as they not only pay to be here, spend their money (or their parents' money) while they live here, but they also work in our hospitals as part of their training. It is a pretty exciting business model for a country, really, if it can persuade foreigners to pay to work there.

The largest number of non-European international students at British universities come from China – over forty thousand in the 2008–09 academic year – followed by India. But, crucially, not nearly as many would have been able to afford to do so if their countries had not become more wealthy by selling us manufactured goods. In order for them to buy expensive items like university educations from us, we needed to spend our money on them in the first place. That is the nature of trade.

Birmingham University is one example of an institution that knows all about the benefits that international students can bring. It has recently celebrated the centenary of the first Chinese graduate to study there. Today, Birmingham has students from 150 countries; international students make up about a fifth of the student population, a percentage share that is not atypical for the red-brick universities. (The institutions with a substantially larger international intake tend to be the London-based ones, such as University College London (34 per cent), Imperial College (38 per cent) and London School of Economics (68 per cent)).

Attracting new students is a year-round job for Birmingham.

The university has a permanent representation in China, the US and India, and uses joint trips with schools, exhibitions, telephone campaigns and roadshows as part of its recruitment programme. China, India, Malaysia and Nigeria are considered the high-priority countries for attracting students, while Brazil and Chile are among the emerging markets. It's an impressive and highly professional set-up, and one that is comparable to the recruitment initiatives of a multinational company.

There is something of a virtuous circle: the larger the international student community at Birmingham, the greater the mix of people, nationalities and cultures, and the more enriched the learning and teaching environment; the more enriched the learning and teaching environment, the more international students want to come to Birmingham. And that's to the benefit of all the students at Birmingham, whether they are from the UK or abroad.

Education is one of our national economic strengths. We are not unique in taking foreign students, but the numbers we teach are very striking. In 2008, the UK had 342,000 non-resident students in tertiary education of one kind or another. Germany had 178,000.

I hope I have persuaded you that we can be proud of our universities. But in looking at our service industries – and, in particular, those that rely on foreigners coming to Britain to enjoy them – I do not just want to claim that Britain has one or two strong sectors. Our nation has gone further and developed an unusual business model as a place where people come to spend money. We act as a host and in that role get to sell services to the many people who pass through.

Let me give you an example. The Shard, the tallest building in the European Union. The building is home to a mix of office space, restaurants, the Shangri-La hotel group (a company that specialises in five-star facilities) and residential apartments.

The Shard is based at London Bridge and its design references London's past: according to its architect, the tower disappears 'into the air like a sixteenth-century pinnacle or the mast-top of a very tall ship. The architecture of the Shard is firmly based in the historic form of London's masts and spires.' But the curious thing is that it has very little of Britain about it. It was designed by an Italian, Renzo Piano, the Genoese architect whose previous work includes the Pompidou Centre in Paris; it has been financed by the Qataris and it is built by labour with a substantial non-British component. (When I visited the construction site, I was greeted with a sign addressing the workers in various languages, most of which I couldn't identify.) The Shangri-La hotel is run by a Hong Kong company, and my impression is that the small number of flats built in the residential section of the building will not be sold to British residents. But there the Shard sits, on top of one of London's commuter hubs.

At this point, you might well be asking yourself what exactly it is that Britain gets out of making itself a country where Lithuanians build Italian-designed flats owned by Arabs for Russian tenants?

While one can see a number of problems with this kind of activity, income is generated from it for the UK and its residents. There are, for example, some taxes that are payable here, and very substantial subsidiary services too. The Lithuanian builder buying a can of Coke at a local newsagent is effectively paying for it with income derived from abroad, so the Coke is therefore an export. Then, of course, British firms supply many of the lucrative services that go with the project. Mace, a London-based firm, is responsible for the tower's construction; Turner & Townsend, a global firm with its origins in Yorkshire, is the project manager. Even when it is all finished, we'll undoubtedly continue to get business: the Russian tenants will probably use the British courts and UK lawyers to fight over their spoils when they get divorced.

I have tended to think of this business as picking up crumbs as others bake cakes on our premises. This is not an original characterisation; it comes from *The Bonfire of the Vanities*, Tom Wolfe's eighties novel recounting the downfall of a financial 'master of the universe'. Bond trader Sherman McCoy is struggling to explain to his daughter what his job consists of. He fails to get his message across, but his wife picks up the theme and explains:

> Just imagine that a bond is a slice of cake. Now you didn't bake that cake, but every time you hand somebody a slice of that cake, a little bit comes off, little crumbs fall off. And you're allowed to keep those crumbs. Yes ... that's what Daddy does. He passes somebody else's cake around and picks up the crumbs. But you have to imagine a lot of crumbs. And a great golden cake. And a lot of golden crumbs. And you have to imagine Daddy running around picking up every little golden crumb he can get his hands on.

That is not a bad analogy for the business model on which London has learned to thrive. All the subsidiary activities associated with the Shard are crumbs that UK residents pick up, and which themselves would form a pretty big cake.

A specific example of a cake made from these crumbs can be derived from the estate-agent commissions earned on transactions between foreign parties that take place on UK soil. Knight Frank, for example, specialises in the very top of the residential market – the super-prime end – and are in charge of selling the residential space in the Shard. They are also the letting agents for the offices. The commissions they earn are an order of magnitude smaller than the value of the property, but are substantial nevertheless. And they handle the affairs of many properties, which all adds up to a good business.

I was shown round one of Knight Frank's central London show houses, on Cornwall Terrace, near Baker Street. Coming in at a cool £45 million, the property is about 1000 square metres and comes complete with a separate mews house, a state-of-the-art air-conditioning system, lights and stereo sound, and an art collection that is included in the price. Tim Wright, the agent who took me round, described how different nationalities look for different qualities in properties: for Middle Eastern buyers, separate accommodation for their staff is important, hence the accompanying mews house; Russian buyers, meanwhile, are more interested in the swimming pool and what Tim terms 'the toys'. He explained to me how the London town house remains a 'must-have' for the super-rich, a trophy to sit alongside the villa in the south of France, the yacht and the art collection. He described how the ongoing success of this market is down to both this continuing demand and the comparative lack of supply: for every ten buyers, there are only one or two properties on the market.

Knight Frank's income is part of the associated earnings that come with these transactions: other examples might be the fees of the interior designer who dressed the house or the property developer in charge of renovating it. For a property like the £45-million Cornwall Terrace house, that is likely bringing in something in the region of several million pounds. And with properties coming back onto the market every five to ten years, Knight Frank can look forward to selling and reselling the houses again and again.

It is a lucrative business, but at some level the idea of Britain acting as a host nation is an odd one. Successful economies tend to evolve in a direction that makes the highest value use of the resources at their disposal, but land is a fairly scarce resource – England is the most densely populated major country in Europe. So offering prime real estate to foreigners in order to create jobs for ourselves as their servants is a peculiar way to make a living.

Although we are relatively deprived when it comes to land, we have moved in the direction we have because we are well endowed with other important attributes. As a nation we have a legal system, a language, a culture and a reputation for competence in the management of property and money. Hence people with those things are happy to have a base in Britain. Our support industries have grown up to serve those people, and those people have come because this is a place to find those support industries.

The history of Britain as an open economy and imperial power helps as well. Just as UK manufacturers have tended to abandon large-scale, low-end commodity production to focus on narrower and more lucrative niches, so our service industries have moved in this direction too. They started out by serving the domestic market, and it was only natural to move on to serving the rest of the world when globalisation made that possible. Economists have given the name Wimbledonisation to the hosting role the UK has developed; we run the best tennis tournament in the world but don't expect to play a very prominent part in the tennis. Even though Tim Henman and Andy Murray have rendered that concept slightly out of date, the idea remains valid as a characterisation of a large source of income in Britain.

Personally, I make the comparison between the London-centred services economy and the Glastonbury Festival. It is an event that has evolved from almost nothing in 1970 (1500 people paid a pound to see T.Rex, Keith Christmas and Al Stewart) into a large industry (137,500 tickets have been sold for the 2011 festival, headlined by U2, Coldplay and Beyoncé, despite a price of £195). What is relevant to the UK economy is the fact that the festival sees a lot of people come into a small crowded space, a lot of money changes hands – most of it between people who do not reside in Somerset – and some crumbs spill off into the local economy.

It is obviously hard to measure the effect of such an industry on one area, but after the festival took a one-year rest in 2006, the local Mendip District Council hired consultants to assess the economic impact of its return in 2007. Their thorough study estimated that the total spending of festival-goers, traders and the organisers amounted to £73 million. The question for us when that amount of money sloshes around, is what proportion drops into the laps of those living where the sloshing occurs? The consultants' report came up with a figure of spending in the Mendip District of £32 million, but this was ludicrously flattered by the inclusion of all of the £25 million spent on the festival site itself, even though most of that would have gone to national suppliers rather than local ones. A better estimate would exclude the on-site spending and thus derive an estimate of the earnings enjoyed by Mendip residents of around £7 million. That implies that about a tenth of the total festival spending makes its way into local hands. That is the Glasto effect and, for me, provides an illustration of the likely order of magnitude of incomes that Britain earns as foreigners pass through London with their money.

However, the story doesn't end there. The report on Glastonbury catalogued the indirect benefits of the event: publicity for Glastonbury, the positive perception of the area, the encouragement of an entrepreneurial culture in the area that resulted from the trading opportunities that the festival brought, to name a few. Even more significantly, there has been development of businesses and skills that have a value beyond the festival itself. The village of Dulcote is home to Serious Stages, one of Europe's 'most experienced companies in the supply for sale or hire of temporary staging, buildings and special structures'. In fact, the report tells us that a small cluster of suppliers and contracting companies that cover festivals on a regional or national scale is developing within the local area, as the marketplace for festivals grows. It is a good analogy of the development of Britain's top-end services; the companies that developed in London can make money by extending beyond. That is perhaps why the UK has four of the top ten global law firms, as measured by *American Lawyer* in terms of revenue.

For all the upsides of this kind of economy – and there is plenty to be proud of – it leaves us in a curious place. At its worst, it sees the British middle class operating as butlers to a global elite. You might have heard of the concept of Status–Income Disequilibrium, or SID for short. It was coined by the American writer David Brooks in his 2000 book, *Bobos in Paradise: The New Upper Class and How They Got There.* Those affected with SID had jobs that came with high status but were only modestly remunerated, a situation that some readers (and authors) might recognise: 'The tragedy of the SID sufferers' lives is that they spend their days in glory and their nights in mediocrity ... if they work in the media or in publishing, they can enjoy fancy expense-account lunches. All day long phone messages pile up on their desks – calls from rich and famous people seeking favours or attention – but at night they realise the bathroom needs cleaning so they have to pull out the Ajax.'

Michael Gove, writing in *The Times* in the pre-ministerial days of 2008, offered a cut-out-and-keep guide to the professions that were susceptible to SID: 'they are researchers and assistant producers in television, editors in publishing firms, newspaper diarists ... almost all art critics, researchers for political parties, senior managers for charities and voluntary organisations, all classical musicians who aren't soloists and every academic who isn't Niall Ferguson or David Starkey'.

As an economy develops and matures, the pay balance can diverge, and some sectors can seem over-remunerated to those who work in other areas. There are other issues involved, but the recent public outcry over bankers and their bonuses is perhaps one example of this. Indeed, such are the potential salaries on offer in the modern financial world that a 2007 article suggested that even a well-paid profession such as law was also beginning to find itself full of SID sufferers, and used a fundraising auction at a private school in New York to illustrate this: 'When a home-cooked meal by a famous chef was being auctioned off, the doctors dropped out of the bidding at $7000, the lawyers at $15,000, and then the bankers, private equity and hedge fund crowd got serious and fought it out among themselves, with the winning bid coming in at $40,000.'

The question is, whether by acting as international host to a wealthy super-elite, the British economy is in danger of this same Status–Income Disequilibrium, but on a much larger scale: creating an economy in which companies such as Knight Frank sell super-prime properties to overseas buyers; where planning permission is granted to foreign-owned buildings such as the Shard; where the City is given a light regulatory touch to make London an attractive place for banks and financial firms to base themselves.

I asked Tim Wright, the Knight Frank estate agent, whether he suffered from SID. He said not, that the disparity between where he could afford to live and the houses he sold was so great that it was a leap too far to imagine living there: 'I think for me because I know it's not a lifestyle that I'm likely to have then I can put it out of mind.' Even so, I'm not sure that everyone shares Tim's professionalism.

As we will see in the next chapter, that's not the only concern to have about the size and nature of our services sector either.

11

Too Much of a Good Thing?

Here's a conundrum. The United States spends more on healthcare than any other country in the developed world – about 16 per cent of its national income. This is substantially larger than France and Germany on about 11 per cent, or the UK at about 9 per cent. In money terms too, the US spends more than twice as much per capita as the three European countries. Yet despite the extra spending, the results are no better than those of other leading economies and, in many cases, are worse: US infant mortality is higher than the OECD average, as is the death rate after haemorrhagic strokes; in 2008, *Health Affairs* revealed that 100,000 Americans die from preventable illnesses each year – the highest number for an industrialised country.

One of the reasons that US healthcare underperforms in some measure is undoubtedly down to the fact that its coverage is less equal than that of many other systems. This implies that, despite high spending overall, there is an under-provision of healthcare for segments of the population, who can expect poor outcomes as a result. This has been a familiar and controversial feature of the US health system and one that President Obama has tried to reform.

But perhaps more interestingly, there is another worry: that US healthcare *over-provides* for other sectors of the population; that it wastes money offering expensive treatments to people that have no discernable effect on outcomes. Could that really be the case? Too much health spending? Well, it certainly seems plausible, according to the Dartmouth Atlas Project, an academic group that tracks variations in Medicare spending per patient in different areas of the US. Its researchers have found significant discrepancies between the amounts that are spent on health and the prognoses of the patients. Here is a report of just one Dartmouth study from the *Journal of Hospice and Palliative Nursing*: 'For example, an elderly person spent an average of 10.6 days in the hospital during the last 2 years of life in Bend, OR, but 34.9 days in the hospital in Manhattan. The variation is even more striking in the last 6 months of life, when chronically ill patients visited the doctor an average of 14.5 times in Ogden, UT, compared to 59.2 times in Los Angeles, CA ... The Atlas research shows that hospitals, regions, and states that use more services per patient do not necessarily have higher quality care. In fact, it is slightly worse.'

Personally, I am not sure whether the elderly of LA are hypochondriacs who waste large amounts of money on needless trips to the doctor, or whether they just have different needs from patients over in Utah. But it is interesting to ask the truly radical question: is it always the case that the more you have of an industry, the better it is? Generally, we regard healthcare as desirable, so the idea of having too much of it seems bizarre. But you probably can, and in this chapter I will try to explain why markets may dysfunction to give too much of a good thing.

Why am I concerned with this issue? Well, it all comes back to the negative associations we have with the service sector in Britain. Many think that we have too many services in general and too many of one category in particular: financial services. It has been heralded as a national champion, a sector in which Britain has a strong international lead and one that earned tens of billions of pounds of export revenue in 2008, as shown in the table in the last chapter. But could it just be a little too large? I'll outline in principle what might make an industry too large for an economy, and ask whether in practice those arguments apply to banking. I'll also ask whether there are other reasons to think that Britain is pushing at the healthy limits in the degree to which it is letting services lead the economy.

But first, what do I mean by too large? What is the right size for an industry? This could be answered in a number of ways, but perhaps the most basic criterion is to compare an industry's contribution to the material welfare of a country with the costs that industry imposes. You might think of an industry being too large if the resources it uses are disproportionate to the value of the output it produces. If it uses £2 billion of labour to produce £1 billion of widgets, then you have too much of it. It's not pulling its weight in the economy. In healthcare, the principle is the same: if a week in hospital costs £1400, you would say that it is overprovision to prescribe a week in hospital if it has no discernable effect on patient outcome.

Any sector can be too big, by this criterion. We could have too big a car industry if we find it employs people at £10 an hour but cannot sell all the cars they make and thus only earns the equivalent of £6 of value for each hour worked. The facts in this case would indicate that there is an imbalance between the resources going in and the value coming out. The solution would be for the car sector to shrink until it can sell all the cars that are made at a price that pays the workers' wages.

At this point, professional economists may grimace and start asking awkward questions about which particular kinds of costs I am referring to, and which measures of output. Fortunately, I do not intend to apply this cost–benefit criterion at any level of precision, so for the sake of a broad under-standing of the issues involved we can proceed without getting bogged down.

In the world of economics textbooks, market forces are rea-sonably efficient at ensuring companies expand and contract to the point at which the resources going in and the items coming out match each other. The reason is quite straightforward. If a company spends more on its inputs than it earns from its outputs, it will lose money. If it loses money, it will tend to shrink or go out of business. On the other side of the economy are companies that expand. They will tend to be companies that are profitable, and the profitable ones are those that sell things for more than they cost to make. The old rule is that resources flow to where they are most valuable, and thus companies or industries that cannot make good use of labour or capital or other resources will lose them to those sectors that can. Textbook economics usually delivers good news and this case is no exception. Do nothing, and the economy will ensure that everybody finds a valuable and productive job.

Alas, we don't live in a textbook and so have to ask why real-world markets might fail, allowing some sectors to grow too big relative to others? How can some parts of the economy succeed in soaking up valuable resources, producing little of value from them and yet still stay in business? Why might some businesses be able to make big returns while doing little good to the rest of the economy? There are, of course, many answers. Markets can dysfunction in lots of different ways, all of which can make industries too big or too small. Governments can also engineer the same results if they want to. But I want to concentrate on one particular issue that can allow over-sized industries to defy the usual economic laws of gravity: the ability they have to make returns for themselves not by creating value but by taking value away from elsewhere.

To understand my point, let's start with an absurd analogy. I want you to imagine that I find a way of erecting a tollbooth on the M1 and applying a charge of £1 to every car that drives through. Let's suppose I am very clever and find a legal wheeze to allow me to do this. I will make about £100,000 a day from my endeavour (assuming few drivers are dissuaded from driving down the route as a result of my toll). If I get away with placing that toll on the M1 and keeping the money I become a rich man, even though I have not helped build the M1, or the cars that drive down it, nor the contents of the lorries carrying their deliveries along my toll road either. All I have done is set up a tollbooth and collected the cash.

Clearly what I am doing is not creating wealth but expropriating it from other people. Now, if I get away with creating a toll on the M1 and I observe that it has been a very successful enterprise from my point of view, maybe I can start a tollbooth programme on other motorways of the UK: the M2, the M3, the M4, right up to the M898 (the tiny little one in Renfrewshire).

I might even sell shares in my business of building tollbooths and collecting revenue. It will look extremely profitable and I'm sure investors will flock to get a piece of the equity. You will remember, though, that I'm still not doing anything very useful. I am not using the revenue from the tolls to build roads or to look after the needy. All I'm doing is creaming off a little piece of the income derived from other people's hard work and keeping it for myself. Yet when business journalists assess the shape of the economy they will be tempted to say that one of our country's best industries is the tollbooth building and operating one. Behold its high level of profitability; the low costs it incurs relative to the huge income it generates; and notice that no other country has a toll business like this one.

When stroppy left-wingers go on the radio to argue that the tolls are simply a drain on the rest of society and do very little good at all, I will retort that they should stop bashing one of our great national success stories. It employs many toll collectors and, moreover, generates export revenues from the tolls it collects from foreign vehicles on our roads. When the suggestion comes forward that the tolls need regulating, I will point out that I pay large amounts of tax to the exchequer and government is threatening to kill the golden goose.

You will see that if I could get away with this toll-charging racket it would be tempting for me to do so, and yet it would be highly socially destructive. In terms of the balance of the economy, it would be one of those industries that was too large. It would be using up some of our national resources to build and operate tollbooths but it would contribute nothing at all to the welfare of the country. The income it made would entirely be at the expense of other industries.

Enough about illusory tolls. The point of the tale is to highlight the possibility that an economy may end up with some industries that are like the rogue tollbooths, which contribute little but have identified and capitalised upon money-sucking niches. What these industries do is very different from what goes on in most of our economy, just as baking a pie is not the same as finding a way to snatch a pie that someone else has baked.

Economists use the terms 'rent-seeking' to describe the activity of taking other people's money rather than creating it yourself. If people find a means (legal or otherwise) of expropriating money from others, they have an incentive to do so. A valid concern in Britain is whether a disproportionate amount of our service economy is built upon rent-seeking.

There are certainly real-world examples of this, which are only slightly less blatant than my tollbooths. My favourite is that of the German chimney sweeps. Although the regulations have been under some challenge, the tradition in Germany has been for each of the 7888 German districts to have its own chimney sweep, who is able to employ one or two helpers. Every property has to have its chimney checked at least once a year by law (at a cost of about €50 to €100). Chimney sweeps have the right to enter buildings even if the owner of the property doesn't want to hire them. To become a fully qualified sweep involves an apprenticeship of about twelve years.

The chimney sweeps effectively have a mandate to tax other people. Nice work if you can get it. Many on the libertarian right regard almost the entire public sector as existing on the back of the same kind of privilege. The government uses its authority to build metaphorical tollbooths that collect money people have earned for themselves (we call those tolls taxation) and in return the government delivers services that people may not want. As a result, those on the right believe, the government sector is too big. It is rent-seeking rather than value-creating.

What my tollbooths, German chimney sweeps and the public sector all have in common is that their size is regulated by law. It is the state that has a licence, or grants one, to collect revenue from other people. I don't want to get drawn into arguments about the size of the government sector or the value of the services it provides; for me the interesting question is whether you might get rogue-tollbooth type activities without the government creating rent-seeking opportunities. Could I get away with my motorway tollbooth if people weren't forced to queue up and pay? If I just asked people to pull over and pay voluntarily, would they do so?

In general, I think we assume not. If people choose to pay for my service they must feel it offers some value to them. What restrains my rent-seeking activities is the fact that in a market economy no one is forced to buy things they don't want, and so when they do buy something it presumably adds value to them. Therefore, you might think, markets outlaw rent-seeking. Or do they?

Suppose I don't build a tollbooth to make money, but I do employ a good lawyer who writes a threatening letter, making a quite unreasonable claim for a small amount of money from you. You can't deal with the legalese and now have to pay up out of court or engage a lawyer to counter the claim. Does that sound so unfamiliar? If the courts find a way of throwing these things out, then fine. If not, we inevitably end up with a large legal industry built on supporting and countering rent-seeking activities. Or imagine I employ a good lawyer to help me avoid taxes by exploiting loopholes in the law. The tax authorities counter this by employing ever more people to frame laws that don't have loopholes. We could use up many of our best brains in this kind of arms race and yet find no one is any richer at the end of it than they were at the beginning.

There are many different versions of the tollbooth business. Suppose I find a neat way of persuading people to buy more of my product than they really need. Then I am attracting business to myself even though it has little value. Here is an example you may find convincing. You go to the car repair shop with a fault in your engine. The mechanic looks at the car and gives you a list of a dozen things that need fixing. Not understanding cars yourself, you ask him to do the work. You don't really know whether all the work was worth carrying out; you have to trust the mechanic has not over-specified the tasks needed. Or in a different scenario, you have damage to your car and go to the mechanic armed with your insurance policy and ask him to repair it. At this point, you probably don't much care whether the mechanic over-specifies; it's not your problem as the insurer is paying the bill. You would have to be quite unworldly to believe that all the work on car insurance repair is actually merited. The fact that more gets done at a higher price when someone else is paying explains why mechanics frequently ask whether it is an insurance job or not.

This is perhaps one step on from the tollbooth. I expect that the mechanic does not just charge money for nothing; he does lots of unnecessary to work to justify his fee. He may even employ an assistant to help with the backlog of cars needing pointless repairs. We end up with a bigger car-repair sector than we really need as a result of these kinds of practices, which are sustained as the industry operates as a burden on the rest of the economy rather than a contributor to it.

Now let's return to the US healthcare system. Has it found a way of extracting cash from the rest of the economy by over-specifying work? It certainly has some of the characteristics that lend themselves to customers buying more than they need. First, it is an expert service, so when you see a doctor you not only get her to treat you, you also get her to tell you what treatment you require. The doctor may have some conflict of interest in that dual role. The second thing about healthcare is that it is not straightforward. There is no mechanical relationship between the diagnosis and the prescription as each case has its own complexities. That's why we go to a medical professional to apply some discretion and judgement. This means it is extremely hard to detect over-specification when it does occur. And a third feature of healthcare is that, generally, we expect someone else to pick up our bills. There is barely a health system in the world that does not involve some element of government or private insurance.

Each of these characteristics makes it more likely that there is scope for money-making at the expense of the customer (or the insurance company) than in most other sectors. If these characteristics are exploited they allow the health sector to absorb a larger proportion of the national income than it merits and, contrary to the spirit of market forces, there is little pressure for the sector to go out of business or shrink; it is quite viable in its over-sized form as the customers keep giving it business. Its large size comes at the expense of the rest of the economy, which has to hand over some of its earnings as high insurance premiums.

There is no open-and-shut case against the US healthcare system. For those who want to argue that it is a conspiracy against the rest of the economy, the challenge is to find a reason why customers and insurance companies remain complicit in allowing themselves to be ripped off. Why don't they control costs by employing something like the National Institute for Health and Clinical Excellence (NICE), which operates in England and Wales, to restrict treatments to those demonstrably worth buying? Or why don't they separate the task of diagnosing from the delivery of services to ensure that there is no conflict of interest? These are difficult questions to answer. In any event, no one would argue that the entire health system in the US is surplus to the nation's requirements. It is merely at the margin there may be problems.

Which brings us to the City, and to the UK financial services sector. There are enormous concerns about its size and levels of remuneration. For many, it has a wonderful business model and creates real wealth. This is a view particularly prevalent in the City itself and I have no doubt it is sincerely held. For others, though, the sector is simply an oversized tollbooth that makes absurd returns which are essentially extracted from the rest of the economy. Unfortunately, most of the usual arguments you hear in favour of the City – the contribution that it makes to the exchequer, or the jobs it creates – do not tell us anything about whether it makes a real contribution or not, any more than those arguments would provide a case for my tollbooths. It is a complicated business working out which of the two prevalent views of the City – the benign or the malign – should prevail.

In the UK, official statistics suggest that the financial services sector accounts for about 8 per cent of our national output. That means that one pound in every twelve we earn comes from a financial service. Of that 8 per cent, about 5 per cent comes from banking and a rather smaller amount from insurance and pensions. It is the banking sector in particular that generates concern, and even before considering possible rent-seeking behaviour there are some good reasons why we should worry about the apparent contribution it makes to the economy because it is very hard to measure the value of what banks do. We can count cars coming off a production line and we can more or less assume that if a customer pays £15,000 for one it is worth £15,000. But it is much more difficult to measure the value-added of a bank. Generally, banks don't have specific charges for their services, but instead earn their living by charging a higher rate of interest to their borrowers than they pay to their lenders. That difference is known as the interest rate spread. The official statistics that make banks look pretty productive are based on adding up the total value of that spread on all the loans in the country. That is the implicit price we pay banks for their services, so it must be the amount by which we value what they do.

That is not, however, an entirely satisfactory way of measuring the banks' contribution. As an example of why, I could point to one of the great statistical ironies of recent years: at the peak of the financial crisis in 2008, when banks were being propped up by governments, the average interest rate spread in the economy widened enormously as risks in the financial system escalated. The result was that the measured output of banks rose considerably. If you believe the official data, our banks hadn't made such a big contribution to the economy for decades as they did in the third quarter of 2008.

Putting aside this statistical problem, the question arises as to whether the returns on the investment activities of banks and other fund managers are to some extent a mirage. Do they extract profits and returns at the expense of the rest of the economy? In principle, it seems quite plausible that they do. The comparison to the car repair shop and the US healthcare system is useful because in financial services some of the same characteristics are apparent. First, the service provided is opaque and incomprehensible to most of the final customers; they thus have to trust experts to invest their money on their behalf. Secondly, even for people who understand the business it is hard to judge the performance of those experts from the outside. How do I know whether my money has been invested well? I can look at the returns that have been made but, crucially, I can't tell what kinds of risks the bank or the professional looking after my pension has been taking with my money. I can't tell whether they are skilful, or have just been lucky. Anyway, if I want to park my money with someone I can only tell how well they have performed in the past, not how well they will invest in the future, and in financial markets the two are often not related.

In addition to all these problems, there is the fact that most of the money sloshing around in the City belongs to someone else. It is their risks that are being taken. Remuneration in these services can easily be designed to take the form 'heads I win, tails you lose' and there is plenty of evidence that such remuneration exists. Paul Woolley, a former financier who now runs the Centre for the Study of Capital Market Dysfunctionality at the

London School of Economics, thinks that the knowledge gap between City insiders and those outside is crucial to the ability of the insiders to cream off disproportionate returns for themselves. In all sorts of ways, the City may have opportunities to look after itself rather than deliver value to customers, who are always one step behind in spotting the poor-value service they are getting. On this account the City charges too much, over-complicates its business, absorbs too much talent and extracts other peoples' money to make a poorly delivered service viable.

Let me give you a few examples. Insiders can sell opaque, dodgy securities to hapless outsiders as they did in the noughties, with complex products that were worth far less than expected. An investment bank that spots a good opportunity can trade in it on its own behalf, leaving the second-best opportunities to its clients. Hedge funds looking after investors' money can take risks with it undetected. If the risks pay off, the hedge fund scores high profits and remuneration; if after a few years the risk goes the wrong way and wipes out the clients' money the previously acquired fees are not repaid.

Quite apart from the argument about whether our financial sector operates by exploiting its own customers, there is another reason to think that it might have outgrown its efficient size: it receives a substantial government subsidy. This argument has been put most strongly by Andrew Haldane, the executive director of financial stability at the Bank of England. His point is that while markets may generally be good at ensuring organisations that don't deliver value tend to shrink or disappear, when it comes to banking governments prevent that happening because the consequences would be too unpleasant to bear. Haldane has attempted to work out the subsidy that large banks enjoy from the implicit support underwritten by the taxpayer. This subsidy is only occasionally handed over in the form of taxpayer cash: in the normal run of things it is a subsidy hidden in the form of a free insurance policy that underwrites the money that large banks borrow from wholesale lenders. Because their lenders know the money will be repaid, the banks can borrow that money more cheaply than they otherwise could. It allows them to earn higher returns and to pay themselves higher wages as well.

For the UK banks in 2007, Haldane calculates the subsidy was worth about £11 billion. That would make it equivalent to about 15 per cent of the value-added of the banking sector. Having a free taxpayer insurance policy of £11 billion obviously makes banking more profitable than it would otherwise be, and it allows banks profitably to suck in resources that in a market economy would ultimately be directed elsewhere. Just as government support allowed British Leyland to sustain itself at a larger size than would otherwise have been viable, the government is helping banks do the same.

That is the case against the City. It has all sorts of implications about the regulation of the activity of the financial sector and the structure of banks, but for me the issue is whether, as a consequence of these potential failures, financial services have remained larger than is healthy for our economy. Have the banks absorbed too much of the nation's talent, and have they spent too much of the nation's sparse savings on building wonderful marble-lined towers for themselves? If they have, we can conclude that the other sectors of the economy – including manufacturing – are a little smaller than they should be. They have been unable to employ the brains they could have used because they can't match the salaries offered by the banks.

You are not going to find a conclusive answer to the question of whether the City is oversized. It is hard to believe that it hasn't to some extent managed to extract returns from other sectors rather than creating them itself, but who can say to what extent that is true? Even if you enthusiastically accept the arguments I have outlined here in principle, it is hard to calibrate them in precise form. Paul Woolley told me that he thinks our financial services should be a third or half of their current size, but the imprecision of that estimate reveals how far we are from knowing the magnitude of the problem.

In addition, the City has a couple of very good defences. Much of what goes on there is not financial services at all. We should never treat the City as a single monolithic industry: rather, it is a cluster of many different activities. There are shipping lawyers, accountants, analysts and other professionals; or companies like ICAP and CMC Markets that provide trading services. They are all earning a living in their own way. Second, we should not forget that what the City does to a large extent is not provide financial services to the UK economy, but host international financial-service activities provided by foreigners for foreigners. If an American bank offers to employ a French person in London selling services to the Chinese, do we want to shun that activity? Do we want to limit the amount the American bank pays to the French person? We have a strong interest in preventing the City expropriating returns from the rest of the British economy, but we have a far weaker interest in preventing London-based institutions making money at the expense of people overseas. In any event, we don't give much taxpayer support to those foreign banks but nonetheless collect a handsome return from them in the form of wages, taxes and rents.

Many arguments and counter-arguments can be made, but my own view on the issue of the City and its weight in the economy is that, ultimately, we should refrain from making judgements about what size it should be and instead should simply ensure that it works properly. That involves eradicating the effects of public subsidy and regulating activities to outlaw any practices that are reminiscent of my motorway tollbooths. We might expect to regulate the international activities less aggressively than the UK-focused ones but they need proper management all the same, if only to preserve the standing of our country overseas. The policy conclusion to be drawn would be that we should not attack the City for the sake of cutting it down to size, but we should not refrain from attacking it in order to keep it large. Just do what needs to be done in order to ensure that it is an effective financial centre.

I suspect that if we do that, if we get the taxation, structure and regulation of the City right, it will inevitably shrink somewhat. I believe that to be true simply because of the strange things that happened as the City underwent significant growth in the noughties. Some of the enlargement of financial services was attributable not to the skills of Londoners at running banks or investing money but to excessive risks taken as banks over-expanded. In addition, international finance came to Britain as it could find a light regulatory touch in London, a touch that is now regarded as too light by almost everyone. The growth over the decade was simply too good to be true. In the table in the last chapter you might have observed that financial service exports from the UK in 2009 amounted to $53 billion. If I tell you that in 2007 the figure was as high as $72 billion and in the years from 2000 to 2002 the figure was as low as about $20 billion, it is clear that an enormous ballooning occurred in a very short period. At the time many said it was down to tighter American regulation driving activity across the Atlantic. There is every reason to think that is the case; certainly the American authorities believe it to be so and it was the conventional wisdom in London at the time. So it appears that government action on both sides of the Atlantic was partly responsible for the growth of that most capitalist corner of the UK rather than the talent of those in the UK. Government action in the opposite direction thus has the power to reduce the size of the City.

As the authorities and the Bank of England attempt to formulate a policy on the City, many will argue that Britain cannot afford to let it shrink or to see financial services move off-shore. There is some good news for the authorities as they ponder on this, though. It comes in the form of one of the oldest economic concepts in the textbook: opportunity costs. These are simply the costs of something that reflect the opportunities foregone. For example, one of the costs of an industry that is too big is that it uses up resources which have high-value opportunities elsewhere. If an industry shrinks the resources move on to those other opportunities. This is vitally important in terms of the debate over the City: economies do not tend to have empty holes for very long. Does anyone really think that the people employed in financial services will remain out of work and under-used if the regulation cuts the size of the City?

Many people think that financial services epitomise the problem with the British service sector. But putting those aside, there are other reasons to think we might have pushed our love of services to the limit. The problem is not our domestic service sector, as we can produce and consume as many services as we want and trade them among ourselves. I can scratch your back and you can scratch mine; both activities are services and the more back-scratching we all do the more we can enjoy. The important question is whether we can earn enough to satisfy our enormous desire for manufactured imports by scratching the backs of foreigners. A reason to be cautious in this ambition is that trade in services implies more pan-national intimacy than trade in manufactured goods, yet not everybody is happy being so close to the rest of the world.

We can buy goods from the Chinese at arm's length but we can't export services to China quite so anonymously. If financial service exports do contract, we will rely even more heavily on exports of other services that usually require face to face contact. That will mean ever greater numbers of foreign people coming to the UK for travel, for study, as a bolt-hole and as a place to live. We will need more open borders to ensure that we have a sufficient supply of people coming here to allow us to sell them the exports necessary to sustain the standards of living to which we have become accustomed. Britain has been very open to the rest of the world – a theme of this book – but there may be limits to the patience of its population. It was interesting that in August 2010 David Cameron gave a speech in which he lamented Britain's failure to exploit its potential as a tourist destination. 'Take Chinese tourists,' he said. 'We're their twenty-second most popular destination. But Germany is forecast to break into their top ten. Why can't we?' The simple answer, according to the Chinese people I spoke to on my visit there shortly after that speech, is that we make it hard for them to get visas to come in. Most other EU countries have a unified visa policy, so one document gets you into them all. Not Britain, which has its own, more expensive, visa. And not everybody can get one. I'm told many Chinese are scared to apply in case they get a refusal stamped in their passport.

I suspect that in a decade's time Britain – if it wanted to – could be selling higher education services to Chinese and Indian students on a scale that dwarfs the current numbers. But not if people are obstructed from coming here. There are plans to clamp down on student visas as there has been such obvious abuse of the system. Bogus colleges clearly existed only to sell British residency to foreigners. Once in on a visa, it was impossible to track them down or get them home. But while it is perfectly sensible to prevent abuse of UK immigration law, it will have undoubted consequences for export-earning industries, particularly the universities.

An obvious example of the effect that restrictions on the

movement of people can have (and that a thriving service needs to flourish) is that on international student numbers in the United States following the September 11th attacks of 2001. Only one of the nineteen hijackers – Hani Hanjour – had entered the United States on a student visa, but the issue had already been controversial and so part of President Bush's response to the attacks was the USA PATRIOT Act which, among other things, paved the way for a substantial tightening of who could come to the US to study. Students from the US Department of State list of countries that sponsored terrorism (Cuba, Libya, Iran, Iraq, North Korea, Sudan and Syria) were to be refused visas for studying a range of courses, such as chemical and biotechnology engineering. The Student Exchange and Visitors Information System put the onus on universities to keep a far closer eye on international students, to electronically log them and inform the Immigration and Naturalization Service of any changes of circumstance, or if the student failed to enrol. The cost of all this was to be borne by the students the scheme was monitoring. Moreover, universities were encouraged to 'self-censor' research reporting on sensitive subjects, and to develop a tiered approach to giving out scientific information, restricting access to those who needed it. Leading up to 2001, the numbers of international students studying in the US had been climbing by about 5 per cent a year; for the 2002–03 academic year – the first year of students applying post the attacks – the rise had all but disappeared. Once all the changes had taken full effect, the numbers of overseas students began to fall. It was not until 2007–08 that international student numbers were back up to pre-September 11th levels. The proportion of students from Muslim countries had fallen very substantially.

Here in Britain, practical issues like visa policy will shape the export industries that the nation develops. Technology, increased affluence and cheap travel have combined to ensure that services have acquired more potential to be globally traded. That has played to our economic strengths in the last decade. How far we go with that is now an important question. There are two responses. First, it can be argued that a nation like Britain has to accept its economic destiny and remain open to the comings and goings of people who spend money here. London in particular is a world city; it is the biggest income-generator we have, and now it has established itself in that role, why on earth would we try to reinvent it? And universities are the export sector of which we can be most proud.

In contrast, the second view is to argue that Britain needs to find an alternative economic model which involves fewer outsiders arriving here, so that the population doesn't find its sense of Britishness so threatened. The logic of this argument derives from my rule in Chapter 2, that successful nations naturally specialise in activities utilising the resources they have in abundance. It is at least odd that a relatively crowded country such as Britain specialises in activities that require high – and increasing – numbers of foreign people residing in it. England is the most densely populated of the major countries in Europe. One sign of the pressures this brings is that in the south-east it is not proving easy to find enough strips of cheap land to build runways to cope with the airline traffic the nation generates. Maybe that just tells us we don't really want to be a global hub.

It is perhaps just a matter of personal taste whether you like being in a cosmopolitan, worldly society where you expect to see anybody from foreign students to Russian oligarchs and American sports magnates; or whether you prefer to live in a more traditional environment. As for the British population, they exhibit some ambivalence in hosting the people who arrive here but appear happy to enjoy the income generated by the industries built on the back of globalisation.

SOME CONCLUDING THOUGHTS

In the last three sections of this book I've tried to explain what the British do to earn a living. We have evolved an economy oriented towards the production and sale of expensive intangibles. Because I can see why it made sense to move in that direction, I take a broadly optimistic view of our productive potential. It seemed like a good idea at the time and we shouldn't be too hard on ourselves for doing things that seem like a good idea. Too many people unthinkingly assume that intangible equals worthless. I hope I have explained why that need not be the case. But I am quite aware of some of the drawbacks of our national business model. Some have always been evident; others have become more painfully so in the years of the financial crisis. So let me conclude this book with some reflections on the task now at hand. To see the challenges facing the UK, there are few better places to go than Sunderland.

I had never spent any time there. Like most London-based journalists, I have usually tended to look upon Newcastle and Gateshead as the big attractions in the north-east, with their contemporary art centres, blinking-eye bridge and excitable nightlife. Sunderland has less to catch a visitor's eye, but is a very substantial city all the same and it was there that I found myself for one of the last filming trips of the *Made in Britain* project. What I quickly realised was that we could have filmed the whole series in that one city alone.

Sunderland was once a great manufacturing centre; the biggest ship-building city in the world. However, that industry went off-shore as lower labour costs were available elsewhere, and by the late eighties it had gone. The glass industry that had existed in the city for hundreds of years also shrank and then closed, as did the coal mines. There was an extremely painful transition, during which old industries died before new industries arrived, prompting a chain reaction of economic and social decline. Crime rose, housing estates fell into disrepair and decent people tried to escape. Family life broke down in many cases (perhaps because if men don't work, women don't bother to marry them). The city lost the sense of identity and civic pride that manufacturing had brought, perhaps explaining why the morale of local people has since come to depend on the performance of the local football team. The eighties were a very low period indeed.

Yet out of despair came hope. A new manufacturing facility opened in 1986: the Nissan plant in nearby Washington, which is the biggest car plant in Britain. Like a lot of new manufacturing – particularly that which built upon the techniques developed in Japan – it was extremely productive and did not need to employ nearly as many people as the equivalent plants a decade or two earlier. But alongside the car plant came new service industries. Sunderland found that it could exploit its pleasing accent, making it a natural location for call centres. With a bit of help from the city council came a development on a green field site, the Doxford International Business Park that now employs eight thousand people, five thousand of whom work in contact centres (the new name for call centres, as they no longer just communicate by telephone call). On the site are British and international companies, from T-Mobile to EDF Energy and Nike UK as well as many financial service providers from Barclays to More Than (part of the Royal Sun Alliance insurance group). As a wonderful symbol of the transition from manufacturing to services, at the centre of the business park is a striking seven-metre stainless steel sculpture called *Quintisection*, which is based on the cross-section of an ocean liner. A few miles away, the city centre has enjoyed something of a renaissance; the university has come to have a huge presence, with 17,500 students (of whom seven thousand are from overseas). Attached to the university is the National Glass Centre, which opened on the north bank of the River Wear in 1998 as a cultural centre, restaurant and visitor attraction (although it struggles to get the visitors it needs). And, of course, one of the city's most striking architectural features is Sunderland AFC's Stadium of Light, which opened in 1997.

It would be lovely to write up Sunderland as the classic narrative of a decline followed by a rebirth into something bigger and better than what had gone before. Unfortunately, the economic story is not quite that simple. For all the improvement that has occurred since the eighties, it is still quite a struggle in the city. While the service economy has gone a long way to filling the hole left by the decline of manufacturing, nobody I spoke to in Sunderland felt that the city could survive on services alone. In addition, the wages paid to people in service jobs often provide less of a living than the manufacturing or mining jobs of yore. In Doxford, north of Sunderland, I visited the offices of 2Touch, an American firm that provides outsourced call-centre services. Quite a lot of the work they do is to cold call members of the public, for example to persuade them to change energy provider. I was told that one of the skills required in this work was 'bounce-backability', because staff could expect to make two or three sales from two or three hundred calls a day, quite a few of which might well involve people telling you to get lost. The buzz and energy level in the office was something to behold; the motivation and drive was high, but it is a very long way from the lucrative and up-market globalised services in the City of London. A long way, too, from the sectors that had made Sunderland rich in the past. The workforce at 2Touch is extremely young and the average tenure is less than a year, and these call-centre sales jobs are unlikely to provide a full replacement for those that have been lost. While it is good that thousands of people can earn a living that way, the area needs a population with skills and specialisms that go much further. Certainly, everybody in Sunderland is glad to have that Nissan plant in the back pocket.

If there is a message from Sunderland and from the rest of the British economy too, it is that when we consider the three different categories of items that the country produces and sells – manufactured goods, intellectual property and services – we need all three in order to flourish. You might see the biggest task for the next decade as getting the right balance between those three. Occasionally people will assert that it is one thing or another that really matters. It is only manufacturing that counts, or the future is services. People endlessly claim that 'moving up the value chain' is important, implying that intellectual property is somehow the supreme form of output. The reason these simplistic claims are so appealing is that they all have a grain of truth. Manufacturing, services and intellectual property matter – it is just that they all matter together. We need manufacturing because not everyone is suited to service work and not everyone can work in the knowledge sectors very productively. For the sake of the population as a whole there obviously needs to be a labour market that provides a balance of opportunities. But we need the other sectors too, as there is no way that an efficient manufacturing sector could usefully employ more than about a fifth of the working population. In any case, we are unlikely to remain rich by specialising in only one of the three sources of wealth. Good manufacturing is built upon the foundations of intellectual property, and intellectual property usually requires some connection to the factory and the physical. At the same time, a strong service economy requires flourishing companies trading internationally to generate things to service.

When you look at the point we had reached by the time of the financial crisis in 2007–08, however, it is clear that the economy's evolution had gone somewhat awry. The tradable sector had shrunk too far. The economy was too oriented towards domestic industries, sustained by imported manufactured goods. That would be fine if we had succeeded in paying for our imports with our intellect and services, but we had not. So we now need to build up the tradable sector, which almost certainly means building up our manufacturing capacity again.

If the financial crisis made anything else clear, it is that we need to save and invest more as a nation. As we do so, a process of rebalancing will occur, shifting towards the manufacturing and exporting sectors.

If a rebalancing does occur, it might help address another important challenge: to find ways of coping with the inequality and regional imbalance that has arisen from the intellectualisation of our economy. When a larger proportion of our output was generated from manufacturing, it naturally tended to disperse itself around the country and employed people of various skill levels. But the key characteristic of the more intellectual industries is their habit of clustering. That has been to the enormous benefit of the places to which they have clustered, in particular London and south-east, Edinburgh and other pockets of the country. But it has not been much use to Sunderland or many other parts of the UK. Not only have they missed out, but clusters elsewhere have made it all too easy for top graduates from provincial centres to migrate to where the top jobs are. This leads to a lopsidedness that leaves some parts of the country at lower incomes and reliant on public-sector jobs, while others are rich but overcrowded.

Quite apart from ensuring that our manufacturing sector is big enough for a nation like ours is the challenge of ensuring that the services sector is not *too* big for the nation My friends on the right will argue that this means we need a smaller government sector because that is the one that is financed by taxes on the successful parts of the economy. My left-wing friends will assert that we need to claw back the power and influence of finance. As an elegant way of avoiding an argument, let me suggest the task is simply to ensure that we get the micromanagement of all parts of the economy right; if we have an efficient government sector delivering services that people want it would be a bit odd to call it a drain on the rest of the economy, any more than our water companies or supermarkets are a drain on the economy. Similarly, if we refine the management of our financial sector to avoid the mistakes of the past and to align its incentives with those of the nation as a whole we could allow ourselves to be relatively relaxed about how big it is.

In meeting the challenge of rebalancing, let me make three observations that have recurred through the work on *Made in Britain*. First is the importance of good universities. Not only are they a large service exporter in their own right, but they also have a significant role in the creation of intellectual property, often for our manufacturing industries. In almost all the smartest and most lucrative parts of the economy university research seems to have played an important role. Britain happens to be very lucky in being endowed with a disproportionately large share of the world's best universities, and if you forced me to tell you of which British export industry I am most proud, I would probably nominate our university sector. If the rule is that we build the best possible economy using the resources we have at hand, the universities seem like one of the most useful, particularly as the demand for higher education is growing very rapidly around the world. It is hard to beat places that combine pure research, applied research and teaching as centres of value creation in the modern world. They represent their own mini-clusters, and have the power to spawn major industrial clusters around them too. In terms of both regional and industrial policy, their role cannot be overstated.

A second observation is that the openness of the British economy has played a major part in shaping our destiny. Not only has it fostered our role as a global commercial services centre but the integration of our companies with those elsewhere has been enormously important in remedying our problems. Just as a deficiency in the quality of football coaching in England has meant that the Football Association has had to go abroad to find a manager worthy of the England team, numerous deficiencies have been evident in the British economy that have been filled from abroad: in the quality of manufacturing management in the seventies; in capital for investment through the decades; and to some extent in labour supply in the noughties. But it has to be said that our relative lack of economic nationalism has had its pluses and minuses. On the one hand, if you have a local bottleneck you are usually better off easing it with whatever solution you can find. On the other, if you can always ease the problem by importing a solution it can make a nation lazy about avoiding problems in the first place. If the England football team can always find good managers from overseas (or if Premiership teams can always get good players from elsewhere, for that matter) why bother to develop talent at home? The lesson is not that we should necessarily retreat from the globalised direction we have followed, but that we should never cease to ensure we are investing in ourselves as well.

My third and final observation is that the development of the economy should not be seen as an event but as a process. Things change, and then they change again: the telex, the fax machine and now email all once seemed like the future, but just as fast as the future arrives something else comes along. If I am right in positing that what successful economies do is take the resources they have to hand, push them into their highest possible value occupations and constantly adapt as the world changes, then we can all expect abstract global forces to shove us around from one place to another.

As an example, people who accept that we have been quite successful at earning a living in recent decades sometimes ask what we will we do when China follows us up market and makes jet engines and creates global brands. They've taken our low-end manufacturing, so it will just be a matter of time before they steal the top-end stuff as well. We will then be left with nothing at all. The good news is that it won't be quite like that. When China becomes a global force in jet-engine manufacture, the price of jet engines will fall and we will move on to other things. Perhaps we will start to make suits again if China doesn't want to do that any more, or maybe China and Britain will each manufacture a mix of the two. I don't know, and nor do I intend to predict what the right response will be. The future is not fixed and there is little value in trying to second-guess it. While it is tempting to think that after one more heave up market we will arrive at the right economic destination, in fact we make one more heave and find that the ideal destination has shifted. This is neither a problem nor is it a prescription; it is simply a reflection of the world as it is.

If it implies anything, it is that the most useful skills of a workforce are the basics – literacy and numeracy – that are important in everything we do and which allow people to transfer from one activity to another as the economy adapts. I'm afraid that is not a particularly original conclusion. All I can say is that, from what I have seen, there are pockets of despair in our economy that need to be remedied, but otherwise there is no need for any shame at the living we earn and no need for there to be any lack of confidence in our ability to meet the challenges that will come along.

BIBLIOGRAPHY

Books

Addy, John, *The Textile Revolution* (London: Longman, 1976)

Allen, Robert C., *The British Industrial Revolution in Global Perspective* (Cambridge: Cambridge University Press, 2009)

Aspin, Chris, *The Cotton Industry* (Princes Risborough: Shire, 1981, new edn 2003)

Bernstein, William J., *A Splendid Exchange: How Trade Shaped the World* (London: Atlantic, 2009)

Beevor, Antony, *D-Day: The Battle for Normandy* (London: Viking, 2009)

Bevan, Judi, *The Rise and Fall of Marks & Spencer* (London: Profile, 2001)

Brooks, David, *Bobos in Paradise: The New Upper Class and How They Got There* (London: Simon & Schuster, 2000)

Crawford, Matthew B., *The Case for Working with Your Hands, or, Why Office Work is Bad for Us and Fixing Things Feels Good* (London: Viking, 2010)

Crump, Thomas, *A Brief History of how the Industrial Revolution Changed the World* (London: Robinson, 2010)

Deane, Phyllis, *The First Industrial Revolution* (Cambridge: Cambridge University Press, 1965)

Farmer, Adrian, *Belper Through Time* (Chalford: Amberley, 2010)

Ferguson, Niall, *Empire: How Britain Made the Modern World* (London: Allen Lane, 2003)

Frank, Robert H. and Philip J. Cook, *The Winner-Takes-All Society: Why the Few at the Top Get So Much More than the Rest of Us* (1995; London: Virgin, 2010)

Friedel, Robert, *A Culture of Improvement: Technology and the Western Millennium* (London: MIT Press, 2007)

Johnson, Steven, *Where Good Ideas Come From: A Natural History of Innovation* (London: Allen Lane, 2010)

Jones, Edgar, *The Business of Medicine: The Extraordinary History of Glaxo, A Baby Food Producer Which Became One of the World's Most Successful Pharmaceutical Companies* (London: Profile, 2001)

Jones, Richard, *The Apparel Industry* (Oxford: Blackwell Science, 2003, 2nd edn 2006)

Lee, Stewart, *How I Escaped My Certain Fate* (London: Faber & Faber, 2010)

Maddison, Angus, *The World Economy: Historical Statistics* (Paris: OECD Publishing, 2003)

McCloskey, Deirdre, *The Bourgeois Virtues: Ethics for an Age of Commerce* (London: University of Chicago Press, 2006)

Olins, Wally, *Wally Olins: The Brand Handbook* (London: Thames & Hudson, 2008)

Sandbrook, Dominic, *White Heat: A History of Britain in the Swinging Sixties* (London: Little, Brown, 2006)

Schonhardt-Bailey, Cheryl, *From the Corn Laws to Free Trade: Interests, Ideas, and Institutions in Historical Perspective* (London: MIT Press, 2006)

Sennett, Richard, *The Craftsman* (London: Allen Lane, 2008)

Trentmann, Frank, *Free Trade Nation: Commerce, Consumption and Civil Society in Modern Britain* (Oxford: Oxford University Press, 2008)

Weightman, Gavin, *The Industrial Revolutionaries: The Creation of the Modern World, 1776–1914* (London: Atlantic, 2007)

Whitehead, Christopher (ed. Phil Coulson), *Proud Heritage: A Pictorial Heritage of British Aerospace Aircraft* (London: Weidenfeld & Nicolson, 1998)

Wilson, Frank R., *The Hand: How its Use Shapes the Brain, Language, and Human Culture* (New York: Pantheon Books, 1998)

Wolfe, Tom, *The Bonfire of the Vanities* (London: Cape, 1987)

Woolley, Paul et al, *The Future of Finance: The LSE Report* (London: London School of Economics and Political Science, 2010)

Yorke, Stan, *The Industrial Revolution Explained: Steam, Speaks and Massive Wheels* (Newbury: Countryside Books, 2005)

Bibliography

Articles

Baumol, William J., 'Macroeconomics of Unbalanced Growth: The Anatomy of Urban Crisis', *The American Economic Review*, June 1967, vol. 57, no. 3, 415–26

———— and William G. Bowen, 'On the Performing Arts: The Anatomy of their Economic Problems', *American Economic Review, Papers and Proceedings*, 1965, 55(1/2), 495–502

Dedrick, Jason, Kenneth L. Kraemer and Greg Linden, 'Who Profits from Innovation in Global Value Chains?: A Study of the iPod and Notebook PCs', *Industrial and Corporate Change*, 2010, vol. 19, issue 1, 80–116

'The Tragedy of SID Revisited', *The Weekly Standard*, 31 December 2007, vol. 13, no. 16

'Chronically Ill Patients Get More Care, Less Quality, Says the Latest Dartmouth Atlas', *Journal of Hospice and Palliative Nursing*, July/August 2008, vol. 10, no. 4, 185–7

'Transatlantic Trends Topline Data 2010', German Marshall Fund of the United States (with the Compagnia di San Paolo, Turin, Italy and others)

INDEX

Index

Fleming, Alexander 155
Fleming, Jon 104
Florey, Howard 155
football 196, 246, 251
Ford Motor Company 148, 150,
    171
foreign currency markets
    devaluation of the pound (18
        November 1967) 52–3, 58
    exchange rates 52–3, 58, 125,
        128, 129–30, 132, 137, 141
    North Sea Oil and 132
    savings levels and 125, 128, 129,
        130, 141
    trade deficit and 24, 27
forestry 19, *21*
Formula One motor racing 117–19
Forsyth, Bruce 55, 56
France 15, 16, 23, 116, 117, 122
    branding and 178, 180, 182
    capital stock 17, 127
    car production 48, 68–9
    clothes manufacturers 66
    consumption in 135
    economic nationalism 3, 8, 51–2,
        63, 67, 69
    foreign ownership of companies
        67
    globalisation and 67
    R&D expenditure 162
    railways 17, 18, 21
    rise of China and 31–2, 66
    savings/investment levels in *126*,
        135
    service economy *208*
    viticulture 42
    working hours 17
France Telecom 178, 180
franchise, electoral 61, 62
free trade 59, 61
    in Edwardian era 64–5

as moral cause 62–3, 64
post-Second World War 65–7
repeal of the Corn Laws (1846)
    59, 63, 64
Tariff Reform movement and 64,
    65
Futurebrand (branding firm)
    178–9

G7 nations 14–15
gas extraction 4, 9
General Agreements on Tariffs and
    Trade (GATT) 65–6
General Motors 48, 151, 190
German Marshall Fund of the
    United States, 'Transatlantic
    Trends' survey 51, 66
Germany 15, 16, *23*, 117, 122,
    211
    branding and 182
    capital stock 17, 127
    car production 5, 18, 20–1, 22,
        48, 49, 151
    chimney sweeps in 231
    foreign ownership of companies
        67
    foreign students in 215
    industrialisation
        (nineteenth-century) 99
    machine tool exports 43
    R&D expenditure 162
    savings/investment levels in *126*,
        130, 133
    service economy 206, *208*
    working hours 17
GKN 69, 70–1
Gladstone, William 168
glass manufacture 146–51
Glastonbury Festival 219–21
GlaxoSmithKline 153, 154–8, 165,
    190–1

Index